ETERNAL STRANGERS

Also by Ursula Bacon

*Shanghai Diary: A Young Girl's Journey
from Hitler's Hate to War-Torn China*

ETERNAL STRANGERS

Ursula Bacon

PRESS™

Milwaukie

M Press

10956 SE Main Street

Milwaukie, OR 97222

mpressbooks.com

Book design by Amy Arendts & Krystal Hennes

Cover photography by Amy Arendts

Special thanks to Aren Kittilsen and Samantha Robertson

Library of Congress Cataloging-in-Publication Data

Bacon, Ursula.

  Eternal strangers : a memoir / Ursula Bacon. -- 1st M Press ed.

    p. cm.

  ISBN-13: 978-1-59582-099-0

  ISBN-10: 1-59582-099-X

  1. Bacon, Ursula. 2. Jews--China--Shanghai--Biography. 3. World War, 1939-1945--Jews--China--Shanghai. I. Title.

  DS135.C5B328 2007

  940.53'18'092--dc22

  [B]

                    2006035097

ISBN-10: 1-59582-099-X

ISBN-13: 978-1-59582-099-0

First M Press Edition: July 2007

10 9 8 7 6 5 4 3 2 1

Printed in U.S.A.

To Thorn, always
and
To my children, Ron and Marly

PART ONE

THE NARROW WOODEN boat pushed away from the golden sands of the North African shore. Oars dipped silently in and out of the blue Mediterranean waters and soon the small vessel was gliding smoothly over the calm sea heading west-northwest. The tall, broad-shouldered man in his clay-colored robe let the oars rest and, cupping one hand over his eyes, David ben Joseph blocked out the penetrating rays of the brilliant late-summer sun. He looked back at the slowly diminishing outline of his homeland. A solitary tear rolled down one weathered, deeply tanned cheek. His lips moved in a silent prayer, asking his God for a safe journey. Huddled in a tight knot beside him were his wife Rachel, his three young sons, and the few bundles of their modest belongings.

What would the future bring? Was there a place to live in peace, to work, and worship God?

Like other Jews, Joseph and his family had been victims of the Diaspora—leaving the Holy Land to scatter all over Europe since 70 C.E. David ben Joseph would never see the land of his forefathers again. Spain was his destination. And as thousands of others like him, he would settle there, work the land, and raise his family.

On other parts of the North African coast, wooden boats were heading east-northeast carrying Jews to unknown lands in

Eastern Europe. These strangers would settle in Turkey, the Balkans, Poland, and as far away as Russia.

The Holy Land became a dream the Jews kept alive in their hearts and passed on from generation to generation—Home, the Holy Land, *Eritz Israel*. They took with them their Torah, their ancient laws, their traditions, and their God—the very core of their existence around which they built their lives.

And so the Jews wandered from land to land, country to country, looking for a place to be accepted, a safe place, a country to belong to—a home—no longer eternal strangers.

But strangers they were. At best the wandering Jews were distrusted by suspicious minds, and ridiculed and ostracized by the bullies of the world. At worst they were persecuted and killed, accused of having crucified Jesus Christ, for worshipping a different god, for living by different laws. In Eastern Europe, brutal pogroms raged from Russia to Poland to the Balkans and sent the strangers fleeing again and again. In Western Europe, in Portugal and Spain, during the infamous Inquisition, the Jews were condemned as heretics, tortured, killed, the survivors sent fleeing to the north into France, Belgium, and Holland, and eastward into Germany and beyond.

For centuries to come the European Jews remained eternal strangers.

Chapter One

FEBRUARY 1918

H E FELL IN love the first time he saw her. His eyes
followed the young woman with the dark hair as she
moved gracefully, dance-like, between the few narrow, rough-
hewn wooden tables and benches in the small, dimly lit tavern.
To the waiting men who came to the tavern for their early
afternoon meals, she carried heavy white plates heaped with
onion-fried potatoes and thick chunks of smoked sausages.
Her faced was flushed from the heat of the coal-fed iron stove
where she and her younger sister, Lucy, prepared the simple
country food.

Carefully, she placed a full-to-the-brim bowl of thick, fragrant
soup in front of the tall, slender soldier in his field-gray uniform.
She brushed a loose strand of hair out of her face with the back of
her hand and was about to return to the makeshift kitchen when
the soldier spoke up.

The passionate tone in his deep, low voice struck a chord within
her. "Just a moment please, I want to talk with you. Please!"

He was overcome with a sense of awe and fascination as his
warm, hazel eyes locked on to her lively, deep brown ones and
searched her face. Like a magnet, the soldier held her glance
and slowly, almost dream-like, she sat down beside him, drawn
by a strange urgency not to let this moment pass. Astonished,

she knew, in that instant, their future together was as inevitable as the appearance of stars on a clear summer's night.

Irene, innkeeper Herman Burger's oldest daughter, had never lacked the attention of eager young men. Serious, more often than not, they pleaded for courting time, painted rosy pictures of a future union, and went as far as asking her father for her hand in marriage. Most of these young men were good Jewish boys from the small garrison town of Lubitz and the small neighboring towns where everybody knew everyone. The hard-working Jewish families from in and around the town pursued their modest businesses, worked their trades, faithfully attended their orthodox synagogue, and lived in a relatively peaceful state with their gentile neighbors.

To her father's surprise and her mother's unveiled disappointment, Irene had politely but firmly turned all her ardent suitors away. She was a dutiful and loving daughter, but when it came to choosing a mate, she had a mind and a vision of the future all her own. She wanted to see the world, to live in a big city. She dreamt of going to the theater, of attending operas and symphony concerts and grandiose balls. In her mind, dressed in silk and velvet gowns, she danced on marble floors beneath glittering chandeliers to the strains of a sparkling Vienna waltz.

She dreamt of the kind of world she never found reflected in the eyes of her suitors. It wasn't that she looked down on her small-town life, it was just that she wanted at least to taste a bigger one. Night after night, she dreamt of a faceless stranger who would sweep her off her feet and take her into that faraway, shiny new world she knew existed. And now, here he was.

"My name is Martin Blomberg," the soldier started a bit haltingly. "I am from Breslau where my parents live. I have three sisters and one brother. I own a printing business. But right now, I am stationed here at the garrison, and I'll probably be shipped out to the front lines any day now. This horrible war is never going to end—just like this miserable winter," he sighed deeply, never taking his eyes off of hers. Before she could say anything, he hurriedly said, "I know this is a bit short for an introduction without references. That can come later. But there's a war on." He paused briefly, his voice trailed off, his eyes were serious.

"Please listen to me, I want to know you, your family, your life. I want to talk with you. I want to tell you what I do; I want to tell you about my family. I want, desperately, to see you." He paused for a second and added, "I'm really quite honorable with honorable intentions." A sudden, quick smile flashed across his craggy face and lit up his eyes with a mischievous twinkle.

She sat perfectly still, looking at him, looking beyond him—looking at her dream. She rose slowly, reluctantly, "Eat your soup," she said softly, "I'll be back." He watched her slender figure weave her way purposefully through the rows of tables and approach the tall, gray-haired man behind the small bar who was pouring generous shots of *Kümmel* and other schnapps into short, stubby glasses.

Irene waited until her father had served his customers, then pulled him gently aside. "Father," she said urgently, "I would like your permission to invite that soldier at the back table for Shabbat dinner tomorrow night. Please?"

Herman Burger looked at his daughter, surprise registering on his face. Irene had never invited an acquaintance, not to mention a stranger, to a Friday-night meal, or any other meal. He had never seen her so excited. He had always admired her cool appraisal of people and events, as well as the logical and practical way she handled them. Watching her growing up into a woman, he had realized how private she was, how secretive about herself and how reticent. Her flushed face, her sparkling eyes, and the passionate insistence in her voice showed a new side of her.

He raised his eyebrows. "Aren't you a bit hasty, my dear? You don't even know if he is Jewish."

"I know. I know. But he could well be; his name is Blomberg. But it doesn't matter. This is important to me. Please, Father," Irene insisted.

"Well, all right," he gave in with a sigh, "but let's not tell your mother that he might not be a Jew. It would be difficult for her to accept him, especially at the Shabbat table."

Irene planted a quick thank-you kiss on her father's cheek, danced off to the lonely soldier in the far corner of the tavern, slid in beside him, and said breathlessly, "I am Irene Burger, the man behind the counter is my father; he owns the tavern. Please come tomorrow for Shabbat dinner. Come at five o'clock. We live above our business on the next floor. Use the door to the right of the tavern, and be on time."

She didn't wait for a reply, but got up swiftly and placed her hands on the table in front of him. She brought her face fairly close to his, and said under her breath, "And don't tell me you're not Jewish."

"I could well be a Jew," Martin shot back. "As a matter of fact, I can be anything I need to be. I want to see you." Again, that mischievous smile settled on his face. His eyes, bright with antici-pation and excitement, never left hers as he reached for her hand and raised it to his lips.

"Thank you, Fräulein Burger; I'll be on time."

Irene's face flushed a deep shade of red. No man had ever kissed her hand. That was something she knew without a doubt belonged to that other world; it belonged to the dream. She whirled away and disappeared behind the six-foot wooden partition that hid the tavern's kitchen activities.

Once out of sight, she leaned against the wall, closed her eyes against the light, turned off the muffled sounds of the tavern, and conjured up the soldier's face in her mind. She saw her vision come to life in his eyes—so clear and so lucid that it left her breathless with excitement. But at the same time a wave of worry wrapped itself around her heart. What if the stranger was not Jewish? What would happen? Her mother would not accept a gentile in the family. It did not matter to Irene whether or not he was a Jew. Her thoughts flashed wildly from one thing to the next, like a flock of sparrows flying against the wind and settling on a tree, only to take off again in search of the next place to land.

The man she had just met, whom she knew, with a certain wisdom, had given a face to the one in her dreams, lived in Breslau. It was not only a big city, but was the capitol of the province of Silesia, some two hundred miles to the north. Breslau was almost as exciting as Berlin or Vienna, she thought. She knew all about the city's opera which was considered the springboard to international fame and that the arts, theatre, and concert flourished there. The city, on the River Oder, was proud of its cultural atmosphere and sophisticated manner.

Irene was twenty-eight years old (an old maid in her mother's eyes) and had never been away from her hometown. But she knew about the world. Since she was a child, she had read everything she could lay her hands on and spent hours studying her father's atlas with the dedication of a treasure hunter looking for a gold mine. She spun her dreams from the pictures she had seen of Paris, Rome, London, Madrid, the Greek Islands, and her busy mind invented the sights and sounds of travel adventures.

"Irene, wake up!" Lucy's voice brought her back to the tavern. "You almost let the fire go out," her sister chided, stoking briskly at the faintly glowing embers, and fed a big shovel of coals to the dying flames. "Are you asleep?"

"It's my turn in the kitchen now," Lucy declared. "Go upstairs and dream some more," she teased gently.

Lucy, five years younger than Irene, was a dear and happy soul, much less complicated than her sister. Her pretty, round face with its friendly brown eyes was framed by naturally dark, wavy hair. She never seemed in a hurry. She walked with slow and leisurely

steps, and looked at the world with childlike innocence. She was
engaged to Max Rosen, her brother Arthur's partner in the dry
goods store, located directly across the square from the Lubitz
Tavern. Max had started there as bookkeeper and eventually
became a partner in the business. Arthur was not much of a businessman and welcomed Max's talent for managing the store's
affairs. In contrast to Lucy's peaceful personality, he was ebullient
and vociferous. Literature and the music of the masters were his
unbridled passion, and he took great delight in introducing Lucy
to the writings and the music of the old masters.

They were to be married the following year. The very thought
of being Mrs. Rosen sent delightful shivers down her spine. In
her state of bliss, she felt a snippet of pity for her older sister's
state of unattachment to a man.

Irene gave her little sister a quick kiss on one cheek, went into
the narrow hall, and climbed the steep and equally narrow
staircase that led to the family's living quarters. Her father had
purchased the historic, three-story house with the tavern and its
small, primitive cement-clad distillery from the former owner for
whom he had worked for nine years. When he married Toni
Friedlander in 1883, he added her small dowry to his savings,
borrowed some money from the local banker, and became the
proud owner of the house and the Lubitz Tavern. He served an
honest drink and wholesome food to his patrons and had earned
the respect of his neighbors. Most of them never gave a thought
to his being a Jew.

Slipping quietly into the large attic room she shared with her
sister, Irene lay down on the chaise lounge, pulled a soft blanket
up to her shoulders, and returned to the look in the soldier's eyes.
She brought back the sound of his voice, felt again his lips
brushing her hand, and began to dream about delicious possibili-
ties. Her thoughts were interrupted by a sharp knock on the door,
followed by her mother entering the room.

Toni Burger was petite and fragile looking, a stark contrast to her strong will and boundless energy. She rarely raised her voice in anger, but there was no doubt in anyone's mind who ruled the roost. She was brought up in a strict, orthodox Jewish home and raised her two sons and two daughters in the same way. It was all she knew. With her own thirty-fifth wedding anniversary approaching, she looked with great concern at Irene, her old-maid daughter, who, as Toni believed, missed the real purpose of a woman's life by not being married.

Irene sat up and petted the side of the wide chaise lounge, inviting her mother to sit. Toni wasted no time in getting to the point of her visit. "Irene," she said, "I have some good news. My second cousin Esther's youngest son, Albert Spanier from Ratibor is in town on one of his selling trips. He is a good boy, handsome and hardworking. He is a clever businessman and well liked. He'll make a fine husband. He is coming to dinner Friday night, and is looking forward to meeting you. His mother told him all about you," she concluded, pleased with herself.

Irene chuckled, "Mother, you have more second and third cousins than anyone I know. By now, I thought I had met them all, including their sons. Well, he'll be in good company," she continued slowly, about to drop the bomb. "I met this interesting soldier in the tavern today. He is from Breslau and is stationed at the garrison. Father gave me permission to invite him to Shabbat dinner."

Toni's face registered surprise. Annoyed, her eyes flew open. Flustered, she asked, "Is he a Jew?"

Irene hoped to sound convincing, "I am certain he is, Mother. His name is Martin Blomberg. That's a Jewish name."

"You should have asked him," Toni grumbled. "Or," she added shaking her head, "at least your father could have asked."

"Mother, I like him. He is different," Irene replied weakly, pleading for her mother's approval.

Toni was quiet for a moment and looked thoughtfully at her daughter. A bit impatiently, she said, "Child, we don't know anything about this man. He certainly is not from around here. Breslau! That's far away. I wouldn't know whom to ask about him or his family. It just isn't right for you. Why can't you be interested in someone we know? What is so wrong with all the ones you have met and sent on their way? They were all good Jewish men. You could have been married for years now, have children. What is it you want?" her mother complained, her face tight and cold.

The question hung heavily in the air like a dark cloud threatening thunder and lightning. Irene held her breath for a moment. How many times had she heard that before? How many times had she tried to explain her dream to her mother and not been heard? "Tradition" was always her mother's reply—the importance of tradition. How many times—in the most respectful way—had Irene explained to her mother that she wasn't looking for tradition? She was looking for new and different things. She was looking for adventure. But all Irene's words had fallen on deaf ears.

The moment in her bedroom had quickly turned into just another one of their mother-daughter disagreements. Nothing ever changes, Irene told herself. She got up, put her hand lovingly on her mother's shoulder, and with a smile she dropped the subject. "Mother, I promised Ana Marieke to help her with tomorrow's dinner preparations. I'd better go. Don't be angry with me, please, I'm just trying myself out." Toni winced painfully and kept shaking her head in disbelief.

Swiftly, Irene escaped through the door, headed for the kitchen and the housekeeper's quarters, knowing well and good that this was not the end of the discussion. Her mother was tenacious about the subject of her daughter's future, and in spite of Irene's constant opposition, held on to it like a dog with a favorite bone.

Ana Marieke was plucking the two Friday-night chickens. She looked up, blew a feather off of the tip of her nose, and said, "Glad you came, I can use your help. My bones are bothering me today." A look of irritation spread over her plain features and settled in her eyes.

When Ana Marieke met Toni Burger twenty years ago, everything changed for her. The peasant girl found a new life away from the one-room dirt-floor cottage of her church-mouse-poor parents, who struggled to eke out a living by raising a few vegetables on less than an acre of barren soil, a few kilometers south of Lubitz. The two women had met at Thursday Market at the Lubitz town square and taken an immediate liking to each other. When Toni mentioned that she was looking for someone to help at the tavern and around the house, Ana Marieke jumped at the chance to get away from home. Two days later, she arrived at the Burgers' door, carrying a pitifully small bundle of her belongings.

When Toni showed the young woman her room under the eaves in the attic with its simple furnishings, friendly light blue gingham curtains, quilt and matching pillows, and a soft rug covering part of the clean wooden floor, Ana Marieke burst into tears of joy.

"I never had a room of my own," she managed to blurt out between sobs, "and this is so beautiful. It's like a room in a castle," she whispered, afraid that the sound of her voice would make the room disappear. To Toni's embarrassment, Ana Marieke curtsied and kissed her hand in gratitude. From that day on, she belonged.

Toni had wasted no time teaching her the intricacies of a kosher household along with some of the strict Jewish laws on which the Burgers' life functioned. She helped Ana improve her limited reading and writing skills to which the young peasant woman took like a duck to water. Ana Marieke had a quick and hungry mind and loved to learn—anything.

She was as devout a Catholic as her mistress was a Jew. Never in all the years had she missed five-o'clock morning Mass, yet at the same time, knew as much about living by the ancient Jewish laws as Toni. Hard working, good humored, and fiercely loyal, she was not interested in meeting a man and getting married. In her free time she read books, and did needlework. She had found a family and a fine home; she never wanted to be anywhere else. In turn, the Burgers deeply appreciated her untiring devotion to the family and couldn't picture life without her.

After Irene had hauled two big buckets of coal for the cooking stove up from the cellar, scrubbed the carrots and potatoes, and rinsed off the dirt, she turned to the older woman with a shy smile. "Ana," she said, "I've met a soldier today. He is not from around here. He lives in Breslau. He is not just nice; he is inter-esting. There is something so different about him. I like him. And," she added with a grin, "you'll meet him tomorrow evening. He is coming to Shabbat dinner."

"What?" Ana exclaimed, sensing trouble on the wing. "Is he Jewish?" Ana Marieke sounded just like Toni.

Irene looked at her and with a touch of steel in her voice said, "Don't tell Mother; but I don't know if he is Jewish, and further-more, I don't care." She dried her hands on a rough linen towel and sat down on a low stool across from the older woman.

"Please don't act like my mother, I need someone on my side. Wait until you have met him," Irene pleaded. "I just know you will like him."

"As to your mother's concern, it's not about liking him. It's about being Jewish," Ana replied sternly.

"Ana, you know I love and respect my parents. I live by their rules. I honor their *tradition*. I never said this to anyone, but this is my life, and each generation has different ideas. I do love my home, but I yearn to leave here and meet the world. I want to see how other people live and think. Change is happening every day.

My parents do not live like their parents did. They no longer live by some of the outdated laws of the Talmud. Why can't I have the freedom to bring about change in my life without hurting others? Does pleasing my parents come before my own needs and dreams?" Irene paused and looked at Ana who was furiously stirring a big pot of potato soup for the evening meal.

"That was quite a speech for one usually so quiet," Ana Marieke replied. "I don't have any advice. You'll do what you need to do. All I can say is, think before you jump. Your dream may become a nightmare," she paused.

Looking at the young woman's troubled face, she added, "I am lucky, I have simple needs. I have no burning desire to see the world. I have found my world right here—safe and small."

Irene nodded in wordless agreement, reached out and patted Ana's strong hands, and sighed, "I'd better go and set the table for dinner. Tomorrow will take care of itself."

Chapter Two

AT THE PRIMITIVE foot soldiers' quarters at the Lubitz Garrison in Upper Silesia, not far from the Polish border, signs of life emerged reluctantly on the bitter cold February morning of 1918. The iron stove that squatted in the center of the barrack crackled and popped loudly, advertising its feeble attempt to warm the spartan barracks—home of war-weary men.

Private Martin Blomberg slowly rolled out of his narrow cot, sat up, and placed his sock-clad feet on the cold floor. He shook himself awake and immediately his thoughts turned to Irene Burger and the excitement of seeing her this very evening in a social setting. He would meet her family, and most probably be subjected to a barrage of questions about himself, his parents, what he did for a living, and above all, he would be interrogated about being Jewish.

While he got dressed, during the morning meal, and as he tackled his daily clerical tasks, he rehearsed how he was going to answer the anticipated questions the Burgers no doubt were sure to ask. He was worried. He wanted to make a good impression and stay as close to the truth as he could. It wasn't easy to explain his background, so vastly different from that of solid citizens like the Burgers. The fact that he was not raised a Jew did not improve his chances when he would ask for her hand in marriage.

And ask, he would. He *would* marry her—indeed he would. He was thirty-two years old, and in all his adult life he had never met anyone who even slightly interested him. He was in love for the first time. He felt like dancing.

He thought of his parents—the strange and puzzling union between Henrietta Flatow, the simple, uneducated, plain country girl and the eccentric, Munchhausen-type, charming big-man-of-the-world. How could he explain his father's wild schemes that were responsible for the fortune he had amassed in rather unorthodox ways, to say the least. And how could he make them understand how he came to call himself Baron Friedrich Wilhelm von Blomberg? Long ago, on a rare occasion of a conversation with his usually non-communicative mother, Henrietta told him, her oldest son, that she knew for certain that her husband had either bought his title, or even more plausible, simply invented it. Invented or purchased was no concern of his. Tall and handsome in his perfect handmade suits and stunning fur-collared overcoats, he looked, acted, and carried himself every inch the aristocrat of lineage and means. The Old Baron, a fascinating blend of questionable business practices and philanthropy, was disappointed that his son Martin refused to carry on the title. He was even a touch offended that he not only questioned the authenticity of his aris-tocratic heritage, but that being a baron didn't mean a lark's song to the younger Blomberg. The old man had shaken his head in disbelief, after all, it was all so real to him. He was Baron Friedrich Wilhelm von Blomberg—"The Old Baron."

Henrietta also told Martin that she had Jewish parents and she was raised in a hit-and-miss attempt at following a watered-down version of Judaism. The latter did not make a lasting impression on her and left her impervious to any religion.

"Your father," she continued in her rough, muffled voice, "has conveniently forgotten that he too has Jewish ancestry in his attic;

quite a few as a matter of fact. We were married in a civil ceremony in Pankow, a tiny hamlet in Saxonia. At that time your father announced himself to be a Protestant; he still does. And whatever notion takes over his mind, becomes his absolute truth. He is a strange one," she sighed. "Some forty years and five children later, I still don't know him. But I am not surprised," Martin's mother told him. "That's how men are."

Martin remembered that rare moment with his mother, whom he thought to be just as strange in her ways as his father—different of course, but quite strange. In the winter. she rinsed her hands in her own urine to prevent the skin from cracking. She was not interested in money and a social life. She never attended the theatre or accompanied her husband in his white tie and tails to an opera in his private box. She owned three dresses; two for "every day" and one for "good." Martin couldn't remember ever seeing her in her "good" dress.

The Old Baron had provided her with a magnificently furnished ten-room apartment. There were the formal salon, the music room, the library, the gentlemen's smoking room, a sitting room, and a dining room which easily could seat twenty guests in comfort. Henrietta never set foot in any of those rooms and kept them locked. Her life played out in the kitchen and in the smallest, least opulent of the six bedrooms. She refused having house-keepers or maids around. She kept house all by herself and never employed nannies for her children.

But most disheartening and sad of all was the cold and stern atmosphere she created in her home, and her inability to display any signs of fondness or compassion for anyone. She had no friends, and not one of her children remembered her ever laughing out loud, or shedding a tear. Like a piece of amber with an insect trapped inside, so were her emotions hopelessly imprisoned and frozen somewhere in the recesses of a hurt soul. Even around her children, she remained alone with herself, detached and somber.

Later, fueled by her intense and neurotic need for cleanliness and order, and her joyless presence, she would drive the Old Baron out of his home and straight into the arms of several friendly, fun-loving, and frivolous damsels. When the gossip reporting him resplendent in full evening attire attending the opera, dining at the *Hotel Vier Jahreszeiten* (Four Seasons), and dancing at chic supper clubs or cabarets—always in the company of beautiful women—reached her ears, Henrietta simply shrugged her shoulders and continued polishing every brass door knob to a dazzling shine.

Martin shook himself out of his reverie. Later, at the right time, he would tell Irene everything about his family before she would meet them. Fortunately, his three sisters and his brother, interesting and lively people, lived the good life and would be delighted to welcome her into their circles.

Tonight would be quite a test for him, he mused. He hoped to pass Shabbat dinner at the Burger home, in the presence of all the family members, with flying colors.

In the late afternoon, he slipped a heavy, gray, army-issue coat over his field uniform and started the twenty-minute walk to the town square and the Burgers' house. He tucked his chin into the upturned collar of his overcoat as he braced himself against the icy, skin-biting, breathtaking winter wind. He shuddered, as he thought of his comrades in their frozen trenches on the front lines. He had been fortunate so far, having been assigned to clerical work away from the blood-soaked battlefields. But with the war going badly for the kaiser and his Germany and the heavy casualties, there was no telling when the clerks and cooks would be sent to battle. War! What a futile, barbaric custom in the neverending parade of human stupidities.

Snow had pillowed softly on the narrow side streets that led to the town square with its small but castle-like city hall, a building with a memory that went back to its beginning in 1732. A wide square of iced-over cobblestones stretched all the way to the sidewalks where narrow two- and three-story houses, each sharing a common wall, hugged the Ring, the heart of the town. Their colorful and well-kept façades, along with the inviting storefronts, were warmed by the last weak rays of the wintry sun and conveyed a picture of stability and modest prosperity.

Martin stomped the accumulated snow from his boots and stepped into the small confectionary shop a few houses removed from the Lubitz Tavern. He was welcomed by the warmth from a small tile stove and the enticing smells of chocolate, vanilla, and almonds. He lingered a moment over selecting a house gift and settled for a large box of mixed marzipan pieces, nougat, and chocolate-covered ginger.

His heart beat a bit faster as he passed the tavern which would remain closed until Sunday morning. Following Irene's directions, he entered through the heavy door into the hallway and rushed up the steep staircase, two steps at a time. A bit breathless, he stopped short at the end of the upper hall in front of the glass and wood door that led to the private quarters of the tavern owners. The big clock in the tower of the city hall struck five.

His knock was quickly answered by Irene who greeted him warmly, with the traditional wish, "Good Shabbat." She wore a simple dress of soft wool that set off the ivory of her smooth skin. He raised her hand to his lips. "Good Shabbat," he replied softly, which made the blush of pink on her face turn a shade or two darker. Martin took off his cap, smoothed back his light brown hair, and let her help him out of his heavy coat.

"Come," she said, her smile deepening, as she ushered him quickly into the modestly furnished, but comfortable sitting room. A wide archway led into the large dining room and offered a view of the festive, sparkling Shabbat table. Still addressing him formally as Herr Blomberg, she introduced the stranger to her mother and father, her brother Arthur, his wife Rosa, brother

Joseph and wife Erna, and of course, to the son of the second cousin, Albert Spanier. The latter, a short, bookish-looking young man with thick, steel-rimmed glasses, dark hair, and a matching mustache, returned Martin's firm handshake and offered a cool but polite, "I am very glad to meet you."

Next, Martin met sister Lucy, who was all aglow holding hands with her fiancé, Max, a vivacious, bright, and jolly fellow, with a head as bald as a billiard ball. Martin liked him immediately, and had the feeling he would get the man's support in his quest to make Irene his wife.

"Good Shabbat," Martin addressed the assembled family, "I am glad and grateful to be here. Thank you," he said and bowed slightly in the direction of his hostess.

Toni acknowledged the stranger's gesture with a faint smile and a nod. She turned to her daughter, handed her the box of sweets, and said to her, "Please take your guest to the table. The sun has set; Shabbat is here."

Quickly everyone was seated, except for Toni. She stood at the far end of the table with its pearl-white damask linens, crystal glasses filled halfway with red wine, white dishes, and antique silverware. She looked at the lovely table with pride. It had taken her almost two decades of saving pennies to acquire the beautiful setting with which to honor the arrival of Shabbat and to celebrate holy days.

With a graceful motion, she covered her head with a triangle of time-aged lace. She struck a wooden match, lit the two white candles in their silver holders, and closed her eyes. With her arms outstretched, she made a circle over the candles. A moment later, in a voice strong and firm, she offered the ancient Hebrew blessing welcoming Shabbat: "*Boruch atoh adanoi alauhenu melech haolom . . .*"

When she had seated herself, the host rose to his feet, raised his glass, and said the blessing over the wine. The guests responded with Amen. Next, Herman reached for the silver basket with the napkin-wrapped challah, the special Shabbat bread, said the blessing, broke off a piece of it, and passed the basket on to his guests.

As if on cue, Ana Marieke appeared with a big tureen of chicken soup which she placed in front of Toni who started to ladle it into the bowls in front of her. With the blessings and prayers said, a lively conversation immediately buzzed among the table. Before Martin had taken a second spoonful of the delicious broth, Herman addressed him with his first blunt question.

"Irene told us that you come from Breslau. Tell us a bit about you and your family."

Martin placed his spoon carefully on the side of his plate. On the inside he chuckled at the not-so-subtle approach that would lead to the discovery of his character, his background, religion, and if at all possible the condition of his teeth. With a touch of his secret mirth reflecting in his voice, he turned to face his host, and replied in a light tone, "I have never been married and live by myself. I have my printing business which I started seven years ago with financial help from my generous father. I employ four master printers and each year I take on a couple of apprentices who then go on to other shops. We print anything from stationery to soccer programs. Blomberg Printing has a good reputation and business comes to us with astonishing regularity. We never stand still." He paused for a moment, and with a big grin added, "I guess I have ink in my veins. I don't sit in a fancy office; I work side by side with my people in the plant; I love being a printer."

All conversation at the table had stopped, all eyes were on him; the family was all ears. He sidestepped the question about his father's profession by simply saying that he had retired from his business activities and was watching over his investments. He briefly mentioned his siblings by saying that his brother Eugene lived in Prague where he managed his wife's transportation company. One sister made her home in Berlin, and the other two lived not far from Breslau.

Between talking, he managed to finish his soup. He was helping himself to the traditional Friday-night roasted chicken surrounded by glazed carrots and potatoes which Ana Marieke passed around on a big platter, when Toni spoke up.

"Tell us about your bar mitzvah and about the synagogue you and your family attend."

Apparently the Burgers had taken it for granted that he was Jewish. He had expected that question and had rehearsed his answer. Blending half-truths with a few fibs, topped off with good intentions, he dove in headfirst.

"Well," he said thoughtfully, looking down at his plate, "this will take some time explaining. I don't wish to monopolize the dinner conversation, so I'll keep it brief for right now."

He raised his eyes, looked at Toni, smiled, and said, "My mother and father come from very different backgrounds. As a matter of fact, I don't know much about them. I don't have the kind of family life all of you enjoy. All I know is that they have had little Jewish training, if any, in their respective homes. In their marriage, my father went one way and left my mother to her own doings. I remember going to the synagogue with my mother a few times as a boy on holidays. But I have certainly not led a traditional Jewish life, not even a reformed one. We all grew up without any kind of religious training, and I can't change that. But I am most willing to catch up on my spiritual education, especially once I am married."

There, he had said it!

With that, he flashed a bright smile and a wink at Irene. No one had to be a mind reader to understand his intentions and one look at Irene's flushed face and glowing eyes sealed the deal. Toni looked at her oldest daughter with worried, questioning eyes; she would have to have a good talk with her. What was this attraction to the stranger? Curiosity? Infatuation? Irene had not paid any attention to Albert, her dinner partner, and had kept her eyes riveted on the soldier's face. What could possibly be wrong with this nice young man, this Albert Spanier? Toni knew where he came from and highly approved of his family. Like her own people, the Spaniers were Sephardic Jews whose ancestors had fled Spain during the Inquisition, wandering here and there, until about 135 years ago when they had settled in Upper Silesia. Toni sighed to herself and thought of her mother's words, "Little children, little problems; big children, big problems."

The conversation at the table turned to the war—this terrible war that raged on in its fourth year, crippling and destroying so many lives. No longer did the German people think of their kaiser with pride and respect. Casualties mounted and the lack of supplies and adequate clothing added to the hopelessness of Germany winning the war. It was only a matter of time and Germany would have to surrender.

After Herman had offered the final blessing, he raised his glass. "To our brave men fighting a losing battle. May God see it fit to bring this senseless slaughter to an end, and may no harm come to our friends and loved ones. Amen." Everyone responded with a firm, "Amen."

After several cups of hot, strong tea along with some of Ana Marieke's delicious apple cake, the Shabbat celebration had come to an end. It was time to leave for the synagogue to attend Friday night services. Martin was unable to join the family; he had to report back to the garrison. He was running late already.

He approached his host and hostess, shook hands, and said, "Thank you so much for letting a stranger come into your home. I shall treasure this special evening, and I hope I may come again," he paused, hesitating for a moment as though searching for the right words for what he wanted to say. He cleared his throat, made a mock bow, and said haltingly, "Mr. and Mrs. Burger, I would like your permission to see your daughter; I think you understand."

Before Toni and Herman could answer, Irene appeared at his side. "If you can get away from soldiering tomorrow morning, come to the synagogue for services."

"I'll be there," Martin replied with a broad smile, "even if I have to desert."

"Young man," Herman interrupted, "we'll talk on Monday. I'll be at the tavern."

Martin replied that he could be there in the late afternoon and followed Irene into the small vestibule where she helped him into his overcoat and handed him his cap. "See you at the synagogue tomorrow. Be on time," she grinned mischievously.

Once again, he planted a kiss on her hand, held on to it, and said, "Oh, I'll be there; on time! I guess I am Jewish after all." The two young people looked at each other as though etching their faces into their memories forever. Reluctantly, Martin let go of her hand. "Goodbye, my dear, good Shabbat. See you tomorrow. And," he added, "we'll plan from there." She nodded with a pleased look in her eyes and a mysterious *Mona Lisa* smile played around her lips.

It was nine o'clock, after Friday night services, when the Burgers let themselves into their home above the tavern, glad to be back in its warmth after their walk in the icy, moonlit night. Irene and Lucy said good night to their parents with a peck on their cheeks and went to their bedroom.

Lucy had hardly closed the door, when she said in a low voice, "You better come clean with me. It sure looks like you're really taken with this Martin Blomberg and he is with you. But you've only known him for two days. Aren't you rushing romance a bit? You better find out something about him. He certainly isn't from around here, and you know how Mother and Father are . . . " her voice trailed off as she looked worriedly at her older sister.

Irene was hanging up her dress in the wardrobe the girls shared, undressed quickly, slipped into a soft flannel nightgown, and looked at her little sister with shining eyes.

"You're right. I feel something in him I've never felt before from any man. And he is more than serious about me. As far as knowing all about him, well, look at you and Max. Just because your fiancé is the third cousin of a third cousin of one of Mother's relatives and is now a partner in Arthur's store, doesn't mean he is a sterling character. The fact is that you like him, love him."

Irene hopped into bed, cuddled beneath the cozy quilt, and before Lucy could reply, she continued thoughtfully, "I have come to the conclusion that the best references, knowing where a man is from, and how nice he appears to be, and to whom he prays, don't really mean that much. Only when you are married and live with a man will you discover what and who he is. That's a risk every woman takes. Courting days are not married days. All we can do is trust our intuition, test ourselves even if our parents disagree."

"Well," shot back Lucy who had settled into her own bed, "our parents only want the best for us. They want us to be safe and happy."

Irene reached for Lucy's hand across the narrow space between their beds and held it in a firm grip. "I know they want the best for us, but they also want the best for themselves. They don't want to deal with having someone in the family whose lifestyle may not match theirs; someone whose beliefs may be different, someone not from the *neighborhood*. They don't want things to change; they want to be comfortable." Irene paused. With a deep sigh she added, "Especially, Mother."

The room fell silent for a while; both young women were lost in their own thoughts. Irene was surprised when her sister spoke up. "You know, Irene, I have been thinking about our family and how we live. We don't have any gentile friends. We don't visit with anyone who is not Jewish. Actually, we know little about people, about the rest of the world. You said once you felt like a canary in a cage, allowed to sing but not to fly. I am beginning to understand what you meant."

"That's right," Irene interrupted. "Everything is fine and good as long as we stay in our cage. But I am going to fly out of my cage one day. I just hope they won't sit *shiva* for me . . . they won't tear their clothes and sit in sackcloth and ashes for eight days. That would banish me from my family forever. In their eyes, I would be dead."

Lucy's mouth dropped open. "No! No! They wouldn't do that," Lucy looked at her sister with eyes drowned in fear.

Irene gave Lucy's hand a reassuring squeeze and turned off the small brass lamp on the nightstand between their beds. "Let's not create problems. Things usually work out if we leave them alone. Let's sleep on it," she yawned. "You know Ana Marieke always says, Man plans and God laughs. Wait and see! Good night, Lucy, happy dreams."

Irene turned on her side, facing the window and closed her eyes, shutting out the cold light of the wintry moon. She started her dream.

Chapter Three

OUTSIDE THE NEXT morning, winter raged on. Thick snowflakes, blown about by a blustery Siberian wind settled on eyelashes and beards, and hastened the steps of the faithful souls on their walk to attend Sabbath services.

There was barely a seat left in the small synagogue that served the Lubitz Jews. The men with their *tallis* (prayer shawl) draped around their shoulders and the *yamulka* (cap) on their heads, occupied the pews on the main floor. The women's place was upstairs in the balcony. Irene had never voiced her dislike of this ancient custom of separating men and women who came to worship—together. Why couldn't the husband sit next to his wife, the father next to his daughter, or the mother next to her son?

Only once had she confided to Lucy that this separation of male and female made her feel as though men thought women to be unclean, that worshiping God was something not done while sitting next to a woman.

Lucy thought about it for a moment, then with a quick grin on her face made light of her sister's concern. "Well," she giggled, "look at it this way: the balcony is closer to Heaven, closer to God." Irene had to laugh at Lucy's humorous simplification of a custom so deeply rooted in orthodox tradition. She informed her sister that she knew for a fact that in big cities, reformed synagogues had sprung up which had eliminated some of the outdated laws of the Talmud, and that men and women sat together during services. She added prophetically that one day she would belong to such a temple.

With prayer books in hand, the Burger women found their seats in the balcony where the unpleasant odor of wet wool hung heavily in the air. Irene slipped out of her winter coat, draped it over the back of the pew, and craned her neck, scanning the lower floor, searching for Martin. He was not there. Disappointed, she leaned back in her seat and waited for services to begin.

But Martin, minus a *tallis*, was there. He sat in the last row of pews near the door, tucked away beneath the women's balcony— out of sight.

The rabbi and the cantor appeared from a side door. The rabbi stepped up to the pulpit and started services by saying a blessing welcoming Shabbat. Prayers and readings from the Torah were intermingled with the chantings of the cantor. Listening to him was Irene's favorite part of any celebration. The cantor of this small congregation had a rich and irresistible, moving voice that seemed to start at his toes, travel upward in his slight body, and emerge as a soul-wrenching sob that contained all the pain and suffering as well as the joy of the Children of Israel. His singing made her aware of a deep connection to her ancestors, a feeling of belonging. At that moment she understood the true meaning of being a Jew.

Irene had been restless during the long service and was more than glad to hear the rabbi give the final prayer. The women gathered the coats and shawls they had shed, and went down the stairs to meet their men for the walk home. Just as Herman joined his wife and daughters in the small lobby, Martin stepped out of the shadow from behind the door. Surprise and pleasure flashed on Irene's face as he approached the Burgers.

"It's been a long time since I've been to a synagogue. This service brought back some faint memories. I am glad you invited me," he smiled at Irene. He shook hands all around, and asked for permission to walk home with them. Herman nodded a polite yes, while Toni wrapped herself in an air of injured resignation. Irene was in a merry mood as she and Lucy, with Martin in the middle, led the way out into the gray wintry Saturday. It had stopped snowing, but the cold wind would not let up as it hurried people along with forceful gusts blowing on their backs.

Martin turned to Irene and said regretfully, "I am on duty today and all day tomorrow. Rumors are flying around like paper snakes. I heard that several trainloads of wounded and exchange soldiers are expected this afternoon. No one is on leave."

Irene just nodded and kept her eyes away from his. She had so wanted to take his arm, but with her parents following behind, she knew it would have been interpreted as making an improper advance. It just wasn't done. Instead she buried her hands into the round coziness of her silk-lined fur muff.

Keeping the conversation going, Lucy told Martin that her fiancé, Max, had been to Breslau once, visiting his married sister and had returned to Lubitz full of wonder and delight about the big city. Passionate about music, he had attended several symphony concerts and a performance of *La Bohème*. In a rare moment when the two had been alone, he had hinted, that once they were married, he might make a daring move and settle in the capitol of Silesia.

"I haven't said anything to my parents about that yet," Lucy confessed shyly, "Mother wants all her children to live in walking distance from home; she won't be happy when she hears about it—if it really happens, that is." She chatted on how much she liked living in a small town, contrary to her sister, who wanted big-city excitement.

Irene had contributed little to the conversation, except to agree with Max who apparently also yearned for the arts and the music Breslau had to offer.

When they reached the entry to the Burgers' house, Martin once again thanked everyone and told Mr. Burger that he would see him at the tavern on Monday. Toni didn't linger at the door, but ushered her family hurriedly into the house. "Come on, come on, it's cold, and Ana Marieke has our noon meal on the table," she said impatiently, barely glancing at the soldier who bowed once more, winked at Irene when everyone's back was turned, and went on his way.

Ana Marieke had heard the Burgers coming up the stairs and was waiting to help them out of their bulky coats and overshoes. "Lunch is ready," she announced brightly. "Go and sit down; I'll bring it before it gets cold."

The conversation during the noon meal was a bit strained. No one mentioned Irene's soldier, and it was only Lucy's light chatter about this, that, and nothing that took the chill off the mealtime. After a serving of the dessert, a stewed cinnamon-apple compote and hot tea, the older Burgers settled down in the living room for some quiet time. Toni obeyed the Sabbath law of not working on this holy day—not even turning the light switches on or off. Ana Marieke had to do that. As had been the custom since Lucy's engagement, the two sisters left to visit their brother Arthur and his family; Max would be there.

No sooner had the girls left the room, when Toni turned to her husband and rushed to say, "I want you to cut off our daughter's misguided romance with this Martin Blomberg when he comes to see you Monday. He very cleverly side-stepped our questions about his bar mitzvah, and about his parents. I bet you five marks that they are not practicing Jews—if they are Jews at all. He is an undesirable suitor for Irene. And," she added stubbornly in a cranky voice, "I refuse to have him back at our house."

With kind and gentle eyes, Herman looked thoughtfully at his wife of more than three decades. Of slim build, she was all of five feet, two inches tall with a full head of cinnamon-brown hair. In spite of a few strands of silver showing, she still looked very much the young bride to him. Raised in a small village not far from Lubitz, the oldest of seven children, she was used to endless chores. Their early years together were times of hardship and penny-pinching. Toni had worked side by side with him to bring the run-down tavern with its aging distillery equipment back on its feet. As soon as the tavern flourished, Toni took on the neglected second floor of the house. She scraped and stripped doors and walls; she puttied and painted and polished until the house glowed with rich warmth and comfort, reflecting the care it had been given.

Toni had raised four children, kept a kosher house, faithfully obeyed the orthodox laws of her God, and never let up on good manners and good grooming. She believed that every one needed to learn a trade, and placed Irene and later Lucy with the local millinery and dressmaker shop for a two-year apprenticeship. Irene took to it like a bird to flight, and emerged a master of the trade. Lucy showed no interest in stitchery, limping along with clumsy hands until the dressmaker came to her rescue declaring her a hopeless case with needle and thread. Lucy was elated. "At least I know how to sew on a button and mend a tear. That's all I need to know," she announced with glee. Her mother put her to work in the business; teaching her the art of bookkeeping. Lucy liked that a lot better than making hats and dresses.

Joseph became an apprentice at the local hardware store and Arthur was introduced to the dos and don'ts of running a dry-goods business. Both young men liked the idea of being merchants and were eager to be on their own. Joseph eventually bought a small hardware store in a neighboring town, and Arthur became a partner, and later sole owner, of Lubitz Dry Goods.

Toni had done well with her children; no one had ever rebelled against parental edicts, nor had they ever gotten into any kind of youthful mischief. They were good children. She was pleased. Her own needs were simple and her demands on her husband were few. In all the years they had been together, he almost always agreed with her and honored her wishes. He couldn't remember having had an argument over something major, ever. But he also knew that she was set in her ways, rarely concerned herself with matters of the world, and was content in her own. Joseph and Arthur had both married young women of whom she approved—as she had of Lucy's choice. This was going to be difficult, Herman imagined. It might even get to a point where he would have to put his foot down and go over his wife's pretty head.

"Toni, my dear," he started slowly, "you will have to look at Irene and the young man in a different light. Please listen to me before you say anything," he said firmly. Toni's hazel eyes sparkled combatively behind her glasses. She was about to interrupt him.

"No," Herman insisted, "please wait and hear me out."

He leaned forward from his comfortable easy chair and reached for his wife's small hands. "Irene has been a model daughter. She was easy to raise, obeyed us, and never gave us a moment of heartache. Now she is twenty-eight years old. And the time has come when she will go her own way, even oppose us. That look of determination in her eyes is not about to go away, and that goes for Martin as well."

He paused for a moment and let go of her hands. Settling back in his chair, he continued. "Listen my dear, I am almost sixty years old, and have been around enough people to know that we cannot judge a man by his religion. We cannot judge a man by the choice of his God and even more importantly, we must not judge him by the kind of parents he has. He is a person all of his own making.

A lot of 'bad boys' came out of 'good homes'—Jewish or otherwise. And, I can tell you without a doubt in my mind, young Blomberg is a decent, good human being," Herman paused.

Clearing her throat, Toni raised her hands as though to ward off any further talk.

"Just one more thing," Herman ignored her gesture. "I am not going to stand in the young man's way to court Irene. If I do, they will see each other behind our backs; they will sneak and lie. I don't want that to happen. I am not a fortuneteller, but Toni, my dear, please get used to it," he predicted with a smile on his face, "and learn to live with it gracefully. This is not the yesterdays where people were locked into a planned life. I remember an old Chinese saying, 'A planned life cannot be lived, it can only be endured.' Our daughter is following her heart. It is her life. We cannot stand in her way; we must let her go."

Toni was dumbfounded for a moment. Not only was this an extraordinarily long speech for her husband, but he had disagreed with her openly and firmly on a highly important matter. Judaism and its practices were indelibly imprinted on her. She was steeped in tradition. She had no quarrel with people of a different faith; she just didn't want her daughter to marry one of them. It was unthinkable to her. Simply unthinkable.

She sighed, shook her head in wordless protest, closed her eyes for a moment to hide the hurt she felt, and finally responded to her husband's challenge in a quiet and defeated voice.

"I am not happy to hear you say that. I'll go along with your wishes. However, I shall have a talk with Irene—mother-to-daughter—I won't threaten and I won't be angry. But I will tell her that I believe in marrying one's own kind; there is a great comfort and a continuity in that. Even if the young man has somewhat of a Jewish background, he certainly has not lived a proper Jewish life. He . . . he's wrong . . . " her voice broke off in a sob and tears welled up in her eyes.

"Toni," Herman said, "we've just been through this. You must not have heard a word I've said." There was a ring of impatience in his voice. "Let me say it once more. It doesn't matter if his god is a seven-tailed comet or a ten-ton rock. He is a fine man. Our daughter has recognized that. And, in her own quiet way, she is going to do exactly what she needs to do. It will only hurt your relationship with her if you continue to be combative and quarrelsome. We can't live our children's lives, nor can we continue ours by living through them. Let things take their natural course, and be happy for her that she found a man she can love. She has certainly waited a long time for it."

Without looking at her, he pulled the soft wool afghan that was draped over one arm of his chair over himself and closed his eyes. "I am going to have a nap," he announced. "Why don't you put your mind to rest as well."

A hush fell over the room. Toni was at a loss. Instead, she reached for her prayer book that lay open on the side table next to the sofa and riffled through the pages until she located the woman's prayer she was looking for. Her lips moved quietly to the words her eyes were reading. Perhaps God would listen.

––––––––––––––

When Germany's arrogant and nearsighted Kaiser Wilhelm, in a moment of misguided loyalty, offered military support to Austria's squabble with Serbia, he started an avalanche of terror and misery that thundered across Europe. World War I was born.

The war was in its fourth year and, not unlike other military installations, unbridled chaos reigned at the Lubitz garrison and at the attached makeshift hospital. Rumors became reality when on Sunday three trainloads of wounded and dead soldiers arrived. They were the unlucky leftovers from the collapsed Eastern Front. The garrison's hospital was filled to overflowing and only those with serious injuries were given a bed. Invading offices and barracks, the rest had to be content with a thin mattress spread on the floor of an already crowded hall or cramped storage closet. The number of casualties was terrifying. The number of injured overwhelmed the few doctors and nurses and soon depleted the inadequate medical supplies. Urgent messages to headquarters for help and supplies went out, but replies were vague and empty. There was no end to the horrors of war—and no end to the war—in sight.

Martin's job was to identify the dead, pull their records, complete the required paperwork to document the untimely end of a life, and send a form letter to the bereaved family. As much as he hated his job, he was almost glad not to be around the moaning maimed to witness their suffering. Slowly, he made his way through the packed railroad cars, collecting identification tags and marking the corpses for shipping to various destinations.

He worked without stopping, and by the late afternoon he felt as lifeless as the dead bodies he had handled. Shaking himself, like a dog shaking off unwanted fleas from its hide, he realized that his nostrils were filled with the stench of dried blood and death. All day, his mind had argued and whirled with unanswered questions about life and about God. He puzzled over who or what made the decision about who lived and who died. Who had the right?

Depressed and sad, he jumped down from the railroad car, leaving the hollow-eyed face of Death behind as he rushed to his barracks. He sat on his cot for a moment, gathering himself for his visit with Herman Burger. He freshened up, put on a clean uniform (one of his father's tailor-made ones), and welcomed the cold, fresh air that accompanied him on his way to the town's center. It was five o'clock by the time he entered the tavern.

The place was humming with the sound of conversation. Men crowded around the bar, and most of the tables were occupied by early diners. He was glad that his favorite table in the far corner of the tavern was waiting for him. Herman Burger was busy filling the empty glasses of his customers with schnapps or beer. Martin would have to wait for the crowd to thin out before approaching him. Irene, however, had seen him at his table and danced her way through the crowd.

"Good evening, Herr Blomberg," she teased, "thank you for coming to the Lubitz Tavern. What may I bring you?" Irene's eyes sparkled with the pleasure of seeing him. He was rather good-looking, she had decided, in a sort of lived-in, bony way. He had strong features and an air of modest confidence about him. His hazel eyes were kind and his sense of humor and lighthearted-ness were catching.

"Good evening, Irene," he replied and kissed her hand. "May I have a bowl of your delicious soup, a piece of bread, and your company—and not necessarily in that order?" he grinned.

"I'll bring your soup and bread, but I can't sit down until the crowd is gone and until you have spoken to my father." She whirled away, her full peasant skirt whipping around her ankles. A white blouse set off her dark hair and smooth skin. She looked lovely, he thought—a bit like a Spanish dancer.

An hour later there were only three customers left and they had been served. Martin put his napkin down on the table, straight-ened up and approached Irene's father, extending his hand. "Good evening, Herr Burger, how are you?" Before the older man could answer, Martin rushed on, "I have been waiting impatiently for this moment. I know I am a stranger here, and it will take some time to prove to you and your family who I am, and that you can trust me with your daughter's hand. You already know that I am in love with her, and now I respectfully ask your permission to visit with her—in the company of a chaperon, of course."

Herman looked at the young man with searching eyes. The memory of having stood in front of Toni's father with the same request so many years ago flashed through his mind again.

He gave a quick chuckle, "I know how you feel, young man. Believe it or not, I've been there, too, and I remember it well." He gave the top of the counter a quick wipe with a white towel, put it down, and said, "Come, let's get off of our feet." He led the way to Martin's table and the two men sat down, facing each other.

Without ceremony, Herman plunged right in. "Against my wife's wishes, Herr Blomberg, I herewith give you permission to court my daughter, Irene, who, I believe, is quite fond of you already. I want to spend some time with you and learn more about you. I am not worried whether or not you are a Jew. I sense that you are not committed to anything, and that it would be easy for you to follow your wife's religious beliefs for no other reason than to please her and us."

Herman stopped to greet two men who had entered the tavern.

"I'll make it short for now. As I mentioned before, you may visit with Irene, but no serious decision will be made until this war is over."

"Thank you, Herr Burger. I am looking forward to the time I will spend with her. I would never consider marriage until I am out of this uniform and able to start married life under normal circumstances," Martin replied earnestly.

Herman sighed and said, "I want to warn you that my wife bitterly opposes a future union between the two of you. Please understand, it is completely against her principles. Try not to be offended by the cool treatment you will receive. Don't let it bother you too much. When she sees her daughter's happiness— when she realizes that you are a fine individual indeed—the ice will melt. Slowly, perhaps, but it will melt. My wife may be somewhat fanatical about her life as a Jew, but she is not stupid, just stubborn."

Herman rose from his chair and offered his hand to his daughter's new suitor. "I have to wait on my customers. We'll talk again soon. I'll tell Irene to join you." Martin shook his hand and watched him stop his daughter on her way to the kitchen, talk to her briefly, and walk to the bar.

Irene looked at Martin from across the room. As their eyes met, they read each others' faces and Irene nodded at him with a smile as big as his. Her face was bright as sunshine as she made her way to his side.

The courtship of Martin Blomberg, the stranger, and Irene Burger, the nice Jewish girl, had officially begun.

Chapter Four

MARTIN WAS THE last to leave the tavern. As soon as he could get away from the garrison for a few hours, he would return and take Irene to Café Bonaparte three doors down from the tavern, where they could visit in full view of all.

Irene and Lucy helped Herman close up for the night and went upstairs. Irene thanked her father profusely for giving his permission to see Martin. Herman held out his cheek for his good night kiss, and then took her gently by her shoulders. "He is as good a man as they come, I am sure of that. But you know that your mother is violently opposed to this romance. She wants a traditional Jewish son-in-law, preferably from the neighborhood."

"Father," Irene broke in, keeping her voice down, "doesn't Mother know that her own sons no longer live her way? Their kitchens are so much hit-and-miss kosher, you might as well call them *trefe* (unclean). The daily morning and evening prayers have gone out the window. The boys keep their stores open on Saturday, and they only go to Shabbat services if there is a bar mitzvah going on. They are living *their* way; but they're still good people. And," she added with a frustration-laced voice, "as much as I love my mother, she cannot expect me, or any of her children, to be an extension of all that she is."

Herman cupped her face gently in his hands and said, "There is no right, there is no wrong. We won't solve this problem tonight, nor any day soon. Be about your way; but don't run. Go slowly. Time and the future are on your side. And for now, get some sleep, my dear. Good night."

Irene gave him a mock salute with the flip of her hand. When she walked into her room, she was glad to find Lucy asleep. Great! She thought—no more talking tonight. Wrapped in her dream and speculating on the future, she fell asleep. It had been quite a day.

Two long days later, Martin walked into the tavern with a tiny bouquet of dried straw flowers in his hand. He approached Irene who was clearing a table in preparation for dinner guests.

He kissed her hand, presented the flowers, and said, "If this were Breslau, they would be red roses. You have no idea how I had to search to come up with these," he grinned.

"Oh, I have no doubt," Irene laughed. "This is a small town in upper Silesia. It is the depth of winter and you want roses? We're not known for our flower shops at any time of year."

She wore a simple tweed skirt with a matching jacket. A rose-colored blouse peeked out from around her neck and added a soft hue to her ivory skin. Ever since her apprenticeship with the dressmaker, she had made her own clothes and those of her mother and sister, as well. She loved to create things with her hands, and when she completed the time-consuming, fine hand-finishing work on a garment, she let her mind roam, imagining the fashion salons of Europe's sophisticated capitols. She saw herself sitting on dove-gray, velvet sofas in posh salons lit by enormous chandeliers, and furnished with sparkling tall mirrors in baroque gold frames. Willowy, sleek models showed off glamorous clothes to an elegant audience of beautiful women. Sometimes she imagined herself to be the designer of the fashion house. At other times she pretended to be a member of the fashionable group of onlookers. Irene had a busy mind, a far-reaching imagination, and a stubborn determination to make her dreams come true.

She reached for a woolen shawl and draped it around her shoulders. Turning to Martin she said, "I'll be warm; we're just going next door. Winter coats are for long walks. They are heavy and they weigh me down."

Martin stood straight as an arrow and offered her his arm. "Shall we go then? Coffee and cakes are awaiting us." Arm in arm, they stood in front of Herman to say goodbye. One look at their bright faces and the glow in their eyes convinced him, without a doubt, that the die was cast. An ancient saying from the mystical depth of the Kabala flashed through his mind: *Seven times blessed and seven times sealed*. Toni's army of objections would not stand a chance against the ironclad armor of their love.

Herman cleared the lump from his throat, ignored the suspicious moisture in his eyes, and said, as gruffly as he could, "Well, go on then. But, Irene, be back by five to help your sister in the kitchen."

As he watched the two young people bounce out of the tavern, he could have sworn that their feet didn't touch the ground.

Warm, chocolate-scented air greeted them at the café. They chose a window table and ordered coffee and eclairs from the stocky waitress, who had a friendly face and blond braids that reached below her waist.

"Well," Martin looked at Irene across the table, "here we are! As the saying goes—alone at last, well, almost. And," he added with that mischievous look dancing in his eyes, "may I just plow ahead and get a few things off my chest?"

"Martin," she replied smiling, "I am just as practical as you are. We are here to find out about each other. So, let's get started."

He nodded and waited until they had been served. With his arms crossed, resting on the edge of the table, he hunched over.

Leaning toward her and keeping his voice low, he began to talk, slowly and introspectively. "I am a simple man. I am not good at diplomacy and clever conversation. You already know why I am here—I am in love with you. I want to marry you. I want to tell you about my strange family. But foremost, you must know that you are *not* marrying my family, you're marrying me. You come first, always." He paused and took a sip of his coffee.

Irene's face flushed with pleasure. "In this case, I like simple. Go on," she urged.

"I really don't know much about my parents, and—come to think of it—children rarely know the true inner workings of their mothers and fathers. So, let me tell a little of what I think I know. Obviously, you will discover a lot more when you meet them."

First he spoke of his mother who remained the peasant girl she had been when she married Friedrich, a young man who had left the poor, life-strangling village to make his fortune. When he returned two years later, his pockets jingling with gold pieces, he asked for the hand of the most beautiful girl in Loden—a tiny hamlet somewhere in Saxonia. Her father was a potato farmer who scrambled to make a meager living on a few acres of over-worked soil, hiring out as a farm hand and carpenter whenever he could. He had fathered nine children, of which Henrietta was the youngest.

"She was only nineteen years old when she married my father and she had no idea of the kind of life he had in mind for her. My father brought his pretty new wife to a huge, ten-room, elegantly furnished flat in a popular residential area in Breslau, expecting that she would embrace the world he had prepared for her." Martin sighed deeply and shook his head. "It didn't work. Except to dust and polish, she never set foot in the carefully appointed rooms. As if that part of the house were only a showcase, and she its caretaker, the doors were locked and she lived only in the kitchen."

He went on to describe his colorful father, who called himself Baron Friedrich Wilhelm von Blomberg. Apparently, no one had ever doubted or challenged the authenticity of his noble heritage. "The man is six foot four inches tall with a true Bismarck face and a matching handlebar mustache. He is dressed by the best tailors in Europe; his shoes and Homburgs come from London and his shirts are handmade. For added effect, he walks with a silver-handled rosewood cane, and makes it his practice to know everybody who is anybody.

"From what I've heard, he has used highly unconventional business practices to amass his fortune and he has gotten away with it. And, although he has become quite the philanthropist in his own odd ways, he still plays his version of the shell game every chance he gets—just for the fun of it. In spite of that, he is well liked in his city and is almost always the center of attention at any gathering."

Martin stopped talking, and while he attacked his eclair, Irene put down her coffee cup and said, "I already like your father. He seems to be quite a rascal and I can't wait to meet him. I have grown up in such a straight-laced, hard-working, no-nonsense, tradition-burdened family, that I welcome some color in my life.

"My parents were quite poor in the first ten years of their marriage. Raising four children and nursing a neglected business back to life was a daily challenge which they faced with reliance on each other and great determination. My mother is a good person, but she never really learned to laugh, to be light-hearted, or to keep an open mind. She judges people by the degrees of piety with which they uphold the laws of the Talmud, study the holy Torah, and live within the walls of orthodox Judaism. Sometimes, I am amazed how well she gets along with Ana Marieke—a devout Catholic. I suppose good old Ana has never been a threat to her beliefs. What little social life my parents have takes place on Jewish holidays, with family and

sometimes folks from around here. At least I meet different
people at the tavern and on market days when I can chat with
the merchants with whom we trade. But that's all superficial. I
don't really know them."

"Well," Martin chuckled, "that will change drastically when
you meet my family. My three sisters all married wealthy widowers
without children and they lead the interesting lives of the privileged. They travel extensively, have villas and flats in France,
Italy, and England, and collect fascinating people like others
collect stamps. You'll have this other world waiting for you." He
paused and looked at his watch. "Next time we meet, we'll pick
up where we left off. We only have a few minutes left before I
deliver you back to your father. So let me ask you this—plain and
simple: Will you marry me when this war is over and when the
time is right?"

Irene looked at him with that secret, quirky little smile of hers
and replied, "You already know that I will. What we are doing
now, and will keep on doing, is to catch up with each other. By
the time we get married, all of our skeletons will be out of their
closets, most puzzles unraveled, and a few secrets shared. Let's
not tell all of it, but keep some surprises for married life," she
blushed and reached for his hand.

"Careful," he joked, giving her hand a quick squeeze. "Lubitz
is watching and you could get the reputation of being a fast
woman."

"Oh, well," she smirked, "let them talk. Gossip is the spice of
small-town life, but no one takes things too seriously here."

He paid the check and they said goodbye to the young
waitress. Hand in hand, they walked slowly in the direction of
the tavern, savoring their time together. At the first stroke of five
from the clock in the city-hall tower, Martin delivered his date.
He was on time.

March roared in full of bluster with promises of spring. A brisk wind scattered the big white clouds around in the sky, making room for the sun to peek through occasionally, helping the people of Lubitz to forget the grayness of winter. But no amount of sunshine could ease the despair and pain of the war that kept on demanding its due in human lives, broken bodies, and economic hardships.

Martin and Irene's courtship came to an instant halt when, just two days after the couple's first *tête-à-tête* at the café, Martin sent word to her that he was being shipped out to the Western Front—not to fight, but to work in several field hospitals' record sections. He would help with the growing mountain of paperwork and keep accurate accounts of the injured and the dead. He promised to write and hoped that his letters would reach her.

Earlier, he expressed his concern for the gradually failing communication systems between the battle fronts and their head-quarters—no different than the broken links in the crumbling supply lines. The lack of food, clothing, medical supplies, ammuni-tion, and equipment would eventually break the spirit of the kaiser's armies. Soldiers were already defecting in considerable numbers. Leaving their units, they took refuge where they could, often hiding out with farmers. Then, dressed in peasant clothes, they slipped back into Germany and eventually returned to their homes.

"Many of the foot soldiers looked almost enviously at the defectors and viewed their disappearance as an act of courage rather than a lack of courage. All of this," Martin wrote in his first letter, "is bringing our armies to their knees. The length of the war has taken its toll. Morale is low, discipline is shaky, and the old 'Hurrah-Hurrah our kaiser' has gone out of their weary hearts. We are losing this war, and our emperor does not want to acknowledge it."

He continued to describe the dismal conditions of the bloody western front and the sheer misery of the muddy foxholes, while expressing his personal views on the folly of war. "Man has not changed much since the Stone Age," he lamented. "We are still killing each other off in the name of God, king, or emperor. Instead of throwing rocks, we have advanced to rifles, guns, cannons, and more. We can now kill with greater accuracy and in greater numbers." The tone of his letters, and the raw despair written between the lines, only increased as time went on.

Irene's missives to him were full of compassion and loving words to heal his wounded heart. She talked about the good side of man—the ordinary man—who despised war and conflict, who wanted nothing more than peace and the opportunity to follow his bliss. She wrote to him about her long-held dream, about the future, and the heartache of his prolonged absence from her life.

Needless to say, Toni was pleased with Martin's absence. Not that she wished him ill; of course not. She just hoped that Irene's infatuation with this stranger, now that he was out of sight, would dissipate like the fog in sunshine. In her daily prayers she even asked God to intervene and make Martin lose interest in Irene Burger. Soon after his departure to the front, she had asked her daughter to join her in the living room where a silver samovar of fragrant hot tea and a plate of Ana Marieke's melt-in-your-mouth butter cookies were waiting.

The two women chatted amicably about daily happenings and about the weather. They even threw in a bit of lighthearted town gossip. When they had exhausted their small talk, Toni refilled the fragile, flowery china cups with tea and started to broach her favorite subject.

"Irene, my dear," she began, a benevolent expression resting on her face, "I've lived a lot longer than you. I have seen a lot more of life and I have watched people fall in and out of love as quickly as the fading of a rainbow. I have seen marriages bloom; I have seen others wither. And," she reached for her daughter's hands, "I know the basic, the most important ingredient for marriage." Her voice rose to a fever pitch, became sharp, and matched the coldness that had crept over her face, "Always, but always, marry your own kind."

She paused for a moment and, before Irene could reply, went on to impart her parental advice. "Listen to me, and listen carefully. Adjusting to married life and making your marriage work is difficult enough—especially in the beginning. But at least, when you come from the same background, you have a great deal in common. That alone makes life much easier."

"Mother," Irene interrupted, pulling her hand away, "I have no intention of being rude. I have always honored your wishes. But this is different. I cannot and will not live my life through you. It is my life; my time to make decisions for myself. Right or wrong, I shall bear the consequences. You and I have been through all of this before and I have not changed my mind. As a matter of fact, now that Martin and I have spent some time together, I am more convinced than ever that he is the man I have waited for. I am at ease with him, as he is with me. I love him."

Toni made signs to interrupt, but Irene held up both hands as though to ward off a swarm of bees. "Please, Mother, hear me out; perhaps you will then understand me better." Irene leaned back against the velvety softness of the sofa and closed her eyes. When she opened them again, she looked straight at her mother. Her voice was gentle, but firm.

"Ever since I was a little girl, I have heard you say that I was different from Lucy. You said that I was a loner, a dreamer—that I was self-contained. You said that I was an obedient child, but stubborn and secretive about myself. All of these characteristics may have just come into full bloom. After all, I am twenty-eight years old."

Irene stopped, and this time she reached for her mother's hands with both of hers.

"Mother," she pleaded, her eyes getting moist, "It makes me unhappy to go against your wishes, but I shall marry Martin. I will always be a Jew, but I believe that there is more to life than rites and rituals. I love, respect, and honor both my parents, but I shall have to break away to be myself. So, please," she added, wiping away her tears with the back of her hand, "allow me to do that, and send me on my way with your blessings. And," she tried a touch of humor and a weak smile, "if I have chosen wrong and I fall on my face, you'll be the first to know. I promise to eat my words."

Toni shrugged her shoulders in helpless resignation, rose from her chair, and straightened her dress. "Well," she sighed deeply, "I've tried my best to plead my case, to make you see reality. Apparently, I have failed. You are my child and I wish you well. Just don't expect me to change my mind and to bubble over with joy and gladness. That is not going to happen any time soon. It may never happen. I shall have to console myself with the fact that I am not the first mother to be disappointed and hurt by the actions of her child." She closed the subject, letting a heavy note of tragedy creep into her voice .

Irene winced for a moment and took a deep breath. Rising, she felt the burden of guilt her mother had just poured upon her make its way through her being and then make its exit. As she reached out and put her arms around her, she felt her mother's body stiffen for a moment, but then relax.

"I love you, Mother," Irene said in a hushed voice.

"It's all right," Toni announced, patting her on her back as though soothing a cranky baby, "Who knows what's going to happen. Who knows what God has in mind for us."

And even though Toni insisted that her mind was not changed and that she was firm in her personal beliefs, Irene felt that the animosity her mother had displayed so openly had just turned into benign resignation. It was a step forward.

Chapter Five

APRIL ARRIVED ON a rainy day and kept the people of Lubitz busy running for their umbrellas one moment, and warming their bones in unseasonably warm temperatures the next. Early spring flowers pushed through the wintry earth as people shed their heavy coats and seemed to smile a little more. Life was easier, but the war kept dragging on, casting its far-reaching shadow of hopelessness, and darkening even the sunniest of days.

At the imminent approach of Passover, Irene and her sister, Toni, and Ana Marieke worked tirelessly, preparing the house for this special holiday. Every corner of the upstairs was swept and scrubbed, getting rid of the tiniest crumbs of breads and cakes. The plain white Passover dishes came out of their storage space to replace the ones used during the rest of the year. The day before the first Seder, the kitchen was attacked once more with broom and mop until Toni was satisfied that even the most miniscule speck of flour had met the dust pan. Stacks of matzo replaced bread; matzo meal and potato starch were used, exclusively, instead of flour. Special food was prepared. Ana Marieke baked delicious Passover cakes and pastries and, finally, the Seder table was set for the Burger family—all eight of them—to celebrate the flight of the Children of Israel from Egypt: eternal strangers looking for a home.

With Passover only one day away, activities had settled down and the house was silent. Irene's evening chores at the tavern were done and Lucy would be serving the few stragglers who came in for a late meal. The tavern would be closed during Passover.

Irene took a hot bath, slipped into a comfortable woolly robe, and stretched out on the chaise lounge in the attic bedroom. By the rosy light of a floor lamp, with its pink silken shade, she reread every one of Martin's letters—all twenty-seven of them. It was one way she felt close to him. She wrote Martin faithfully every day and practiced courtship by mail. It would have to do for now. Interestingly enough, writing about her feelings, her emotions, and her views on life, led her on a new path to self-discovery. She was astounded at the passion with which she reminisced about their magical meeting and talked about her love for him. She recognized a heightened strength in her convictions and purpose. She could watch herself grow.

Toni, on the other hand, stood still. She was the first to see the daily mail. She never commented on the letters her daughter received from her suitor, nor did she ever inquire about him. Gingerly, between thumb and forefinger—as though in danger of being contaminated by a dreaded disease—she handed Irene the envelopes. Toni had not brought up the subject of her daughter's intention to marry the stranger again, which was all right with Irene. Her silence was a blessing of sorts. Any further discussions on the subject would only lead down the same dead-end street and nothing would have been accomplished.

It had taken fifteen days for Martin's last letter to travel a mere two hundred kilometers. The roads from the east into Silesia were rendered almost impassable by the rain-fed mud that kept building into a swollen river of mire, trapping anything on wheels and anyone traveling on foot.

In his letters, Martin rarely dwelled on his work and the war— "Enough said already," was his comment. He wrote of the wonder of having found his future wife and of his deep love for her. He talked about his intentions of becoming a "Good Jew" for no other reason than to ease the strain between mother and daughter. "It doesn't matter to me which road I take," he wrote. "I believe there is only one destination. As long as we honor life, as long as we are kind to each other and the world around us, we will pass muster with whoever is in charge."

In plain and simple terms, he shared his innermost feelings with her, something, he confessed, he had never done before. "I realize that I have seldom talked about myself, but as I am writing to you, the floodgates of my thoughts have opened and keep spilling out all over this paper. One can only do that when feeling safe and comfortable with another person."

In turn, Irene wrote to him about her childhood and the early dream which, over the years, had taken on shape and form and had turned into a clear and precise vision. "The very first time we met," she wrote, "I saw my dream reflected in your eyes. It was a strange sensation—something like having wandered aimlessly about and, finally, finding the way home."

Wise for her years, she appreciated the separation which gave them both an opportunity to let their thoughts walk on paper. Their words revealed the key to their being; a documentation of themselves—something that might have been more difficult to accomplish face to face.

One of his letters was much shorter than the ones before. He apologized for being brief, going on to explain that he had been on duty for twenty hours and was desperate for some sleep. "It isn't the long hours that are so tiring. It's being in the never-changing atmosphere of pain and suffering. It is the pitifully inadequate conditions in our field hospital that leaves me with the energy of a wet rag. Help is so short," he said, "that the men from the administrative sections have been ordered to take over as nurses aides after their own work is done. That makes for a long day and night," he wrote, and went on to lament the fact that he was not the best nurse. "I cannot stomach the sight of blood and I could weep when I see the wounded and maimed bodies—and those vacant eyes of shell-shock victims. There is nothing left of their former selves. All that for the glory of the kaiser." He closed on a cheerful note, however. Rumors were afloat that the Lubitz soldiers would return to their garrison the moment their replacements arrived. "Not a moment too soon," was his comment, to which Irene heartily agreed

She envisioned him walking into the tavern with that mischievous look in his eyes and that irresistible grin on his face. She would be alone in the kitchen, of course, and would dare to fly into his arms. What a delicious thought. She believed that some of the tight-laced courtship etiquette, still being practiced, should have gone out with the bustle and high-button shoes.

"It is so restrictive, so Victorian," she complained to Lucy. "How can two people really get to know each other when they are always in the spotlight, always in the presence of others, being watched and overheard? It's time for change, time for parents to let go. People, our age especially, should be on their own.

"Look at you," she took a deep breath. "Unless Max is invited here, you meet him at Arthur's house for tea. The only time you are alone with him, for even a few minutes, is when Arthur returns to his store and Rosa has to go to the bathroom."

"You're funny," Irene giggled. "But I don't mind. Max and I are going to be married for a long time and we will soon get to know each other. I am not as curious as you, nor as thorough. I don't stew and chew over things as you do. I think I am more content with the way things are," she looked, somewhat questioningly, at her older sister.

Irene thought for a moment. "I guess you're right," she replied slowly, examining herself ruthlessly as she spoke. "I am not necessarily discontent, I would just like to see change in some social customs which have outlived themselves. What was 'good taste' fifty years ago has been abandoned along with the fashions of that time. Each generation will express itself in new and different ways. I believe we should take the best from the past and improve on it. It's not a revolution of turning our world upside down, it's just replacing a worn-out piece of elastic with a snappy new and springy one."

Lucy laughed out loud. "You should hear what you say. Though you may be right. I'll have to think about it. I like the sound of it."

"Lucy," Irene's eyes sparkled, "let me approach this in another way. How many times have you heard our mother and our father say how different things were when they grew up? How strict their parents had been and how little freedom they had? On and on we've heard stories comparing 'then' to 'now.' When we come into our own, we'll do the same thing. We'll just do it in purple."

Irene stopped to answer the soft knock on the door. Ana Marieke walked in with a tray in her hands. "I just finished the Passover baking," she announced, "and when I heard you talking, I thought we should have a midnight tea party and taste the freshly baked pastry. What are you doing up so late?"

"Oh," Lucy replied, "Irene wants to change the world. You came at the right time, we haven't gotten very far."

Ana Marieke took the chair away from the dressing table, placed it between the two beds, and sat down with the tray in her lap. "Here," she said, handing out cups of hot tea, "try the macaroons and the lemon sponge cake."

From the first day she came to live with the Burgers, Ana Marieke, the three-year-old Lucy, and the eight-year-old Irene took to each other like birds take to flight. Ana nursed them through their childhood illnesses, let the girls "help" her in the kitchen, and listened with an open heart to their growing pains.

More so than their two brothers, the girls became the children she never had. She stood by silently, not taking sides, watching Irene's struggle to leave the nest with a man of whom her mother did not approve—and observing Toni's stubborn refusal to give an inch.

Ana made a jerky little bow in response to the sisters' raving compliments about the pastry, then refilled her teacup. Facing Irene, she said, "I know what you two have been talking about. It's been on my mind, too. I don't like to see what's happening between you and your mother, but I understand both sides. When I first came here, I was overwhelmed by the passion with which your mother taught me the intricacies of keeping a kosher household. For each ancient law, for each rule, she explained the meaning to me. She impressed upon me how important it all was to her and to her family." Ana paused for a minute. Her face was soft as her eyes reached back into the past.

"I remember my surprise when she explained the reason for having three sets of dishes in a kosher kitchen: one set from which to eat dairy products only, one for meat, and, of course, the ones for Passover. She taught me how to bury a plate in ashes for a certain length of time when it had been contaminated by incorrect usage. I learned all about *kosher* and *trefe* and I follow the law to the extreme degree," Ana paused. Then she beamed, "If I weren't such a good Catholic, I'd make a fine orthodox Jew."

She became thoughtful for a moment and turned once more to Irene. "Your mother's beliefs are threatened because you made it clear that finding love with a good man is more important than tradition. You do what's right for you, Irene, but be gentle with the feelings of others. Let's put it to rest for now and not talk it to death."

Ana Marieke got up, returned the chair to its place, and picked up the tray. "I had better go to bed now. It's past midnight," she sighed, "and I go to five o'clock mass. I'll pray for you."

She patted Irene on the shoulder and, with a familiar gesture just like old times, she tucked her into her quilt. "Good night, happy dreams, and remember to be kind to each other."

Lucy had already fallen asleep. Grateful for Ana Marieke's presence, Irene smiled to herself and closed her eyes. She turned her thoughts to Martin as she waited for slumber to embrace her.

——————————

It wasn't until mid-May that Irene heard from Martin again. Confiding in no one, she kept her worries about his well-being to herself. She had no best girlfriend with whom to share her misery and she did not want to burden Lucy with her fears. Not that she was looking for answers or sympathy, she just wanted someone who would listen. But there was no one. So when Toni handed her an unusually thick envelope from Martin, a mountain of fear and phantom worries dropped from her heart. She slipped the letter into the pocket of her apron.

Reading his mail was almost like having a date. And even though the envelope threatened to burn a hole in her apron, she would wait until her day was done before savoring its contents. From the beginning she had established a routine for their date-by-letter event, and it never varied.

Alone in the bedroom, she shed her work clothes, washed her face, brushed her hair, dabbed a drop of *eau de cologne* on her wrist, and slipped into her cozy robe. She was ready.

Released from the confines of the envelope, eighteen pages of his writings tumbled onto her lap. She smoothed out the pages, put them in order, and began to read slowly, cherishing every word—making her visit with Martin last as long as possible.

"I am on night duty in the main ward tonight," Martin started out, "all is quiet—for a while, anyway. We received some medical supplies yesterday—sleeping pills among them. Our patients are finally getting much-needed rest, and, in turn, so do we.

"Let me answer your question about why I chose to become a printer. It will give you another insight into my father's wicked ways and my mother's hopelessly twisted and old-fashioned thinking. Please don't give up on me because of what I tell you about my parents, dearest. Remember, you are *not* marrying my family.

"I don't understand why my mother refused to participate in the life my father provided for her. She never stopped thinking, living, and acting like the dirt-poor peasant girl of her past. Apparently, she did not believe or appreciate that she had a wealthy husband, nor did she believe in education. As soon as each of her children completed tenth grade, she yanked us out of school and placed us into an apprenticeship so that we could learn a trade. And typical of the times, my three sisters became apprentices in a large dressmaker establishment. Mother decided that my brother, Eugene, and I should be printers, and marched us into a small print shop in downtown Breslau. Since we were both in the same class in school—my brother had skipped a grade—we started working at the same time. Eugene hated printing, but I could not have been more satisfied with her choice. I loved it. On Fridays, Mother appeared at our print shop, as well as at the dressmaker's, and collected the pitifully few marks we had earned in our lowly state of employment."

So began the telling of the strange events orchestrated by the Old Baron. "When my father heard of his children's fate, he immediately pulled one of his countless shenanigans out of his homburg—behind his wife's back, of course. He wanted his children to continue their education not in a public or even private school, but in a setting of his choice. He also wanted them to be introduced to social graces, art, literature, music, theatre. They would learn about the world of fashion and the lifestyles of the privileged.

"He appeared at the two places of our employment and, leaving a bundle of money behind, he swore our employers to secrecy. He told the owners that he intended to have his children return to their school and he gave them instructions to pay his wife the weekly earnings of their apprentices, and keep the rest of the money for themselves. He would return every month to fill their pockets—provided that his wife remained unaware of this new arrangement.

"Earlier, in one of his complicated and mysterious dealings, he had added the Golden Ram, in Breslau, to his collection of small, elite hotels. Acquiring hotels was one of his passions."

Irene stopped reading for a moment, dropped her hands into her lap, and envisioned the mischievous grin she was certain would have lingered on Martin's face when he wrote those words. After savoring the picture in her mind's eye for a moment, she picked up the letter and continued to read.

Martin went on to write that his father took over the Royal Suite in his Golden Ram, converted one of the large bedrooms into a comfortable school room and hired two tutors. "The girls and my brother were thrilled with that arrangement. But I loved my job, and I really wanted to be a printer. With some pleading and gentle persuasion, I convinced my father to let me attend his school three days a week and work in the print shop the other three."

He described how he had successfully avoided Madame Negri, a lively, petite *Parisienne*, who came every day to teach French and give piano lessons. "Foreign languages have never been my strength," he confessed, "and as much as I love music, Madame Negri had me declared 'hopeless' when it came to reading notes and learning to play the piano. Just the same, the five of us lived quite the life.

"Of course, as you may have guessed by now, my mother discovered the big secret by the third week, and from what I remember, there was a heated discussion between my parents.

The end result was that my father had his way, and my mother, bitter and resentful, retreated deeper into the vacuum of her existence. Where before, her attitude was impersonal and distant, it then turned to ice and she became unapproachable. Living at home was not pleasant."

Continuing to read, Irene learned how, two years later, Martin's father started to travel all over Europe with his children and their tutors, often staying away as long as three months at a time. The Old Baron showed his offspring London, Paris, Rome, and Madrid. He played with them on the French Riviera, blissfully cruised the Aegean and the Greek Islands with them, and saw to it that his daughters, especially, met the right people. And they did. "The next time we talk, I'll tell you all about them.

"I went on a couple of trips with my siblings, which I enjoyed," Martin wrote, "but I tired of it and, as uncomfortable as home was, I stayed put and completed all the requirements to become a full-fledged printer. I then went to work for a larger printing house, and, within the year, my father—unbeknownst to me—had bought the business. Typical! Well, dear one, you know the rest: Breslau Printing and Publishing has been mine for six years now."

Before he closed, he again mentioned that replacements were on their way and that he and his comrades would soon return to Lubitz. What he didn't tell her was the fact that each time he was sent to the front lines, he flirted with death and danger. Some of the makeshift field hospitals had been hastily abandoned as the German army retreated, and some of the dead and dying had been left behind enemy lines. Never certain of the enemy's exact position, often receiving outdated information from reconnaissance patrols, German rescue missions were caught in enemy fire. Those who were not killed were captured. It was on one of those night patrols that Martin and his men came face to face with danger.

In the black of night, a detail of six men crouched its way across a deserted battlefield and silently crawled through rows of abandoned, blood-soaked trenches. Coming out of a hollow, the hospital tent they were seeking loomed dark against the midnight landscape, one side leaning dangerously close to the ground, threatening to collapse. Martin was just about to signal his detail to enter the tent, when suddenly a man's deep snoring announced the presence of life.

Six men hit the ground and froze. The wit of the group whispered to Martin. "Do you know the difference between a Frenchman's snoring or a German's?"

Martin was in no mood for jokes, nor was he eager to discover who was who, and turned back. Ducking down, they retreated just as the tent came awake with the sound of loud voices speaking French.

It had been a close call, but it wasn't the first time. Many times, Martin and his men ran for cover—bullets flying around them like a swarm of angry wasps with the enemy at their heels. Once, six men went out on patrol and two came back. Martin was one of them. Each time a bullet whizzed by his head, each time he heard the warning whistling of a grenade about to explode nearby, and each time a comrade was hurt or killed, a burning rage boiled on his insides and tore at his heart. He cursed the war-making rulers of the world whose self-importance ignored the pain and misery their actions brought upon the rest of the world.

Carefully, Irene folded the tightly written pages, tucked them back in the envelope, and added it to all the other letters in their hiding place. She turned out the light and, before she fell asleep, her imagination took flight once again, and she traveled right along with the Old Baron and his brood. She walked the Champs Élysées, visited the Louvre, popped over to London, and stopped in Rome to visit the Forum Romano.

The make-believe hotels and villas excited her beyond antici-pation, and with unerring certainty, she believed that in her new life doors would open that she never knew existed.

She couldn't wait.

Chapter Six

ANA MARIEKE APPEARED in the tavern's kitchen carrying two shopping baskets. "Here," she said to Irene, handing her one of the baskets. "It's Friday market day, and a beautiful morning at that. Summer's here and you need to get out of the house. I told Lucy to take over for you, and we had better get going. With the shortage of food, there's no telling what we can find to buy."

Irene greeted her with a smile and feigned resignation, "Oh, well, I guess I'll go with you. After all," she joked, "You have been ordering me around all my life." She took off her apron, grabbed the basket, linked arms with Ana Marieke, and marched out into the sunshine.

It was late June, summer had arrived, and every inch of soil had been planted with vegetables. The flower boxes beneath the windows of the houses facing the town square had been turned into tiny vegetable plots. Onions, carrots, radishes, beans, and peas had replaced the geraniums and the pansies.

Lately, the number of vendors who displayed their goods in makeshift canvas-covered stalls, or under simple umbrellas, had shrunk as had the abundance of goods offered. The fun of bargaining had gone out as the war increased demands on the food supply. It was a seller's market. A few plump, fluffy chickens chattered from their wire cages, red-combed roosters crowed importantly, snow-white ducks and geese squawked and quacked, announcing their presence. Brightly colored crochet tea cozies and egg warmers, handmade gingham aprons, knitted caps, scarves, and mittens, lived in harmony with small crates of eggs, jars of thick cream, and freshly churned butter wrapped in pieces of clean, moist linen. Potatoes, root vegetables, and burlap sacks of dried beans vied for attention. A knife sharpener, a cobbler, and a tinker plied their trade next to an onion-and-herb dealer who shared a stall with a man selling tinny, little wind-up toys.

People milled about and stopped to gossip, lamenting the war, comparing prices and the size of a turnip. Over the years Ana Marieke had made friends among the vendors who always saved something for her. After she bought eggs, butter, and potatoes, she headed for the woman from whom, for as long as she could remember, she bought the Burgers' Shabbat chickens.

"Dorothea, how are you?" she greeted the round, apple-cheeked woman. "Did you save your best chickens for me?"

"Yes, yes," chirped the woman, displaying a toothless grin. "Always the best for Ana Marieke and her family." She released the latch on one of the two wire cages next to her, grabbed a big, squawking, brown-feathered hen by her feet, and holding down its wings, offered it to her customer. With knowing fingers, eyes closed in concentration, Ana slowly probed the warm body of the loudly protesting chicken.

"I'll take this one and one more just like her. There will be eight for dinner tonight."

"Could you possibly make that nine for dinner?" a male voice broke in.

Irene's head flew around, and she let out a funny little yelp of surprise. "Martin, you're back!" She dropped her basket, eggs and all, to the ground, and walked straight into the weary-looking soldier's arms—right in front of the citizens of Lubitz. And they were looking. Heads turned, faces smiled with approval, and the market chatter around them stopped to observe the scene.

To Ana Marieke's great relief, Irene stepped away from her soldier, but held on to both his hands. "You're back," she repeated with wonder in her voice, "and all in one piece!" Irene's eyes glistened with tears of joy. "And," she added breathlessly, "you must come to dinner tonight."

Before Martin could say a word, Ana Marieke greeted him warmly, but in the same breath, quickly suggested for him not to come to Shabbat dinner. "Be a bit more diplomatic, Irene," she chided, "don't drop this on your mother without a warning. You know she's not fond of surprises; especially not . . . not . . . " Her voice trailed off as though lost for words.

Martin shook her hand, and with great warmth in his voice he said, "Thank you, Ana Marieke, I'll take your advice. I fully agree with you. Irene, my dear," he looked with great longing into her flushed face, "let's give your mother a little time to get used to the idea that I am back in town, and that we will be seeing each other. I would not be comfortable coming to your house tonight. Besides," he grinned, "Fate has its way. I go on duty in less than one hour from now, and I will be working into the night. As soon as I have a few hours off, we'll go to the café house on the square and pick up where we left off."

While Ana Marieke concluded her purchase of the two lively chickens, reminding Dorothea to be sure and bring her best hens to the next Friday market, Martin quickly explained that he had gone to the tavern looking for her. "Lucy told me where to find you. She said that she wished she could be here to see the reunion. She's quite the romantic soul, isn't she?"

"Not more than I," Irene replied giddily, her face washed in happiness.

Ana Marieke carefully bound the feet of the hens together with a piece of string, popped them into the big basket, and kept one arm protectively over them. She turned to the quietly chatting couple. "Irene," she said, "I'll take the hens to the butcher while you and Martin stroll on home. Please take the basket to the kitchen. I'll be there shortly."

She said goodbye to Martin, expressing once more how glad she was that he had returned to the garrison unharmed. She gave Irene a friendly pat on the back, and headed off in the opposite direction to have the chickens slaughtered in the proper kosher way.

Arm in arm, Martin and Irene walked leisurely through the crowds. Unaware of the hustle and bustle of Friday market, they had eyes for each other only. At the tavern door, he raised her free hand to his lips, let go of it reluctantly, and said, softly, "I have thought of you every moment of every day. Thinking of you, conjuring up pictures of our future together, was the only thing that kept me sane in the middle of the insanity of war. I just hope that it all ends soon and that some of us are left whole enough to be able to start life all over again."

Touched by his words, Irene shyly confessed that she had read and reread his letters every night. "I missed you terribly and I ache to spend more time with you. Please don't make me wait too long."

She watched him walk away and slowly opened the tavern door. She brushed past Lucy with a smile and a quick hello, and climbed the stairs to the kitchen to drop off the basket. On her way back down, with Martin's affectionate words resonating like a song in her heart, a huge wave of excitement and happiness rose up from her toes, invaded every pore in her being, and cloaked itself around her. Overcome by the powerful feeling, she sat down on the bottom step, wrapped her arms around her knees, and let her head come to rest on them.

In the silence of that moment, she realized with great clarity that it was not the promise of a life of adventure and of privilege that Martin represented, which made him so attractive to her. Suddenly, she experienced a deep knowing that it was his genuine love for her, his simple ways, and a feeling of bottomless safety to trust him with her heart, that overshadowed the mundane. If she never saw Rome, Paris, or London, if she never danced at great balls, if her dreams remained just dreams—she would still want to be his wife. It was a true and honest feeling that would last for a lifetime.

When she re-entered the tavern, Lucy had lunch under control. "I'll be right back to help you, Lucy. I just want to have a quick word with Father."

Lucy chuckled, "You look as though you just found the pot of gold at the end of the rainbow, saw an angel, or—met Prince Charming," she teased. "I think I know which one of the three put the magic on your face."

"Of course, you know, silly. And I can't wait to tell you all about it."

Irene walked over to the bar where Herman Burger was stocking a shelf with bottles of kümmel, anise, and plum schnapps. "Father, can you sit down with me for just a little while? I need to talk to you."

Herman Burger looked over the rim of his glasses at his oldest daughter. With a smile in his eyes, but managing a stern, fatherly tone, he said, "As if I didn't know what you want to talk about. Let's get started. It's market day and the early lunch crowd will be in soon."

They sat down at the nearest table, facing each other. Irene sighed. "I'll make it brief, Father. Martin has returned to the garrison. As you know, we have kept in touch with letters during his absence and I did get to know more and more about him. Everything I've learned, I like. The same certainty with which I have turned down a dozen or so men who were interested in me, now serves me again. And I rely on that inner knowing. Father, with all respect and love for you and Mother, and even against her wishes . . ." Irene halted, tucked her hand under her father's, and continued softly, but determined, "I am going to marry Martin Blomberg. I shall wait until this war is over, as you requested. I will be patient. But after that, I am going to be in a hurry." Irene looked at his face, anxiously searching for a sign, a good sign.

Without hesitation he replied, giving her hand a reassuring squeeze. "I've known that from the first time I saw the two of you together. I have already told you that I believe he is a fine man, good for his word, honest, and fair. Considering all odds, I believe you will have a good life with him; and that is enough for me. As far as your mother is concerned, I know that her child's happiness will eventually overshadow the stubborn resistance she harbors now."

The tavern door opened, letting in a bright burst of sunshine and the first lunch guests. Herman rose from his seat, greeted the newcomers, patted Irene's shoulder, and added. "Let it rest for now. Give it time. I trust your judgment as much as I trust my own. I won't fight your battle with your mother for you, but I am certain you two will find a way to solve the problem."

Relieved, Irene sat for a moment longer, her mind turning cartwheels. She was overwhelmed and grateful for her father's understanding and his approval of her decision to marry the stranger. She was no longer deeply worried about her mother's reluctance to accept the inevitable. Her father was probably right. Resistance would eventually give way to acceptance—reluctantly for sure, but acceptance just the same.

Four days after their brief meeting at Friday market, Irene and Martin met at Café Bonaparte. Dressed in a freshly pressed uniform, clean shaven, and smelling slightly of lavender, he looked a bit more rested and relaxed, she thought. As though reading her mind, Martin started to tell her about the harrowing months at various field hospitals.

"It's hard to describe the conditions of a hospital, the mood of a worn-out army of desperate men, and the pain and the stink that go with it, without tearing out one's hair," he started out, slowly and hesitatingly. "But I don't want to use the little time we have to spend together talking about the war, so let me say it again; war is horror personified. No one, but no one, should be subjected to such inhuman circumstances.

"I'm not telling you anything new; rumors are flying about like chaff in the wind. It's time for the kaiser to admit his defeat: the war is lost."

He reached for her hand, "Now, tell me about you."

Irene looked out of the window for a moment, then leaning forward, close to him, she said in a low voice, "I was in that strange place which I had described to you in my letters. I led a kind of stand-still life while you were gone. Days, weeks, and even months passed, but I was standing still. Waiting. Waiting for the future to happen. I had this odd feeling that I was outside of myself, watching time go by, and not participating in life. Just waiting."

She stopped, searching his face for an unspoken understanding. "I know that sounds crazy, but now that you are here, I am back in the moment, back in the swing of it. All of sudden, my future is becoming a destination. Am I making any sense?"

"Of course you make sense," he replied quietly. "Hearing what you say, I realize that I, too, spent my days at the front in a vacuum, working zombie-like, but waiting. Waiting to return to you."

With their heads close together, between sips of strong coffee, they whispered about the wonder of their serendipitous meeting, their feelings for each other, and their impatience to begin a life together.

"It is all meant to be; we're meant to be, I'm sure of it," Irene announced, leaning back in her chair. Martin nodded happily, "In that case," he replied with a twinkle in his eyes, "let me get the formalities out of the way. Irene Burger will you marry me?"

"I thought you had already asked, and I had accepted," she teased. "However, let this be your formal moment. Martin Blomberg," she continued in a mock-serious tone, "I will marry you." They both laughed at the game they played, and shook hands to seal the bargain.

"I know you have to leave again, Martin, but I must tell you how much I loved the stories about your family. They are an extraordinary group and I can hardly wait to meet them—especially, your father."

"You don't know the half of it yet," Martin interrupted, shaking his head, "You've got some interesting surprises coming your way, that will set your mind spinning. I just hope you are going to see the humor of it all, and are prepared to like my father, in spite of his exotic conduct. Basically, he is a good man—just full of mischief. He still plays his games, but in the end, he always manages to redeem himself. It's just the way he is."

Martin rose to his feet, left some money on the table, reached for her hand, and pulled her up. "I'll walk you to the tavern and then I have to hurry back to duty."

They walked out into the late-afternoon blue of the warm summer day. Children ran their colorful hoops on the sidewalk. Others whipped their small, wooden tops swirling with a piece of string attached to a stick. The trick was to keep them spinning before they lost momentum and dropped. People strolled leisurely around the square, greeting each other and stopping to chat.

Lubitz seemed quiet and peaceful on the surface. But the town's people worried. They worried about the safety of their men fighting a war that seemed to have no end. They worried about the decline in business and they worried about keeping food on the table. The monstrous appetite of the German war machine was depleting the supply of marketable goods along with the population of young men.

As always, Irene watched Martin's long strides carry him away from her, and only when she lost sight of him, did she re-enter the tavern. The place was beginning to fill up with customers and she hurried to the kitchen to help Lucy and Ana.

"Well," Lucy greeted her, "how was your rendezvous? What's new?"

"Nothing is really new. He described briefly his time at the front lines, and his sadness over the wounds of war—the stupidity and futility of it all. And then, we just talked and talked about us until it was time for him to leave."

Irene slipped into her apron and got out the dishes and the silverware, ready to serve the evening meal to the patrons of the Lubitz Tavern. She was anxious to be done with her work, impatient for the day to end. She cherished that time just before drifting off to sleep, when she would go over every word and every feeling she and Martin had exchanged.

Chapter Seven

IRENE AVOIDED BROACHING the subject of Martin to her mother. In her mind she had rehearsed how she was going to tell her that the stranger was not going to go away. She would have to tell her that, contrary to Toni's wishes, she was going to marry Martin and that her father had given her his blessing. She kept changing her script from day to day, until finally, she tossed it all out. She would let the words happen when the time came. And then the time did come.

A few days after her date with Martin, celebrating his return to the garrison, Irene was in her room putting the finishing touches on a silk blouse she was making for herself. There was a sharp knock on her door and Toni walked in. Dressed in a simple navy blue frock, with a white collar circling her slender neck, she looked every bit the prim and proper *Hausfrau*. She carried a small tray with two cups of tea and a few slices of Ana Marieke's raisin-filled pound cake.

"Peace offerings," Toni joked a bit feebly, putting the tray on a small table and pulling up a chair to face her daughter. "We haven't had a moment to ourselves lately, my dear. When you are not working, you seem so preoccupied, so removed. You leave the dinner table with a polite 'good night,' and shut yourself in your room. I've stood in front of your closed door many times, tempted to knock and come in. But I stopped myself each time. I had an odd feeling that the door wouldn't open. Today," she sighed, "I just couldn't wait any longer, so here I am."

Irene put her sewing down, got up, walked over to her mother, and bent down to kiss her cheek. "I am glad you came in. I guess I have been avoiding another mother-daughter talk because I wasn't sure what I was going to say. I am ready now . . . as ready as I'll ever be," she reached for her cup of tea and sat down across from her mother.

"Well, then tell me," Toni began, "what is going on in your young life?"

"Not so young any more, Mother," Irene laughed softly, "I'll be twenty-eight in a few weeks. I am an old maid, but I am going to change that."

Slowly, she put her cup down. "Mother, I agonized for days about how I was going to talk to you without hurting your feelings, without causing a break in our family, without bringing unhappiness into this house. There is no easy way to say it, but I'm going to marry Martin when the war is over. I know you are concerned about his family and about not knowing anything of them. He has a Jewish mother and a part-Jewish father, but he was not raised a Jew. He didn't even know that he was Jewish until a year or so ago when his mother finally had a brief talk with him.

"His family is about as different from ours as the North Pole from the Sahara Desert. But then, as Martin said, I am not marrying his family, I am marrying him," Irene stopped and read her mother's expression.

Even though Toni's face still bore that same stubborn, closed expression Irene remembered so well, there was a faint sign of resignation in her eyes and in the slump of her shoulders.

Toni cleared her throat and glanced past Irene at the far wall of the bedroom, as though searching for new words to an old subject. Finally, she folded her hands in her lap and said, "I have not changed my mind about wanting a good Jewish man for you: someone whose family we know. But I also understand, and you have made it very clear, that I cannot live your life for you. I suppose that I should be pleased you are happy and that you believe you have found the man of your dreams. But, sometimes a dream is short-lived and reality is altogether different. So please, don't ask me to embrace your stranger as a member of the family, just yet. But on the other hand, I shall not sit *shiva* for you either."

Irene shuddered a bit at the mention of the ancient practice of a family mourning the dead. For a moment, she pictured her mother sitting in ragged garments, dusted heavily with ashes, sobbing and tearing out her hair for the required eight days. It was a demonstration of grief as old as the first temple in Jerusalem—a dramatization of personal tragedy when a loved one died or was ostracized for betraying the Talmud and the traditions of Judaism. Members of a family who married outside their Jewish faith were considered dead and banished from memory once this ritual was completed.

Bringing herself back from the disturbing thought, she heard her mother say, "You are my child, and I love you. I just wanted you to have the same things that have given me comfort and purpose all of my years. We are Jews." She poured herself a fresh cup of tea and rushed on.

"Throughout time, Jews have suffered. We have been ostracized and punished for our faith. We have been persecuted and killed; but we have persevered. And that is a holy gift for me. That is why I live by the laws of the God of the Jews, and by the traditions which have survived along with our people. Each time we water down the laws of our God, each time someone turns his back on Judaism, the chain weakens. That's all I have to say."

"I don't want to argue, Mother, but I must point out something you may have forgotten. You just spoke of watering down the laws of God and weakening the chain. But people do change the laws of God. Two things I know of: Your mother shaved her head and wore a wig, according to 'God's law.' Your mother, at the end of her menstrual cycle, still went to the *mikveh* (the women's bathhouse) to be dunked under, and prayed over, by the rabbi. You follow neither of those rituals. My grandfather laid *tvillem* (a prayer ritual) every morning, something my father no longer practices." Irene looked at her mother with questioning eyes.

Flustered and annoyed, Toni snapped sharply, "In case you haven't noticed, we neither have a *mikveh* here in Lubitz, nor a wig maker. We have to do without. So don't be smart with me."

Weak as Toni's excuse was, Irene did not challenge it. An oppressive silence filled the room. Finally, Irene straightened her back, sat up tall in her chair, and, in a low and pleading voice closed the subject. "I am so sorry to disappoint you, Mother. But Father has given me his approval to marry Martin and while I would like yours, as well, and I do respect your reasons for not doing so, I will follow my heart in this matter. I don't know what else to say except that I love you. You are my mother and all I wish for is that you trust me and give the future a chance."

Irene got up just as Toni rose to her feet. Once again, she put her arms around her mother and held on to her. She didn't let go until she sensed a certain resignation, and could feel the stiffness leave her mother's body. "Thank you, Mother."

Toni smoothed down her dress, picked up the tray, and, with a forced, almost painful smile on her face, she patted Irene's cheek and replied in a noticeably curt manner, "Don't thank me yet. Let's wait and see. Who knows what the Almighty God has in mind for us."

The door closed behind Toni. Irene was left standing in the middle of her room with a mix of thoughts and emotions scurrying about in her mind. One thing was certain, she was glad the mother-daughter moment was over and, according to her mother, the subject of Irene's future had been laid to rest on her part. Toni had turned the matter over to God—her God.

Irene picked up her sewing. She loved those quiet hours when she could create something pretty and useful with her hands while her mind had the leisure to roam at will. She slowed down her mind, dwelled briefly on her mother's almost imperceptible signs of letting go and giving in, and turned her thoughts to Martin and the war. It too would have to end; everything does. She consoled herself with a sigh and a prayer.

Three days later, a young soldier appeared at the tavern and asked for Irene. He handed her a letter from Martin and left hurriedly. "The garrison was in an uproar," he mentioned under his breath on his way out. "Young, green recruits arrived almost daily, and before they could even complete the most basic training, they were packed like sardines into dirty, old railroad cars." Their destination was, of course, the front lines.

In his brief note, Martin had hastily scribbled that he was ordered to accompany the trainloads of replacements bound for the western front. On the return trip, the train would carry the dead and wounded. "I'm something between a record clerk, a nurse, and a nanny," he wrote. "Most of the recruits are so young, they don't even shave yet. There is barely enough time to teach them how to load and clean their rifles and how and when to use the bayonet. Those poor chaps are nothing more than cannon fodder."

Though left unsaid, Irene recognized Martin's frustration and could feel his misery. He closed his letter with warm and loving words, painting a picture of happier times to come, but it was not enough reassurance to ward off the dark and oppressive feeling of empty hopelessness that lingered in her mind. She worried about Martin's safety. How long would his luck last to dodge the bullets in a war zone? What if . . . ? What if . . . ? She closed her eyes, shook herself free of fear, cast out the phantoms of doom, and let peace take over her heart. "Tonight," she announced to herself, "I shall wish upon a star, maybe even two."

Once again, their courtship was continued through letter writing, but the correspondence did not travel by mail. It was hand-carried by several of Martin's comrades on their occasional visits to the Lubitz Tavern. Irene kept an eagle eye out for letter-bearing messengers and always kept one for him in her apron pocket—just in case.

His notes to her were brief. He wrote of his anticipation to be relieved from duty for a few hours on each return trip to the barracks. But more often than not, the train's whistle wailed mournfully as the transport of wounded and dead soldiers passed the Lubitz station and creaked and clanked on to other destinations.

"Nothing has a ring of truth to it," he wrote. "All we do now is mop up the mess left by the collapse of the eastern front, pulling out all stops to support the armies in the west. Turmoil reigns and clouds the sunniest summer day."

She had not seen Martin for more than eight weeks when an officer from the garrison left a thick letter with her father. "Well," Herman joked, handing her the envelope, "I guess we won't see you tonight. You've got a whole book to read."

"Thank you, Father," Irene planted a quick kiss on both of his cheeks and hastily stuffed the letter deep in the pocket of her apron, as though she was afraid she would lose it. "You're right. I shall keep my date with Martin tonight. I don't get to visit with him often anymore," she teased, and made her way to the kitchen.

It was her turn to prepare the evening menu for the tavern's guests. When the last man had left, and all of the dishes were washed and put away, Irene grabbed an apple and rushed up the stairs to her room. Lucy was playing the regular Thursday night game of dominos with their parents and Ana Marieke, leaving Irene with the room all to herself. She got ready for bed, slipped between the cool linens topped by a light summer blanket, and propped herself up against a small mountain of thick feather pillows. She slit the envelope open and started to read.

He was on a train with more than two hundred sick and shell-shocked soldiers, headed for a large field hospital somewhere in Thüringen. He excused himself for the uneven writing due to the rattling and swaying of the train running on worn-out tracks. "I have an hour to myself," he wrote, "and I couldn't spend it any better than in sharing my thoughts with you." He went on to tell of his desperation to save the lives of the seriously injured. There was a shortage of medication and adequate surgical care was not available

Then, turning to a cheerier subject, he described his sisters whom she would meet when she became his wife. "All three are tall and slender and look so much alike they could be triplets. Helene is kind and gentle and a bit on the serious side, while Ida is an adventurous and highly curious soul. Antonia, the youngest, is the most lighthearted and 'ready-for-anything' of the trio. To use my wicked father's word to describe her is to say, 'With her, you can steal horses.'

"Then there is my only brother, Eugene—casual, relaxed, and slightly irresponsible—who more or less manages my father's uniform and boot factory. Helene categorizes him as someone who stopped growing in kindergarten, because he was having such a good time."

At the end of the letter, he mentioned that his commanding officer had promised him a few days off in September. With the revolution in Russia in full swing and the new Bolshevik government's withdrawal from the war, battles on the eastern front had ceased months ago. However, thousands of soldiers had to be reassigned and re-shuffled, and the sick and the wounded needed to be transported to hospitals.

"We'll do a lot of catching up at the Café Bonaparte. We'll stay until they run out of apple strudel," he promised.

Gently, Irene refolded the pages of the letter and tucked it away with all the others. Tomorrow, she would read them again. Back in bed, she watched moon shadows dance through the filmy curtains of the open window, play on her blanket, and follow her into her dreams.

———————————

Autumn quietly announced itself with a snap of crispness in the air that began to change the color of the leaves. With Rosh Hashanoh and Yom Kippur just days away, Toni and Ana Marieke turned the house and kitchen upside down. The whole Burger family, including Max, would be together to celebrate the Jewish New Year. A week later—according to a tradition as old as the hills—they would fast on the Day of Atonement, spend the day at the synagogue, and, after sunset, break the fast at Toni's table.

Not hearing from Martin for several weeks, Irene had a difficult time feeling festive. The sun was shining on this first day of the New Year. Dressed in their best attire, people milled about in front of the small synagogue. Happy faces greeted each other with a hearty *Leshono tauvo*—Happy New Year! Irene forced herself to return the cheerful greetings and good wishes with a pasted-on smile. Happy New Year? For a tiny moment, she had lost her bearing and her balance. An ocean of doubt and sadness washed over her and left its mark.

But, as quickly as those dark thoughts had invaded her heart, they vanished into thin air when, one day before the celebration of *Yom Kippur*, Martin walked into the deserted tavern. It was early afternoon and he hadn't bothered to change. He wore a creased and crumpled uniform that matched the weariness in his face—and was mirrored in the way he carried himself.

"Martin, you're back," was about all Irene managed to say, and, without taking her eyes off of him, she held on to his arm and led him to a table. Before she could say another word, he reached across the table and clasped both of her hands.

"Irene, dearest," he said in a rough voice that sounded as though he had eaten dust for days. "Please forgive me. I didn't take time to clean up, nor did I ask permission to leave the barracks. It doesn't matter anymore, it's almost over. We can count the days now. A huge Allied offensive was successful at the western front. Allied troops broke through the Hindenburg Line at several places. The fighting spirit of our troops is broken, and at the home front, unrest is mounting. We've all had enough. We are defeated . . . " his voice trailed off.

"Oh, Martin, I know from rumors that it is bad," Irene replied. "Our local newspaper is so pro-kaiser that the reports are biased and veiled with lies. But among the people, there is growing resentment of the war and of the kaiser. Abdication is the word on the street."

Martin cleared his throat and said, "I don't know much about politics in this country. I can only guess that chaos will spread for lack of responsible leadership. The Socialists, the Nationalists, the Communists, and all the other parties will be fighting like mongrel dogs to come out on top. And, of course, it's the people who will suffer again. Well," he straightened up and, giving her hands a reassuring squeeze, continued. "Enough of that. Let's be selfish. Let's talk about us. First, how are things at home, Irene?"

She sighed and grinned at the same time. "I think my war at home is over, too. Mother and I had another talk. She has not changed her mind, but she told me she will not sit *shiva* for me if I marry you, and that is a great relief. I feel she is no longer quite as unbending as she was in the beginning and, of course, we have my father's blessing. I feel free to do what is right for me—for us—and to trust myself."

Just then, the back door opened and Herman Burger walked in. Martin rose to his feet as the older man greeted him warmly. They shook hands and sat down.

"Well, young man," Herman said jovially, "you don't look too bad for all the horror you have experienced. I want to hear all about it. If you would be so kind and bring us a cup of hot, strong tea, Irene," he asked, "that would be wonderful."

Irene nodded and left for the kitchen. She glanced back at the table, looked at the two men she loved so deeply, and felt as though she was walking on air. Contentment and happiness embraced her like a cozy quilt, as she thought to herself: "All's well that ends well. Yes, all is well."

Chapter Eight

EVERY INCH OF Ana Marieke's kitchen table was taken up
with the fixings for the *Yom Kippur* dinner. At one end,
Toni was cleaning vegetables and on the opposite, Ana shredded
her noodle dough into paper-thin strips. "Soup noodles" she
called them. The two women were chatting like good friends
do, when Irene walked in and pulled up a tall wooden stool to
the table.

"Any work left for me?" she inquired.

"Not right now," Ana Marieke replied, "ask me again when it's
time to clean up."

"I have some good news: Martin is back," Irene announced,
furtively looking at Toni. "Father invited him for *Yom Kippur*. I
hope it is all right with you, Mother?"

Toni did not look up from her chore, but after a moment of
stony silence, she shrugged her shoulders and said, "Why ask me?
Your father did the inviting, and I'll live with it."

What went on in Irene's head and what came out of her
mouth were two entirely different responses. "Thank you,
Mother. Martin appreciated the invitation. It will be his first
Yom Kippur celebration, and he is anxious to be included," was
her polite reply. Her feelings, however, were stung from the
bitter and guilt-evoking tone of Toni's words. She fought

against the unspoken accusation that her news had besmirched and ruined the holy day for her mother.

Ana Marieke came to the rescue and said matter-of-factly, "Well, it's a good thing that there is always enough food for an extra mouth and enough room at the table for one more."

Irene sent Ana a grateful look for her quick attempt to ease the strained atmosphere. "What's for dessert, Ana?" she asked, quickly changing the subject which had long been exhausted for her.

"As if you didn't know. It's your mother's favorite poppyseed and apple cake concoction—a *Yom Kippur* tradition in this house. By the way, the apples are in that basket behind you. Why don't you peel and slice them. I'll do the rest."

Irene bounced off of her stool and cleared a space at one end of the kitchen table, grateful for the opportunity to keep her hands busy and for a reason to stay in the kitchen. Ana Marieke handed her a peeler. "Here," she ordered, chopping away on her noodle dough with practiced strokes, "Start at the top of the apple and keep the peel in one piece until the end. It brings good luck. And we can all use some, what with the world in trouble."

Toni remained behind the wall she had erected around herself—unavailable, face stern, voice silent, scraping and chopping at her vegetables with sullen vigor.

Ana and Irene talked about the war. They speculated what the country would be like when peace was restored among the fighting nations. Would there still be a royal house? They agreed that political parties were going to be at each others' throats, squabbling and fighting to gain control over a broken people. Ana Marieke, a voracious reader of history books, kept abreast of current happenings and was well informed. She liked nothing better than a lively discussion on past or present issues.

"Who would even want to keep on running Germany?" Irene asked.

"There are enough power-hungry egos in the political world," Ana replied, "who are convinced that they not only *have* the answer to the problems, but that they *are* the answer. We will have more unrest, more uncertainty, and more unhappy citizens," Ana sighed in sadness. "So much damage has already been done; it's hard to imagine that more is on its way. And it's all for the glory of some self-appointed political savior."

Lost in their thoughts, the kitchen fell silent. When Toni was finished with her chore, she placed the vegetables in a large colander, washed her hands in the kitchen sink, and said to no one in particular, "I'm done for now. I have some reading to do for *Yom Kippur*." She left the kitchen, taking her dark and stormy cloud with her.

Irene looked at Ana Marieke and shrugged her shoulders. "Nothing has changed," she shook her head.

Ana Marieke spread the noodles on a wooden board to dry and dusted her hands free of flour. She turned to Irene and with a fine edge of steel in her raspy voice, "I've told you before and I'll tell you again—for the last time. Leave it alone, put it to rest, and let the future happen. No matter what you want, and no matter how you approach your mother, she won't come around until she is ready. Change," Ana Marieke said with emphasis, "does not come from without, it comes from within."

It never ceased to amaze Irene how this simple peasant woman, raised in a one-room, dirt-floor hut and with less than six years of hit-and-miss schooling, was so wise, so bright and shiny. Never intrusive, her judgment was always fair and her observations analytical. On top of that, she was fun. "Oh, Ana Marieke," Irene said in a low voice, "what will I ever do without you? Who's going to straighten me out?"

"You'll be fine. You'll do the same thing I've done: you pay attention to life's signals and learn along the way," she replied cheerfully. "Life is going to straighten you out. In the meantime, help me get Dorothea's best chickens ready for the roasting pan."

Clean-shaven, his uniform pressed, Martin appeared at the Burgers' on the eve of *Yom Kippur* bearing a large bouquet of flowers. Lucy and Max, Arthur and Joseph and their wives, had already assembled in the living room. Stiff and impersonal, Toni greeted the stranger briefly. She handed Irene the flowers and tuned her back on him to talk to Rosa, Arthur's young wife. Toni inquired about her grandchildren, little Susie and Erwin, who were at home in bed with the measles.

Undisturbed by his hostess' frigid reception, Martin shook hands with everyone, smiled, joked with Herman, and generally turned his charm on high. Irene watched him in lively conversation with her brothers, who bombarded him with questions about the war, about Germany's rapidly failing economy, and the uncertain future they all faced. Typically, the men clustered in one part of the living room while the women congregated in the other—together, yet worlds apart.

When everyone was settled at the table, Toni lit the Shabbat candles and said the blessing. She then lit the four *Jahrzeit* candles in memory of Herman's and her parents. The four candles in their plain glass cups were not to be extinguished for twenty-four hours, or until they went out on their own.

After Herman said the blessings over wine and bread, Ana Marieke brought in the two big platters with roasted-to-perfection chickens, and all the trimmings. Irene and Martin sat across from each other at the far end of the table. Irene wondered if it was an intentional move of her mother's not to mingle them within the family. She shrugged her shoulders imperceptibly; perhaps she was reading signs that weren't there.

After demolishing Toni's delicious apple-poppyseed dessert, the men draped their prayer shawls over their arms, the women grabbed their prayer books, and everyone set off for the short walk to the synagogue in the crisp, clear air of the fall day. Martin had been given a *yamulka* and a *tallis* by Herman, and kept his place among the men. As always, the men led the way, the women followed behind.

The heavy oak doors of the synagogue closed with a muffled thud a few moments before sundown. The Eve of *Yom Kippur* had arrived—the Day of Atonement, the holiest day of the Jewish year. It was a day of fasting and of setting things right with God.

In the somber, candle-lit synagogue, the cantor's rich voice started the service with the singing of the celebrated *Kol Nidre*. The ancient, haunting, and soul-touching melody of supplication filled every inch of the synagogue, moved many of worshippers to tears, and reached deep into the hearts of everyone. Upstairs, sitting with the women, Irene hunched forward as though to get closer to the prayer and the meaning of *Kol Nidre*. To her, in every sobbing note, in every pleading sound, there rested centuries of suffering as well as the Jews' unbreakable bond with their faith, with their God. Irene glanced at her mother. Toni's face seemed to glow with an inner light and a blissful rapture that linked her to another place—a holy place.

When the service ended, and after countless *Gut Yontifs* were exchanged among the congregation, the Burger women caught up with their men for the walk home. Martin turned to Irene for a hasty goodbye and a brief thank-you for his hosts. He was overdue at the garrison, he explained, but would be at the synagogue for the day-long services tomorrow, if at all possible.

Yom Kippur—the service that would last until sundown, was filled with prayers of regret and grief. Twice, there were the readings from the Sefer Torah, and *Kaddish*, the memorial prayer for the souls of the departed, was recited. During *Neilah* (the end), the worshippers made their final peace with their God and their consciences. When dusk arrived, the *shofar* sounded a last mournful note and the Shabbat of Shabbats had come to an end. During the long and tiring day, Irene had looked in vain for Martin in the crowd of praying and swaying men. He had not been there.

Back at the house, with Martin's gift of flowers in a crystal vase, Ana Marieke had set a festive table with platters of cold chicken, slices of beef, chunks of dark bread, and crisp rolls. It was time to break the fast. No one commented on Martin's absence. After all, he was a soldier and there was a war on. Everyone talked about the holy day.

Toni elaborated on the beauty of the *Yom Kippur* services, and praised the cantor's rich voice and his singing of the *Kol Nidre*. "I feel whole and close to God again," she said. "I feel a part of our people's past. Today I was there. I was at the Temple in Jerusalem; I was worshipping with the Children of Israel. I know who I am, and I know my God. And that," she addressed Irene, "is what I want you to have. This knowing, this feeling of belonging supports you and gives you all the strength you'll ever need."

Irene looked at her mother and heard the passionate plea in her voice. In a small and almost child-like tone, she replied. "Thank you, Mother. It was a beautiful day for me, as well. And," she added with a smiling grimace, "it was a long day, too."

Ana Marieke who was about to clear the table, worried where the conversation would lead to, when Lucy came to the rescue.

"Ana, what a wonderful meal. Thank you. If I eat another bite," she groaned comically, "I shall fall asleep in my chair, and won't help with the dishes."

As if on cue, everyone agreed to the condition of overeating, thanked Herman and Toni profusely, added their good wishes for the new beginning, and prepared to leave.

After the young Burger families and Max had left, Irene and Lucy helped Ana finish clearing the table and pitched in washing dishes. Lucy chatted about her upcoming wedding and her hope chest, which was filling up nicely with towels and linens. Irene was quiet—a million miles away. Her hands dried plates and glasses automatically, while her mind was busy day dreaming about the future and mentally speculating, for the hundredth time, what her new life would be like.

Two weeks later, Irene sat across the table from Martin at their usual rendezvous, Café Bonaparte. Circling their arms around their steaming cups of Russian tea, they held hands and talked in low voices about their feelings for each other, grateful for the moment. When the young waitress came to refill their cups, Irene pulled her hands away from his and Martin started to tell her the current news—some rumors, some truth—which came straight from his commanding officer.

"From the day I met Major von Stueben at the garrison, he has never treated me like the no-rank foot soldiers. He always took me into his confidence. He trusts me. He is well informed and this is what he told me today." Martin took a bite of his pastry, sipped his tea, and continued.

"I am excited, Irene," he rushed on. "Things are finally happening that are going to shape and change our lives soon. Stueben told me that Field Marshal Ludendorf has informed the German government that the war is lost and it is necessary to agree on armistice. Apparently, everybody has disputed the terms of surrender so far. Obviously Germany, the surrendering country, doesn't have the upper hand in these negotiations. The terms for armistice are going to be stiff and costly and will no doubt include our kaiser's abdication. That's not a great loss. After all, His Majesty got us into this mess solely for his own glory," he sighed.

Martin went on to say that von Stueben had also mentioned—rather grimly—that on top of Germany's woes of near economic collapse and political turmoil, an epidemic of influenza was raging, claiming more lives than the battlefield. "In Berlin alone, in just one day," Martin shook himself, "more than 1,600 people died, and it isn't over yet. So, be careful, dearest," he urged, "stay away from crowds and wash your hands often."

Irene had, of course, been aware of some of the news, but always questioned the reliability of the sources. Now, confirmed by Martin's account, she said, "Father and I talked at length last night after we closed the tavern. He knows it's over. But, he also said, we are going to face another kind of war. He believes that we will have a rampant inflation coupled with unrest and minor revolts brought about by ambitious politicians fighting to gain control of the *Reichstag*. He is so sure about his predictions," Irene grinned, "that he took his money out of the bank and bought gold."

"Good!" Martin's face lit up. "My father exchanged his *Deutsche* marks for Swiss francs and has been banking in Switzerland since last year. He did the same with my savings, and has been overseeing my business as well. He loves to wheel and deal. I swear he was born on a pushcart. God only knows what he did with my print shop," Martin chuckled. "I just hope he hasn't expanded it, made it big. I like it the way it is—busy and profitable, but manageable."

"Your father sounds like a combination of a parade and Robin Hood. I can't wait to meet him. I have a feeling we are going to get along like a house on fire."

"That won't come as a surprise to me. I know a lot more about you than you think. You have a touch of that pushcart characteristic yourself and the gift of humor to laugh about it. I'll have to watch you closely." They both laughed at the prospect and added another dimension to their relationship. Each time they were together, they discovered new things about each other, and they liked what they discovered.

Quiet and self-contained, Irene was coming out of her shell in Martin's presence. They shared the same sense of fairness and believed in the goodness of life. They laughed about the same things and there was an air of wholeness and simplicity about them.

Martin looked at his watch. "I don't have much time left; I'll have to leave soon. But before I go, let me tell you the plan I've made for us. Think about it, see if you like what I dreamed up."

Martin's face was one big smile. "Here it is! The day of armistice is the day we shall announce our engagement—another historical event. We'll never forget that date," he joked.

Slowly, as though checking the validity of his idea, he began to outline the immediate future. He would return home at once, take care of business, and then send for her.

"In order to follow some form of etiquette, I shall invite you, and Lucy as your chaperon, to come to Breslau to meet my family. Sisters Antonia and Helene are a lot of fun and they will take you under their wings. I don't want to be engaged for a year, like Lucy and Max. Let's get married. I also don't want our wedding to be a problem. If your mother still resists the idea, she won't join in the celebration, and that would make you unhappy. Personally, I don't need a big wedding feast. I would like to sneak away with you, get married by a justice of the peace, surprise everyone with the *fait accompli*—and," he grabbed her hands, "run off to Italy or any place you choose. What do you think of that?"

"You are a man after my own heart," Irene announced happily. "I knew that the moment we met and my intuition hasn't let me down. I like your plan. Let's just run away. In all my life, I can't remember ever throwing my cares to the wind and acting on impulse. I have never felt especially burdened by anything, but at the same time, I never felt free to follow a whim."

"I'm glad I came along," Martin, teased. "But I do want to be more than a whim."

"How about a forever whim?"

Martin nodded, eyes shining, and rose to his feet. "That's good enough for me."

At the tavern door, they shook hands solemnly. "We have a deal," Irene announced, businesslike.

"Oh, yes, we do! Just as your father said, seven times sealed and seven times blessed," he grinned, kissed her hand, and was gone.

In a tranquil state, Irene walked through the tavern, politely greeted the few schnapps-drinking customers, and proceeded up the stairs to the family quarters. She spoke briefly with her mother and Lucy, blissfully unaware of the softest of smiles that played around her full mouth and just stayed there. No one but Ana Marieke noticed. "You look like the fox who found a way into the hen house," she commented when Irene appeared in the kitchen. "What happened?"

"Oh, Ana, I never could keep a secret from you. I'll fix us some tea and then I'll tell you."

The big kettle that sat on the cooking stove was singing at a low boil. Irene filled the old Russian glass cups with freshly brewed tea, while Ana Marieke contributed nut-stuffed butter cookies to the impromptu tea party. "So," Ana prompted, "is it story time yet?"

"As if you haven't guessed. I met Martin for coffee and we talked about how and when and what we are going to do. According to him, armistice is only days away, and that's when we announce our engagement. I know you won't say anything to Mother, but we plan to simply get married by a justice of the peace in Breslau, as soon as Martin has his business affairs in order. What do you say to that?"

Ana raised her eyebrows and shrugged her shoulders. Her response was laconic. "I am not surprised, it is your time. You are finally ready to fly and you're going to leave the nest. You don't need my advice, but I will just say to you: It is your life to live and you will do a good job. Of that, I am certain. Now you must stop trying to please the world. Martin is a fine *Mensch*, and I need say no more."

"You always make things come out right, Ana. I treasure you." She walked around the table, embraced the dear woman, held on to her tightly, and kissed her cheek. "Thank you."

———————————

Like an untamed witch's brew, rumors boiled up all over Lubitz. Newspapers reported events, then refuted them in the next edition. Customers who frequented the tavern came in with their own version of the "facts." But rumor finally culminated into the bitter truth. Succumbing to Hindenburg's warnings about his safety, Kaiser Wilhelm abdicated and sought political asylum in Holland. On November 7, 1918, German delegates passed through the Allied lines, met the Allies in a railroad car in a forest near Compiegne, and opened negotiations for an armistice. The German delegates were given seventy-two hours to accept the terms and pay the price for defeat. Refusal to do so, the Allies stated, would lead to the resumption of hostilities. After frantic negotiations, at five o'clock on the morning of November 11, 1918, the Germans finally signed the armistice.

The long-awaited news was flashed to the world with record speed: the armistice would come into effect at eleven o'clock that morning. And the world breathed an audible sigh of relief.

At four o'clock that afternoon, Martin appeared at the tavern. Not looking left nor right, he marched straight into the kitchen where Irene was cooking. Without a word of acknowledgment to anyone, he reached for her right hand, slipped a slim gold band on the ring finger, and raised the cherished hand to his lips. "The war is over, and we're engaged," he shouted triumphantly. He may not have won the peace, but he had won the love of the woman he knew to be his destined life's partner in the moment he first turned his eyes to her. Irene simply walked into his arms, raised her face to meet his, and just stayed there. The onions in the skillet burned to cinders.

Glowing with happiness and grinning broadly, the newly engaged couple appeared before Toni and Herman Burger. Irene held out her hand with the gold band. "Mother, Father, we are engaged."

"Well," Toni snipped, "you certainly didn't waste any time. The war has been over just a few hours and here you are. What is the hurry?"

Herman saved the moment by laughing out loud, embracing his daughter, and congratulating Martin, saying, "Toni, come. Enjoy the moment and help celebrate the inevitable. These two were, unquestionably, meant for each other, and I, for one, wish them all the joy in the world. And in time, my dear, you'll get round it, too."

Toni managed a watery smile, a swift kiss on her daughter's cheek, and a weak *mazeltov*. Herman walked into the dining room and returned with glasses on a silver tray and a decanter of brandy. Lucy and Ana Marieke had been waiting in the wings it seemed and, as if on cue, they appeared in the living room just in time to toast the elated couple.

"*Mazeltov*, good luck and a long and happy life." Herman raised his glass, wrapped one arm around his wife's shoulder, and, with that gentle gesture, brought the reluctant mother of the bride into the circle of wellwishers.

Ana Marieke looked pleased. Lucy was all giggles and chatter and immediately proposed a double wedding.

"Dear parents," she announced gaily, "you could get rid of both of us on the same day."

"We'll have one wedding at a time," Toni interjected, cool and calm. "These two are barely engaged, and you would have them married off before the stardust settles. I'm sure that much water will have gone under the bridge before their nuptial day."

Irene had anticipated her mother's cool response and was not hurt by Toni's lackluster manner. Martin was all smiles and good humor, thanked his new family for their good wishes, and announced his plans to have Irene visit his family in the company of Lucy as soon as arrangements could be made.

He turned to Toni, managed an exaggerated bow, and said, "Madam, my family and I would be delighted if you would accompany your daughters to Breslau. It would be an honor to entertain you." He had hoped to pique her curiosity about the Blombergs.

Toni shook her head. "Oh, no, thank you. I don't believe all three of us could get away at the same time. We have a business to run. And, at any rate, all this is certain to be a long time off."

Not wanting to cause any ripples, neither Irene nor Martin replied. Time indeed, Irene thought to herself, would take care of it. The worst was over, the rest would be easier. Irene felt a surge of confidence rise that blended and matched her happiness. She held on tightly to Martin's hand.

Lucy, of course, was beside herself with excitement over the prospect of traveling to Breslau. She cornered Martin and asked him a string of questions about the big city. When Herman announced that he would have to return to his place behind the bar for a while, Martin took the hint and said goodbye. Irene walked him to the door.

"I'll be by tomorrow to tell you when I can go home," Martin assured her. "Since I am not a member of the regular army, and now that all order and protocol are out the window, I expect to be able to leave at will." He kissed her quickly and vanished into the quiet darkness of the cold and rainy November night.

Irene had curled up on the chaise lounge in her room when Ana Marieke arrived, carrying her usual goody tray. "I brought you something to eat because I have a feeling you won't be joining your parents for dinner tonight. I am sure you want to be alone with your thoughts." She sat down on a corner of the chaise and patted Irene's hand. A wistful, loving expression hovered on her face. "Well," she said, "I think it went rather well this evening. Lucy is ecstatic, your father is pleased, and your mother is getting used to the idea. She isn't ready to give up her role of the opposing authority just yet, but give her time. Right now she is enjoying her part in the drama of her daughter's life." Ana Marieke chuckled and got to her feet. "Time for me to put dinner on the table. Don't stay up late. Tomorrow is going to be a busy day. Everyone will be at the tavern to toast the end of the war. Good night, happy dreams."

"Thank you, Ana. I won't last long tonight. All of a sudden, I feel exhausted from the anticipation, the excitement, the happiness. I'll be asleep the moment my head touches the pillow. Good night, my dear friend." Irene never made it to her bed; she fell asleep on the chaise.

Ana was right. By noon the next day, the tavern was crowded with townspeople, and soldiers from the garrison as well. While Herman poured schnapps, Lucy, Irene, and Ana worked in the kitchen, served their patrons, and washed tray after tray of glasses and dishes. Herman had recently hired a young man by the name of Hans Gustav to run the distillery but, by early afternoon, he had to pitch in to pour drinks and clear tables. At the end of the night, the till was overflowing. The Lubitz Tavern experienced its best day ever.

Just before closing, Martin rushed in looking for Irene. He bounced into the kitchen where she was at the sink. "No time for ceremony," he announced breathlessly. "A train leaves in less than an hour for Breslau and I just found out that I am on it, in the company of Major Stueben, no less. I am no longer *Feldwebel* (Private) Blomberg; I am a *Herr* again."

He reached in his coat pocket and handed Irene a piece of paper. "Here are the addresses of my apartment and my business. I've been told that the postal service is one of the few bureaucracies that is working. I'll write as soon as I walk into my living room," he promised. "And," he added, including Lucy, "as soon as regular train service is restored, I expect both of you to travel. And if this takes too long," he grinned, "my father, no doubt, will acquire a railroad to avoid the delay."

After quickly saying goodbye to Ana and Lucy, he grabbed Irene's hand, "Come, walk me to the door."

On his way, he shook hands with Herman and, once outside in the darkness of the night, he took Irene into his arms and kissed her goodbye. "I have to go, *Liebchen*. But I will see you in Breslau, soon. And," he said in a self-assured tone, "the next time we meet, we won't have to say goodbye. We've done enough of that, already."

Irene clung to him. Not entirely trusting of the future, she was reluctant to let go. But, with one more kiss, he propelled her gently through the tavern door, closed it behind her, and was out of sight.

The next rendezvous would take place in Breslau.

Chapter Nine

THE ONLY SOUND in the attic bedroom was the busy whirring of the sewing machine. Irene's dark head was bent over her work and her nimble fingers expertly guided the slippery silk under the fast-moving needle, making a perfect seam. Since the day Martin left Lubitz, she had been creating new wardrobes for Lucy and herself, in anticipation of their visit to Breslau.

"We have to dress appropriately," she announced to Lucy, "and look our very best. I don't want us to feel out of place—like peasants from the province."

Irene had gone to visit the dressmaker from her apprenticeship days, whom she knew to keep abreast of fashion trends from Paris to Berlin. There she leafed through the pages of *Haute Monde*, *Illustrirte Zeitung*, and a selection of clippings, searching for ideas to copy and adapt. With the final designs pictured in her mind, she found what she needed to accomplish her goals in the huge trunk of a traveling notions and fabric salesman who never failed to call on her during his regular visits to Lubitz. Her unerring eye for color, texture, and quality, her sense of style, and her photographic memory were uncanny. By the time she finished a dress, all of that natural talent blended with her ability to recreate any design, and resulted in fashions that could well have come from a famous salon.

Tightlipped, Toni commented on her daughter's creative efforts in a whip-like tone. "I hope your new husband will appreciate your talents. You'll be saving him a lot of money making your own clothes."

Disregarding her mother's snapping, Irene responded laughingly, "You're right, Mother, he is a lucky man."

She had vowed to herself not to take the bait when her mother threw out the line with a barbed hook on it. She would remain cheerful, keeping the peace at any price. And, it worked. Mother and daughter lived in the silence of their convictions. Time would be the witness to the outcome of events but, one thing was certain, the younger woman mused: in the end, everybody would win and no one would lose.

Martin's first letter to her from his home arrived one week after his departure from Lubitz. His voice resonated within her as she read his words of love and commitment, making her heart dance with joy. He wrote that, thanks to his father's supervision, his business had not suffered from his absence. The Old Baron had brought in new accounts, kept the presses running and the small staff content. But true to his style, he had "acquired" a brand new Italian press that had more bells and whistles than a circus parade.

"I think he really had a good time playing boss, because he keeps coming in every day," Martin observed. "But sooner or later, some interesting opportunity will present itself and lure him away. I enjoy having him around. He is a bag of surprises, as well as a tidal wave of energy and mischief. There is never a dull or dreary moment. I finally have come up with a proper title for him: He is an 'Acquisition Specialist.'

"Wait until I tell you his latest coup. Believe it! While I was away, he 'acquired' a beautifully furnished, private railroad car—mahagony and brass, fine art and Oriental carpets—along with a handsome, white-gloved butler and a white-clad, tall-hatted chef.

This latest jewel in his crown is sitting on a dead track here at the train station, just waiting to be hooked up and go places. I am certain he will find a way to have his railroad car attached to the train you, my *Liebchen*, and Lucy will be taking. You'll be traveling in style. When I asked him where and when and how. . . he just grinned wickedly, and mumbled something to the effect of . . . *'yours is not to reason why . . . . just enjoy the things I buy.'* He has now added glib poetry to his repertoire of outrageous explanations."

In his next letter, Martin touched on the change that accompanied the armistice, and which he described as "troublesome as Medusa's head." The end of the year 1918 saw the collapse of imperial dynasties and great empires—the German Hohenzollern, the House of Habsburg in Austria, the Romanovs in Russia, and the sultans of the Ottoman Empire. "We all will have a lot of adjusting to do," Martin proclaimed. "Our world will never be the same." He kept the rest of his letter on the light side. He hinted at the surprises he and his sisters had waiting for her and mentioned his father's eagerness to meet his new daughter-in-law-to-be.

With every mention of the Old Baron's escapades, which Martin shared with her, Irene's curiosity rose to ever loftier heights. What would he think of her? Would she like him? The Old Baron seemed to be the hub of the Blomberg family wheel, the center of attention and the master of ceremonies. Irene was in a hurry to find out. Ana Marieke had told her several times not to hurry the future. "All things will come to you in good time: never wish the hours away," she counseled. "There are no refunds for time passed, so be patient."

Irene practiced patience regularly, but she never did get really good at it. Sometimes she felt like a racehorse straining at the gate, ready to run with the wind toward the finishing line. Each time Martin discussed details of her upcoming visit, Irene was

ready to grab her coat and hat, and just go. Even the preparations for Chanukah, her favorite holiday, were only milestones
measured in time passing. Seven days of celebration, seven days
of gift giving; family gatherings all had a veil of unreality about
them. Outwardly she portrayed that pleasant, thoughtful, and
calm young woman everyone loved. On the inside, she was
something between a volcano on the verge of erupting and a full
blown tropical storm.

Finally, on the 28th of January the waiting was over. Martin
sent a telegram: "Train leaves Lubitz on January 30, 1919, nine
o'clock in the morning. Board private Blomberg car. All arrangements completed. Next stop Breslau! My heart is waiting. Martin."

That night, at the evening meal with her parents and Lucy,
Irene read Martin's telegram, all but the last sentence. "I have
talked to Ana Marieke," Irene addressed her father, "she and her
cousin Bertel are only too glad to cover for Lucy and me at the
tavern. We'll be gone no more than ten days."

Disregarding Lucy's happy shriek of delight, Toni cut in
sharply, "Ten days," she objected with an icy glare in her eyes.
"That's too long. I won't allow it."

"Now, now, Toni," Herman raised his right hand in her
direction as though to ward off a swarm of approaching locusts,
"let's not set a time limit here. Neither one of the girls has ever
been away from home and it's about time they get a good look at
what lies beyond Lubitz. And this is a wonderful opportunity.
The girls have level heads on their shoulders. They'll know when
it's right to stay and when it's time to leave. I want them to enjoy
themselves and come home with lots to tell. I rest my case." He
leaned over closer to Toni and added firmly, "I am sure, dear
heart, you will come to the same conclusion."

Toni managed a weak smile and rose to her feet. "We'll see,"
she snipped. "Right now I'm going to the kitchen to check on our
dessert and tea."

The room fell silent for a moment. "I wish Mother would make it a bit easier for all of us," Lucy mused. "First of all, we're pretty grown up and, secondly, we're not doing anything wrong."

"Stop worrying about your mother. She'll get there in her time," Herman closed the subject and greeted Toni, bearing a bowl of lemon mousse, with an enthusiastic, "Sweets to the sweet. Enjoy!"

Later, in her attic bedroom, Irene started to pack the two suitcases she had borrowed from her brother, Joseph. Humming a familiar Strauss melody, she waltzed between the wardrobe and her chest of drawers. She ceased her whirling for a moment to stop in front of the full-length mirror and hold up one of her new dresses, for effect. Gently, she folded and fitted each thoughtfully created outfit into the depth of the suitcase, between protective layers of tissue paper.

When Lucy walked into the room, she took one look at the half-empty wardrobe, took in the open, overflowing suitcases, and gasped, "Irene! We're only going to be gone ten days, two of which we spend traveling. Your side of the wardrobe is empty. You have packed all of your clothes. Why . . . Irene?" Suddenly, a knowing look flooded her face. "You don't intend to come back— you never told me," she whispered hoarsely.

"Shhhh," Irene placed a finger over her lips, "I was waiting to tell you on the train. I didn't want you to know anything so you wouldn't have to lie to Mother, in case she decided to ask you if I am up to something of which she would not approve." Irene grabbed Lucy's hand and pulled her down on the chaise, beside her.

"Listen, my dear, dear, Lucy. I don't want to be married on Mother's terms, or at her timing. It would only put a strain on all of us. Martin and I agreed that shortly before you return home again, we will get married in a quiet civil ceremony—no gown, no veil, no fanfare. If I were to ask Mother to be present at my wedding, on my terms, she would not accept. So, why create more unpleasantness?"

Wide-eyed, Lucy listened to her sister's secret plans and, in the end, promised to faithfully keep her confidence. "Cross my heart," she vowed. "Actually," she giggled, "You know I like a bit of intrigue and secrets." She put her arm around her sister's shoulders, gave her a firm squeeze, and whispered: "We've shared them all of our lives—but never one this important. Mother is going to be furious with me when she finds out that I was in on it. But," she said with an air of confidence, "I can handle it. And, furthermore," she tilted her head and shrugged—"I've got a secret of my own which I've been dying to share with you."

She faced Irene, "Guess what? Max has been corresponding with several companies in Breslau, two of which have offered him well-paying positions as their accountant. Right after we are married in May, we will be moving to the city, as well." Lucy could hardly contain her excitement as she pulled Irene to her feet. The two of them danced around the room to the tune of an unheard polka, stifling their little-girl laughter until Ana Marieke appeared. Entering, she wanted to know what the noise was all about.

Never able to keep anything from Ana, the two sisters took their faithful friend into their confidence. Ana Marieke didn't crack a smile, but her blue eyes were filled with amusement. "So, what else is new? I've always known what the two of you were up to before you did it."

Relaxing, healing laughter broke out between the three women as they embraced in a circle and shed a few tears—happy tears.

Two days later, Joseph, fascinated with automobiles, proudly transported Irene, Lucy, and luggage to the quaint Lubitz depot in his latest set of wheels. The train had just pulled on to track number one of the two at the quaint little Lubitz station, and all eyes were on the last railroad car, agleam with its prominent brass crest sitting above the large brass letters, *FW BvB*. Wearing a handsome morning coat and striped pants, a distinguished-looking man greeted the travelers, helped them up the steps, and ushered them into the velvet and mahogany interior of the Old Baron's private car.

"My name is Kurt, I am here to serve you and see to your needs. Your luggage is already on board, please make yourselves comfortable." He bowed, helped Irene and Lucy out of their winter coats, and disappeared once his important passengers had settled into facing, deep green velvet chairs placed beside one of the windows.

"This is absolutely astonishing," Irene uttered in a low voice. "It's a millionaire's living room on wheels—silver, crystal, paintings, fresh flowers, and all."

"I'm almost speechless," Lucy confessed, looking with her big eyes at the lavishly furnished railroad car. "You must feel like Cinderella—this train—and Prince Charming waiting at the other end of the line."

"Oh, Lucy, I do. Indeed I do!" Irene's voice was choked with excitement.

The station master blew his whistle and the locomotive replied with a long, woeful "hooooot" as the train slowly moved out of the station. Irene pushed down the bottom window and, with Lucy at her side, waved goodbye to Joseph.

"You girls have the world by the tail," Joseph shouted, wildly waving a white handkerchief and grinning from ear to ear. "Have a wonderful time; don't worry about anything. Take care! *Auf Wiedersehen!*"

"*Auf Wiedersehen!*" Lucy and Irene waved back at their brother until he was out of sight. Kurt re-appeared, closed the window, handed Irene an envelope, and announced that he would be serving a "second breakfast" shortly.

"If this is any indication of what your married life will be like, Irene," Lucy shook her head in wonder, "you will be traveling first class from now on. Just don't forget your poor relatives in the province," she said with a smile.

"Oh, silly! These are the Old Baron's trimmings. Martin is far from being wealthy. Besides, I am not impressed with money. You know that. Life is about people, not wealth."

Irene opened the envelope and retrieved a brief note from Martin.

"What does he say?" Lucy asked eagerly.

Irene blushed. "Don't be so nosy. He is just wishing us a good journey. Etc., etc."

"The *etc., etc.* is probably the best part," Lucy teased. Irene put on her Mona Lisa face and snuggled deeper into the luxurious softness of her velvet chair.

The click-clack sound of the train's wheels, and the occasional swaying motion, were a new sensation for the two sisters. The first and last time they had been on a train was more than twenty years ago when the Burgers attended the wedding of Toni's youngest sister in Racibórz, less than an hour from Lubitz. Neither Irene nor Lucy remembered the event nor the train ride.

Kurt rolled a snow-white, linen-draped table between the two chairs and, with a theatrical gesture, flipped a napkin across each of their laps. The "second breakfast" consisted of paté, smoked salmon, and a variety of sausages and cheeses all artfully arranged on a silver platter. Warm toast and freshly baked rolls hid between the folds of a linen-lined basket. He poured coffee into thin china cups and wished his guests *bon appetit*. Then, pointing to a dainty bell with a carved ivory handle, he said, "*Mademoiselles*, please ring for me to serve you." With that, their "personal servant" bowed again and left.

"Well," joked Irene, as she helped herself to some salmon, "there is nothing wrong with the service on this train."

"It's a good thing Mother can't see us now," Lucy said sheepishly, plopping a large dollop of paté on a piece of buttered toast.

"Remember her last words before we left the house? 'Be sure to eat kosher!' And all of this display is about as un-kosher as it can get."

"And God won't strike us dead," Irene quipped, assuredly. "Lucy, just think. The kosher laws were health laws created for conditions that existed thousands of years ago. The world has changed a lot since then. Those laws have no practical meaning anymore. In these modern times, they simply represent rituals." She looked thoughtful for a moment and took a deep breath.

"Another thing, Lucy," she continued, "doesn't this prove that when we are left to ourselves—as grown women—we make our own decisions? We create ourselves. We try ourselves out. We choose our own limits and boundaries, and at the same time allow ourselves to experience new things?"

"Well, of course you're right," Lucy mused. "Right now, I feel like a bird let out of the cage. Being around you has rubbed off on me and, all of a sudden, I'm getting curious about people and about the world. I think I've discovered that I want to learn about life face-to-face, and not have it interpreted for me by others. I'm ready for a little adventure, too."

"Welcome aboard," Irene laughed, "Now that we settled that, let's look at the countryside. We have never seen it before."

Kurt had silently removed the remnants of breakfast, poured fresh coffee, and discreetly vanished. Outside, heavy, gray clouds did nothing to bring color and life to the small villages, the modest cottages, and the winter-barren fields that rushed by.

The train made four brief stops at modest little stations, not unlike Lubitz, unloading passengers and boarding new ones, exchanging cargo for goods that were bound for villages and towns ahead. Everywhere people gawked and pointed at the imposing private railroad car. Inquisitive, some people walked up to the impressive vehicle to peek through the windows. When they encountered the two passengers, they smiled and waved and their greeting was returned, in kind.

"I feel like visiting royalty," Lucy laughingly commented, as she waved her white hanky at a cluster of curious faces staring at her. Irene grimaced, "Just don't let it go to your head, Your Majesty. It's only temporary."

Each clack of the wheels brought her closer to her destination. Irene closed her eyes in an attempt to settle down and take control of the excitement that brought butterflies to her stomach and jitters to her very being. With every kilometer she traveled, she moved farther and farther away from her beginnings. She remembered Ana Marieke's words of wisdom when she said, "Take the best of the past with you and improve on it. Make it right; make it work for you." Irene already missed her.

She had dozed off when Kurt appeared, advising them that they would arrive in Breslau in about fifteen minutes. Pointing to a brass-trimmed door at the front of the car, he announced the location of the ladies' salon. "Perhaps the young ladies would like to freshen up. You'll find everything you need in there," he bowed and was gone.

Entering the small salon, Irene was stunned by the very air of luxury that greeted her. The elegant space was painted in a soft blue with ivory trim, and furnished with crystal-dripping light fixtures that gave life to the huge, gold-framed Venetian mirror that hung on the wall. The marble-topped washstand was graced with flacons of perfume, bottles of *4711*, jars of cream, and powder puffs resting on Coty face-powder boxes. The final touch included silver-edged combs and brushes and a stack of small linen towels, all awaiting her ladyship's pleasure.

Irene ran a comb through her hair, washed her hands, and tried a little powder on her face. Carefully placing her hat on her head, she returned to her seat by the window without saying a word. And then it was Lucy's turn.

When Lucy emerged from the "salon", she was absolutely beside herself. "This is unreal," she stammered, "this is a fairy tale, a dream, a fantasy. Any minute now, I'm going to wake up in the distillery, down on my knees, scrubbing the floor."

"Lucy, just enjoy it. I am sure there is more of the same still to come. Breathe in the magical experience. This is just the beginning of a wonderful adventure."

Outside, the landscape had changed as they approached the capital of Silesia. Gone were the cottages and winter-still fields. In their place were large brick buildings, factories, and ware-houses pointing to the industrial activities of a growing city. The train had slowed down considerably. It hooted and whistled as it made its way through a maze of railroad tracks, finally settling on the one that would bring them into the depot.

Irene pulled up the window again. Unaware of the blast of ice-cold air that struck her face, she leaned way out, looking for a familiar figure. And then her heart flip-flopped and missed a beat as he came into sight. When the train stopped, Martin, with a tall woman at his side, were only a few feet away from the Old Baron's home on wheels.

Hurriedly, Kurt helped the girls into their coats and gave them a hand down the steps. On the platform, Martin dropped the huge bouquet of roses he carried as he opened his arms for Irene to walk in. Letting go of her with one arm, he draped it around Lucy and included her in the welcoming hug.

He reached for Irene's hands but kept her at arm's length. "Let me look at you, *mein Liebchen*. I've had a terrible time the last few days trying to conjure up your face in my mind's eye. Something was always missing. Well," he concluded with great satisfaction, "nothing is missing now."

He turned to the tall woman who had remained silently at the sidelines—an amused, warm look on her face. "Antonia, this is my Irene, the light of my heart, and this is her sister, Lucy. Ladies?" he bowed with exaggerated drama, "may I present my youngest sister, Antonia, Baroness von Warteburg. But, be at ease, don't let the title impress you. She is as friendly and as comfortable as an old pair of slippers."

"Welcome, welcome," Antonia reached out a slim hand. "I am so glad you are finally here, Irene. This brother of mine has been impossible to live with for days." Irene looked at Antonia's strong face which was the female version of Martin's visage. They could have been twins.

"I've not been exactly patient, either," Irene laughed at Antonia. She was immediately at ease with this elegant woman whose clothes spoke French and whose jewels must have originated from some maharani's hope chest.

Martin retrieved the roses and handed them to Irene with an apologetic grimace, but never let go of her hand. Antonia linked arms with Lucy as they made their way out of the bustling railroad station to the biggest Mercedes they had ever seen, sidestepping an army of porters, travelers, and a string of baggage carts.

"Your suitcases are on their way to the Hotel Golden Ram. You'll be staying in the family suite," Martin announced as he tucked the girls into the car, "courtesy of the Old Baron, of course. It is the same suite," he added, "that Father had converted into a school for us a long time ago."

"Oh, yes!" Irene nodded, "I remember the story. I know all of your letters by heart." She gave his sheltering hand a firm squeeze.

"We're taking you through the heart of downtown," Antonia explained, "so you can get a good look at our city." Handsome buildings, imposing storefronts, well-dressed people, automobiles and streetcars greeted the visitors with new images. Antonia pointed out the State Opera House, a major theatre, a museum, and the elegant apartment buildings guarded by their tall, liveried doormen. They passed Breslau's park where its wide tree-lined waterway was solidly frozen, much to the delight of skating children, ice-dancing couples, and a cluster of dangerously

tottering beginners and their teacher. Antonia cracked the
window to let in the strains of the "Skater's Waltz" that wafted
through the air.

The car turned onto a broad street and came to a stop in front
of a handsome, five-story building. A huge green awning
sheltered two silver-haired doormen in midnight-blue, brass-
buttoned, and gold-corded uniforms. No one could miss the
words *Golden Ram Hotel*, executed in prominent shiny brass
lettering, on the awning's wide overhang.

The doormen rushed up to the automobile, lending white-
gloved hands to its passengers. Then, with great flourish, they
threw open the oak-and-carved-glass double doors that led to the
well-appointed, black-and-white marble foyer of the Old Baron's
home away from home.

Irene gasped at the enormous, sparkling chandeliers that
duplicated themselves in the rows of ebony- and gold-framed
mirrors. Six-foot palms in Italian terracotta pots, and child-size
vases filled with ferns and long-stemmed roses, denied that
winter reigned outside.

Antonia and Martin waved a friendly greeting to the two
distinguished-looking men behind the registration desk and
followed the uniformed valet up the wide, gracefully curving,
red-carpeted staircase to the first floor. Halfway down the broad
corridor, the valet opened a door and stood back as the four
entered the family suite

"This is even more grand than the railroad car," Lucy
exclaimed as she took in the French furniture, the soft silks, the
tapestries and paintings, the yards and yards of brilliantly colored
Persian carpets, crystal bowls, handsome silver pieces, and
delicate porcelain figurines.

Antonia, amused by Lucy's outburst, replied briskly. "Our
father has impeccable good taste and always manages to find the
money, and the right people to execute the spending of it. When

I was a small child, I thought he was a magician, or maybe even God. And you know what," she looked at Irene and Lucy with mirth. "Sometimes, I still believe that."

Martin led Irene and Lucy to a small settee and sat down in a facing chair. He sighed, "I might as well tell you the whole story of how he acquired this hotel. Not only is it amusing, but it portrays my father at his naughtiest."

"Quite some time ago," Martin related, "the old man gathered twelve street bums and herded them to the Hotel Golden Ram. He asked for a private dining room and ordered a sumptuous dinner for thirteen—nothing but the best: paté, caviar, pheasant with all the trimmings, and a flaming dessert. Champagne or wine accompanied each course. When the last drop of brandy was consumed, the manager of the hotel presented my father with the bill. The Old Baron studied the bill, divided the total by thirteen, reached for his wallet and paid one thirteenth of the bill, to which he added a handsome tip.

"Now here comes the good part," Martin chuckled. "The manager looked at the money, looked at the bill, and supposedly said, 'Herr Baron, there are thirteen in your party and you paid for only one . . . ?'

"'My dear young man,' my father replied. 'You're in the hotel business, aren't you? If you can't tell a paying guest from a bum, you have a problem.' And with that, he rose from his chair and left. A month later he bought the place."

"He is quite a study in mischief." Irene burst into laughter.

"Oh yes, that he is," Antonia shook her head. "He does some exotic dealings; and we don't know the half of it. It's a game with him. But somehow, he always vindicates himself by his generosity and comes out on top. What he doesn't know is that we are on to him. We know about his double personality. It is harmless, though, and he carries it off with great elan."

"There are lots of stories about him and you'll eventually hear them all, my dear. But for now," Martin paused, "let me tell you of our immediate plans for you. We have every intention to overwhelm you," he grinned mischievously. "And we are showing you our best side only."

He explained that a maid would unpack their suitcases, and told Irene to ring for anything they needed. "Explore your quarters, rest up, and change for high tea. I'll come for you in about an hour and a half. You'll meet my sister, Helene and, of course, the Old Baron. I couldn't keep him away any longer." Martin hugged Irene and followed Antonia to the door where he turned around. "I don't mind leaving you for a little while, Irene," he joked softly, "I know where to find you."

Irene, who had walked him to the door, gave him a quick kiss on his cheek and teased, "Don't ever be too sure of anything. Girls possess strange powers." She gave him a playful push out the door and closed it behind him.

"Well, Lucy," she embraced her sister. "Here we are, and here we go."

In their quick tour of the suite they discovered two large, elegant bedrooms with twin beds, each topped with light-as-a-cloud satin quilts and matching *plumeaux*. Lucy let out a shriek of delight when she stepped into the marble-clad bathroom with its huge white tub, fluffy towels on brass racks, a mirrored dressing table, and chaise longue.

"Oh my!" she managed to breathe. "It even has two faucets: one for cold and one for hot water. Just look," she tugged at Irene's arm, "this place is even better stocked with toiletries than the ladies' salon on the train. Too bad," she added with a sigh, "that no one lives here."

"Right now, we live here, little sister. We shall make good use of all the lovely things and thank our host profusely," Irene said. She placed the rubber stopper in the tub's drain, turned on the hot water, opened a large glass jar of bath crystals, and dumped a handful of lavender fragrance into the steaming water.

"When in Rome," she giggled, "do as the Romans. I for one shall have a bath and meet our new world, squeaky clean."

"So, m'lady," Lucy ordered, "get going; I'm next."

Chapter Ten

AT FIVE O'CLOCK sharp, Lucy answered the knock on the door of their suite to let Martin in. Irene, in a simple dress and matching jacket of a burgundy silk, held out her cheek for Martin who promptly turned her face around and kissed her soundly on her full lips.

Lucy, dressed in a rose-colored gown, stood by laughing. "What's a chaperon to do? This is all new to me."

Martin let go of Irene and kissed Lucy's hand, "You'll just have to learn as you go along, my dear. But," he took a deep breath, "before I forget, I better deliver something. Irene, Lucy, turn around please," he ordered. He reached into the right pocket of his suit coat, retrieved a magnificent triple strand of flawless, matched pearls, dropped them over Irene's neck, and secured the diamond and ruby clasp. From his left pocket, there came a single strand of large pink pearls which he placed around Lucy's neck.

"Now, ladies, go look in the mirror."

One look, and both Lucy and Irene were speechless. Finally, Irene managed a hoarse, "Oh! My dear God! They are breathtaking!" And when Lucy recovered her voice, she couldn't stop chatting and thanking him. "I have never seen anything so beautiful," she muttered with tears in her eyes. "This is so, so, so extravagant. I'll treasure my gift forever." While the girls owned a few modest trinkets, neither of them had ever been near anything that could be called fine jewelry.

"Believe me," Martin responded, "It is my pleasure. Irene's pearls are a belated engagement present and yours, Lucy, are what I call a 'just-because' gift to enjoy. Now, let's get going. Our people are waiting."

When Irene reached for her coat, he slapped his forehead with the palm of his hand in mock despair. "How thoughtless of me. I forgot to mention that we are staying right here in the hotel. We are having high tea in one of the private dining suites. You won't need your coats."

Arms linked, the trio slowly descended the stately staircase. Halfway down the stairs, Irene's heart missed a beat. "I have been here before," she told herself with great wonder. "I am walking down the staircase of my dreams." She had the odd sensation that her feet never touched the ground—just like in the dream.

Martin's voice brought her back. "Here we are," he announced. One-story double doors were held wide open by two waiters, bringing a beautifully appointed room into view. Soft violin and piano music floated out to meet them. Irene had barely crossed the threshold when a tall, silver-haired man in white tie and tails and with a prominent handlebar mustache—no doubt who *he* was—rose from his chair and strode directly toward her.

Before Martin could make the introduction, the Old Baron embraced Irene, kissing her on both cheeks. "My dear," he beamed, "you are finally here. I am delighted. You are just like Martin described you and I could have picked you out in any crowd. Welcome, welcome! I had no idea my son had the good sense to find someone so lovely. You've made an old man very happy."

Irene held his glance and felt a compelling urge to laugh out loud and never stop. "I think I've got your number," she told herself. "Indeed, I do!"

Instead, she executed a mock curtsy. Poised, with a hint of amusement in her voice, she acknowledged his welcome. "I am delighted to be here, and after learning so much about you, I have been eager for this moment. Martin told me that you stand out in any crowd," she teased. "And he did not exaggerate."

"Oh my!" The Old Baron's expression on his face changed to woeful. "Don't believe everything my son tells you. You need to hear my side. Please." His mischievous smile was identical to Martin's, which had so captivated her. The Old Baron turned to greet Lucy with flattering compliments, making quite a fuss over her and oozing irresistible charm.

Lucy, wide-eyed, flustered, and unusually quiet, admired— almost envied—her sister's ease and the poise with which she handled herself among these strangers in a setting that was so new, and almost foreign to the two girls. Irene belonged, she thought.

Her sister contributed to the lively conversation, bantered, teased, and acted as though she had grown up in a salon and not in a small town tavern. Lucy was in awe. How did she do it? All that confidence, all that charm, when she herself felt so awkward. She wondered if one had to be born with the gift of gracefully rising to every occasion, or could it be learned? She would have to practice.

Antonia introduced the girls to her husband, Erich, and to Helene. Both had come to the city to meet their new sister-in-law. Helene, every bit a Blomberg in looks and bearing, was elegantly dressed, pearls gleamed at her throat and diamond rings sparkled with miniature blazes of rainbow colors, with every move she made. Her face bore a strong likeness to her siblings. Like Antonia, she was tall and slender, with wavy light brown hair and hazel eyes that brimmed over with intelligence and compassion.

Helene's voice was deep and serious. "I gladly join in the general consensus that we are all happy to meet you. Lucky

Martin, lucky us." She went on to explain that she had left her husband in the clutches of a nasty cold, and conveyed his greetings.

Irene kept pinching herself to make sure everyone and everything was real. It was, indeed, too good to be true. "My luck is hanging on as well," she replied, "I think I have surely walked into a wonderland."

"Irene," Antonia quipped, "remember, there is no fairy tale without a witch. Just wait until you meet our mother."

"Antonia, you're terrible," Helene scolded. "Mother is just different. She . . . is . . . " Slightly embarrassed and at a loss for words, her voice trailed off.

With diplomatic precision, Erich, Baron von Warteburg, saved the awkward moment by bending over Irene's hand and then Lucy's, warmly welcoming the soon-to-be members of the family. Trim and fit, he barely came up to the top of his statuesque wife's head, but somehow managed to look taller. His face was broad with high cheekbones, and his ivory skin gave contrast to the darkest, friendliest eyes. His ebony black hair was streaked with gray, and solid silver had settled in at his temples. Erich was a distinguished-looking figure, yet had an approachable and open air about him.

Irene was seated between Martin and the Old Baron. The latter explained that his formal attire was due to the fact that later that evening, he would attend a gala performance of *Swan Lake*. "Martin is not wild about ballet, but he will escort you to see this magnificent event next week. I don't want you to miss Galina Rostokovsksy's superb performance. She used to dance with the Royal Ballet in Russia, but fled her homeland when the Bolsheviks took over. She is exquisite. We are so fortunate to have her here."

During the sumptuous parade of food, accompanied by champagne, Antonia laid out their plans for entertaining their visitors. Overwhelmed when she heard what was in store for them, Irene was certain that Antonia and Martin must have been privy to her life-long fantasies.

"We're going to leave you alone tonight to rest up, but starting tomorrow, we will squeeze as much into a day as possible," Antonia announced gleefully. Martin excused himself stating that he was working on something important the following day, and would not see Irene until the early evening. He acted rather mysteriously and was vague when questioned about it.

Antonia paid no attention to him, instructing the girls to ring for breakfast the next morning, and to be in the lobby around ten o'clock. "Martin is returning to his flat tonight," she said, "but Helene and Erich and I are staying here at the hotel—just three doors down the hall."

The best way to see downtown was on foot, Helene declared, adding that the weather, although cold, should be dry and sunny.

"We're pretty good on foot," Irene broke in, enthusiastically, "Lucy and I have had a lot of practice. We will enjoy the walk!"

Helene was in charge of evening events and told Irene that the Old Baron had acquired the use of the royal box at the State Opera House. "You'll see *La Bohème, Madame Butterfly,* and, on the lighter side, there is a performance of *The Merry Widow* straight from the stage of the Vienna Opera House. You might want to attend a concert or two and we shall definitely spend an evening at our famous cabaret which, supposedly, is every bit as good as the one in Berlin."

"And," Antonia added breathlessly, "we are going to take you to Helene and Karl's little country place. And later in the week Helene is going to take you for a visit with Mother. She'll tell you all about it."

"Martin," Antonia asked, "when are you going to tell Irene and Lucy of your plans?"

"I thought I'd leave the best for last." He reached for Irene's hand, "and I'm not going to tell—yet. I know you like surprises, *Liebchen*." He looked at her with joy and mirth, "And you'll just have to wait until the time is right."

"Well, I may just have to stay longer. I couldn't possibly leave a surprise behind. Lucy," she turned to her sister, "do you agree?"

"Oh, of course," Lucy grinned, "I don't want to miss it either, but it had better be a good one!"

"Well, that's settled then," Martin bantered. "I'm relieved."

At this, the Old Baron interrupted. Putting out his chest and sounding miffed, but in a jesting way: "Have my thoughtless children left me any time with my new daughter-in-law, or do I have to polish up my dueling pistols? I have a few things up my sleeve, as well."

"Oh! Father, there's no doubt in our minds about that," Antonia burst out with an infectious gale of laughter, which made the rounds of the table. When she had caught her breath, she patted her father's right hand with its big signet ring. "You'll have your share of her, of course. We just want to have some time with Irene and Lucy so that we can prepare them for your 'up-the-sleeve' surprises. They can be rather, hmm, unnerving, shall we say?"

"Here you go again," the Old Baron protested mildly, rather pleased with the assessment of his escapades. "Always making me the villain. I am certain that you will approve of what I have in mind. In any case," he sighed in playful resignation, "You'll be there to supervise. But," he added with a devilish grin, "you'll have to catch me first."

Delighted beyond description, Irene took it all in. She may have been the picture of poise and calm on the outside, but on the inside she was shivering with excitement. Her mind tumbled and whirled, trying to keep up with the kaleidoscope of changing shapes and colors that never ceased. But some of the excitement had escaped, leaving a deep rosy blush on her cheeks and a shower of starlight in her eyes.

"Irene, Lucy," Erich interrupted, "If all this gets to be too much, protest! I just hope my dear wife and her sister will give you a moment or two to breathe. It's a bit overwhelming sometimes to meet their crowded schedules. I just wonder if they have also planned to take you out of the country," he joked.

"No, no!" Antonia shouted, with tongue-in-cheek, "that comes later."

The Old Baron got up from the table, champagne glass in hand. "It's time for me to leave," he announced, "but before I go, I would like to propose a toast. Fill your glasses and join me. To Martin and Irene—health and happiness, and the good sense to enjoy it. *Prosit!*"

And then he raised his glass to Irene alone, "I can see now how you stole my son's heart. You stole all of ours tonight. Welcome!"

Irene rose to her feet, hugged the old Baron, fluttered a kiss on each of his cheeks, and said, to his delight, "Speaking for myself, you, Herr Baron, do a good job of stealing—hearts that is —yourself."

That brought everybody to their feet. Roaring with laughter, glasses clinked and champagne spilled as they walked the Old Baron to the door.

"Father, you've been had," Antonia gasped, holding her aching sides.

The Old Baron bowed deeply, "I surrender and say good night." With great dignity, his full evening cape billowing out behind him, he made a dashing exit worthy of any villain leaving center stage.

Everyone lingered over mocha and brandy for a while, and had the best time getting acquainted. It was almost midnight when Helene suggested that it was time to end the evening. "Irene and Lucy have had a long day. Let's call it a night."

Martin accompanied his guests to their rooms. "Happy dreams, Irene, my dear. I know mine will be wonderful. I'll arrange to have dinner here with you tomorrow night. Helene and Antonia will run your legs off in the city all day and you'll probably be only too glad to stay in."

When Irene finally put her head on the pillow, she didn't have a moment to sort out the day. She was asleep before Lucy turned out the light.

Chapter Eleven

THE OLD BARON relaxed his big frame against the soft leather seat of his car. Herr Schmidt, the chauffeur, was driving him to one of the bi-weekly get-togethers with his cronies, at the venerable Rathskeller. He was reliving the excitement of the last evening—of meeting his son's bride. He was delighted with Martin's choice. Baron Friedrich Wilhelm von Blomberg—man of the world—was captivated by her quiet, unassuming manner, her intelligence, her quick sense of humor, and of course, her lovely features. He sensed an immense strength and a passion for peace in her demeanor. He couldn't wait to tell his friends about her.

When he entered the musty, fifteenth-century tavern, he headed straight for the Stammtisch (a special reserved table) where the sacred inner circle of old friends—"Troubadours of Commerce"—as the five wealthy businessmen referred to themselves—met twice a week without fail. He was the last of the troubadours to arrive.

"So! Don't keep us in suspense," haughty Sigfried Count von Laite demanded, "tell us all about your new daughter-in-law."

The Old Baron flipped open the lid of his tall tankard, took a sip of the cool, dark beer, and dabbed at his mustache with a white handkerchief, ready to give his report.

"Irene Burger was born a lady. She is lovely, just lovely. Bright, charming, and poised. She is self-confident in a most becoming, modest way. She has a way of looking at you—through you—that is rather awesome. There is an air of calm and peace about her. And, I believe, she can soft-talk a tidal wave into retreat," Friedrich bragged to his friends.

"She is good for Martin," he concluded with deep satisfaction in his voice. "She isn't one of those fashion-crazy, spoiled, horsey debutantes with a long line of blue-blooded ancestors and little blood of their own. Just the same, her bloodline goes back to Spain and the Inquisition," he boasted.

"But she is a Jew, and anti-Semitism is alive and well," Count Sigfried offered, brushing a non-existing speck of dust from the lapels of his well-tailored, dove-gray suit. "And," he was shaking his head, "in our world that is a serious flaw; a handicap, you might say," he sighed. He snapped the pewter lid of his stein shut with a bang and looked expectantly around the table for support of his opinion.

"Sigfried," Horst von Brunnen turned to his handsome friend, whose patrician face was framed by a halo of silver hair, "you seem to have forgotten your grandmother, Hannah, God rest her soul. Your grandfather married a Jewess because he was broke and she had money. Lots of money. And there was your Jewish aunt Rosa, whose dowry came in handy when your uncle dropped his gold ducats at Monte Carlo."

"Well," Count Sigfried replied, thoughtfully twirling the long ends of his mustache between his thumb and forefinger, "that was different. Hannah was an American and nobody here in Germany knew she was Jewish. A lot of people guessed and gossiped, but grandfather denied it whenever the subject came up. He explained away her ivory complexion, her dark eyes and hair, by saying she was part Indian; a princess at that, he insisted. And," he added smugly, "my grandmother is a long way back, and long gone. Who would even remember?"

Old Friedrich, who had played the role of a Protestant aristocrat for nearly fifty years and had no memory of being anything
other than that, replied that he did not consider Irene's background a problem. "Even if my son doesn't use his title, she will
be Baroness von Blomberg. That's good protection. At any rate, I
am immensely pleased, and when you meet her, you'll see why."
He mentioned that he planned a reception for the newlyweds
upon their return from their honeymoon.

The talk at the Stammtisch turned to politics, the state of the
economy, and back to politics. They all agreed that the future
looked far from rosy, and they speculated about what party and
which individual was qualified to govern Germany. There seemed
to be no favorite. The banker discussed the fragile post-war
economics and advised his cronies to exchange their marks for
Swiss francs, or buy property. "I'm afraid we cannot stop a major
inflation coming at us," he voiced his fears, "and in order to save
your assets, buy real estate, buy art." For the last twenty years, these
influential men had done business together, had profited highly
from combining their large assets in business ventures, and, at the
same time, contributed to the growth of the city.

The Old Baron was the first to leave. Sometimes his friends
were too serious for him. They worried too much. He had been a
gambler all his life and had played at winning without fear of
losing. It had worked for him. Once settled in his car, he tapped his
chauffeur gently on the shoulder with the tip of his cane, "Herr
Schmidt, please take me to Fräulein Charlotte's house. I need a
little laughter." The Old Baron smiled to himself. Among her many
attributes, Fräulein Charlotte knew how to make him laugh,

———————————

Antonia and Helene left no detail to chance when they planned
Irene's introduction to big-city life. The next five days were

packed full of new sights, sounds, and surprises, all of which
Irene stored away in her mind until she could sort them out
and relive them. Performances of La Bohème, Tosca, Swan
Lake, an evening of provocative and witty acts at the cabaret, a
tea dance, and romantic dinners left her glowing and grateful.
Lucy remained big-eyed, overwhelmed, and quietly enchanted
No wonder Max wanted to live in Breslau, she thought to
herself; he had had a taste of it. Most definitely, there was the
concern about the big city's recovery from the wounds of war.
Germany's uncertain future cast dark shadows over the
attempt to bring back the sparkle and glitter of the good life
enjoyed in the pre-war years.

But throwing concerns and worries into the wind, Antonia and
Helene took the girls on a whirlwind tour of what Breslau had to
offer. They introduced them to Gerstel, their favorite dress salon,
went window shopping at the "family" furrier, the art and antique
galleries, and the French shoe and glove boutique. After a stop at
Hammels, the jeweler, they went in to the Café Hutmacher where
everybody knew everybody, and where the music and the food
were superb. When appetites were satisfied and thirst quenched,
the four of them visited Breslau Printing & Publishing. Martin,
beaming from ear to ear, proudly showed them around and introduced Irene and Lucy to his staff. Irene was greatly impressed
with the orderliness of the plant, the cordial atmosphere, and the
pleasant manners of the people who worked there.

The final stop was at Martin's flat in a five-story building on
a quiet, tree-lined avenue not far from downtown. "I helped
him refurnish it last year," Antonia remarked, as they walked
into the large, comfortable living room. "I replaced some of the
depressing bachelor dreariness with lights and colors. A few
pieces of art, some silver and crystal here and there, made all
the difference. I'll be happy to assist you with the changes you
may want to make, and take you shopping until you find your

way around." Irene loved the tall windows, handsome furniture, and colorful Persian carpets. As she walked from room to room a warm sense of belonging, a sense of home and comfort sheltered her.

When Irene asked about visiting their mother, Helene, after a deep pause, answered slowly, as though weighing every word. "I saw Mother the other day and told her about you and Martin, and the upcoming festivities in which she is included. She was unresponsive—unapproachable—and said something to the effect that she would prefer to meet you at another time." Helene assured Irene not to take this personally. "Don't let it worry you, please. It has nothing to do with you. It's Mother. It's just the way she is. She was relieved when I left a few minutes later. I had disturbed the silence of her emptiness."

Irene let it rest. She thought that one difficult mother in her life was enough for the moment. She would gladly wait before facing another one.

And, of course, there was Martin. He showed up in a shiny, newly purchased automobile, complete with chauffeur and plaid lap-robes. "I can't have my wife running around town in this cold weather," he explained. "And," he added with a grin, "I have to stop borrowing my father's car. I think I'm cramping his style."

It was late afternoon, on the sixth day of their visit, when Martin—as arranged—appeared at the girls' hotel suite, followed by a waiter pushing a white-linen-draped cart with a samovar of tea and a silver tray piled high with mouth-watering petit fours. A second waiter placed a bottle of champagne in an ice bucket and set three glasses on a side table.

"I really can't wait another minute to tell you what is happening tomorrow and the day after, *Liebchen*," his voice crackling with excitement. Lucy made an attempt to rise and leave the room, but Martin held her back. "No, no, my dear; please stay. You've been part of this all along."

He turned to Irene, grabbed her hands, pumped them up and down a few times like a little boy might do, cleared his voice, and said. "Here it is! Tomorrow afternoon we are driving to Schloss Warteburg where we will spend the night. The next day, precisely at noon, we are getting married in a civil ceremony. Ida and her husband Werner are coming by train from Berlin, and my brother Eugene and Father, of course, will also be there. Antonia and Erich have made all the arrangements, everything is in place, and I," he ended breathlessly, "I am beside myself with happiness."

Irene nodded wordlessly, eyes shining. Lucy had the good sense to ignore the teacups and poured champagne into the three glasses. She raised hers spontaneously, somewhat surprising herself about coming out of her shell.

"To my beloved sister, to life, and *mazeltov*." Glasses touched, champagne bubbles danced, and tears of joy were blinked away.

Irene finally found her voice. She embraced her sister. "I know I have disappointed my mother. There is nothing I can do, nor will I talk it to death. Just tell her that I am happy; tell her about our visit, and meeting our new family. But please, don't plead my case. You go about your life. I shall write to her."

Martin explained that he and Irene would leave on their honeymoon right after lunch—drive back to Breslau, board the Old Baron's railroad car, and head for romantic Italy. Antonia would take Lucy to catch the train for Lubitz.

"This time, Lucy," he apologized, "you won't have a private railroad car, but you will travel first class."

"Oh dear, dear," she bantered, "I don't know if I can be expected to handle that."

"I'll leave you to your packing now." Martin rose from his chair. "Tomorrow is going to be a big day—a day of great joy!"

Having bumped over a half-frozen, unpaved country road for twenty miles after they left the main highway, Werner, the chauffeur, drove Martin's silver-gray Mercedes through the tall, wrought-iron gates of Schloss Warteburg, honking his horn a few times, announcing his arrival.

Huge chestnut trees, their bare branches touching, lined both sides of a wide driveway like watchful sentinels. Werner brought the car to a stop in front of the three-story, brick-and-stone building where the Warteburgs had made their home for generations. Turrets, broad chimneys, and leaded windows gave the old *Schloss* a medieval look.

As Martin helped Irene and Lucy out of the car, the massive brass-trimmed front door flew open and Antonia, with Erich at her side, stepped out onto the terrace to welcome their guests. Large lanterns lined the stone steps that reached up to the house and broke the dim light of the late afternoon dusk with their flickering candles. Irene and Lucy were ushered into the spacious hall with its marble floor, where a red-carpeted curved staircase led to the upper two floors. A huge bouquet of tea roses, nestling among lacy ferns in an elegant crystal vase, sat on a round table in the center of the hall.

"Welcome. Welcome to our home," Erich's voice boomed over the hustle of servants carrying luggage up the stairs. "We've never been happier than playing host to your wedding," he greeted Irene and his brother-in-law with great warmth.

Antonia took over, showing the girls to the third-floor guest rooms. She opened the door to a cozy chintz-and-flowers bedroom with windows looking out at the sprawling formal gardens in back of the house, now covered with pillows of snow. "Your room, Lucy, is connected to Irene's by this door, and is its twin in every way."

"Oh, how lovely," Irene spoke in a barely audible voice. "I'm overwhelmed with everyone's kindness and generosity. I have run out of ways to say thank you. I do feel like Cinderella! I'm having such a wonderful time."

"And so you should," replied Antonia. "This is your moment. Live and enjoy every breath of it."

Before Antonia left, she told her guests to rest until it was time to dress for dinner. "We will join the family in the first-floor drawing room at six o'clock." She pointed to a crystal bowl filled to the brim with marzipan, nougat, and dark chocolate pieces. "These should hold you over until dinner. The candy comes from Sarotti, my favorite place for sinful nibbling." She grinned, snatched a piece of candy, and whisked out of the room.

Stretched out on the chaise longue, next to the crackling fire in the baroque white-tile stove, Irene closed her eyes in an attempt to nap. But sleep wouldn't come to her busy mind. Behind her eyes she watched the parade of events from the last days march by. Everything felt right. Walking into a world so far removed from that of her parent's home had been as natural to her as breathing. She admired the liveliness of these bright people, the conversations that sparkled with ideas—challenging and thought provoking. She had discovered her love and need for music and her appreciation for art and treasures. She felt at home.

When Irene and Lucy walked into the formal drawing room that evening, new faces approached, eager to meet them. The men in their black-and-white evening attire presented a stark contrast to the colorful gowns of the ladies and their glittering jewels. Ida Bohne, Martin's middle sister, was as striking as the other two. Werner, her husband, a slender man of medium height, had searching gray eyes and an unruly shock of reddish-brown hair which gave him a boyish look.

Carl Schreiber, Helene's distinguished-looking, white-haired husband with his patrician face and gentle hazel eyes, greeted

Irene warmly. "I talked Antonia into letting me be your right-hand dinner partner tonight, so that I can have a chance to get to know you better. My wife told me a bit about you and she is truly taken with you—and so happy for Martin."

Eugene introduced himself with a playful grin on his handsome face and announced, "How lovely to meet you. However," he teased in mock concern, "are you sure you know what you're getting into—marrying my brother, I mean?"

"Only time will tell," Irene laughed. "And you," she added, "are exactly as Martin described you: a man looking for trouble."

The Old Baron appeared all smiles and turned to Eugene, "Watch out for that one, son. Not only can she look right through you, but she also lets you know what she sees. I shall have to watch my steps."

Irene and her sister were drawn into the circle of jovial banter and lighthearted conversation like moths to the light. It was as though an unspoken agreement existed between the family not to mar the festive occasion with talk about the hard times facing their country, the early signs of inflation, and the ominous cloud of political revolt that sailed over everyone's head. The subject was not brought up.

Arm in arm, Martin and Irene walked into the dining room after Heinrich, the butler, announced that dinner was served. Soft violin music filtered into the chandelier-lit room from the wide hallway where Antonia had stationed the musicians. Champagne flowed and course after course appeared like magic from Schloss Warteburg's kitchen, known for its fine cuisine. After dinner, Heinrich served strong mocha in delicate Sevres demitasses, along with rich amber-colored brandy in chubby snifters.

The evening flew by, candles flickered good night, and one by one the guests retired and headed up to their third-floor guest rooms.

Martin held on to Irene's hand for a moment longer. "I won't see you until our noon wedding, Irene," Martin said regretfully. "Antonia warned me to stay away. But, after that, you're stuck with me," he hugged her good night.

"I'll just have to grow accustomed to it, but I'm sure I'll manage." Irene's eyes glowed.

No one mentioned the absence of Martin's mother, nor did anyone express regrets that Irene's family was not attending the festivities. Irene kept chasing the waves of guilt and sadness away with great regularity, determined not to let negative thoughts ruin her wedding. The bond between her and her parents ran deep and strong, but her devotion to Martin, and the life they were about to share, was of ultimate importance. It was the future. It was her dream come to life.

February the thirteenth, 1919 dawned under gray, wintry skies. By nine o'clock a weak, but determined sun, aided by gusts of blustering winds, began to chase away the clouds and a clear, blue sky greeted the noon hour. Overnight, magic hands had turned the drawing room into a lush garden. Greenery and palm trees hovered in corners and large, marble urns filled with tea roses formed a half circle where the simple wedding ceremony would take place.

At noon sharp, Carl Schreiber escorted the bride, dressed in an elegant light-blue afternoon dress, into the drawing room where Lucy, Martin, and the guests were already waiting. Carl kissed the bride lightly on each cheek and took his place next to the groom. The justice of the peace, a portly gentleman in a dark suit, appeared from the back of the room, stepped into the circle of roses, and faced the couple. The ceremony, void of frills and poetic words, was over in ten minutes, ending with the signing of papers after which the justice of the peace pronounced the couple man and wife. Martin slipped a fabulous sapphire-and-diamond ring on Irene's hand and kissed the bride. "Martin," she choked on her breath, "the ring is so . . . so beautiful. And I," she looked bewildered, "I have no gift for you . . . I wish . . . "

He simply squeezed her hand and turned to their guests, who showered the newlyweds with good wishes, congratulations, hugs, and kisses. Heinrich and his helper offered frosty glasses of champagne. At the end of a round of rousing toasts, the wedding party followed Heinrich into the dining room and found their seats at the festive lunch table. As soon as everyone had been seated, the Old Baron tapped his wine glass with a fork, waited for the chatter to die down, and rose to his feet. He cleared his throat importantly, as though to make sure he had everyone's attention.

"I am no different from other parents who want their children to have the best in life. I would like to add one more gift to the ones you have already received. But, there's a bit of history that goes with it. I shall be brief. Having lived in a big city most of my life, I developed a strong urge to have a place in the country. And, as good fortune would have it, I was able to acquire a charming little country estate—not far from here, just one day before it was to go under the hammer. Over the last fourteen months, with the help of fine craftsmen and helpers, the manor house, the gardens, as well as the land, are being restored to their original state. That restoration will go on for some time. A wonderful family of eight, the Burdachs, live in cottages on the grounds and have taken care of the estate for years. These people are pure gold and Marienhall is a little jewel. However, when I spent several days there, in the peaceful quiet of the countryside, I quickly came to the conclusion that it was not really a lifestyle I could embrace. I missed the heartbeat of the city."

He paused for a moment, and directed his glance at Irene, who sat at his left. "And when you, my dear, came into my son's life, I knew why I had held on to Marienhall." He reached into the inside pocket of his morning coat, retrieved a white envelope, and handed it to her. "This is the deed to Marienhall and all its lands. May the two of you live there in peace and harmony. May you be a good steward of the land, and may God bless Marienhall."

The Old Baron had a suspicious glistening of moisture in his eyes as he embraced his son and his new daughter-in-law. The silence of the room turned into a tower of Babel, with everyone talking and laughing at the same time.

"Hear, hear!" Eugene shouted, "Father has been at it again. This time he has outdone himself."

"Not at all," the old man laughed, pleased with himself. "I've just been lucky." He turned to Irene and told her that upon her return from their travel, he would like to have the privilege of showing the "gift" to her, and Martin, by himself. "I so hope, my dear, that you approve and that you'll fall in love with Marienhall as I have. There is still much to be done, including furnishing some of the rooms. But that is your task," he patted her hand. "You need to put your own finishing touches to the old place and make it yours—all yours."

Irene was stunned and slow to find her voice. Choking back tears of joy and surprise, she rose and took his hand. "Once again I don't know what to say," she confessed. "For now, I shall simply offer my thanks." She kissed him on his cheek and sat down again.

"That will do nicely, my dear," the Old Baron assured her. "I've said it before and I'll say it again, you have brought great pleasure to an old man."

Just before dessert was served, Irene and Lucy slipped away to go upstairs where Irene would change into traveling clothes. Both girls quickly finished packing, and were soon ready to leave.

Lucy held on to her sister. "I shall miss you," she cried, letting tears flow freely. "I am sure," she sobbed, "life will be gloomy at home. Mother will be . . . well, she will be Mother."

"Just think, Lucy," Irene interrupted, "in less than three months you will be married, and most probably be on your way to Breslau. Martin and I will come to your wedding, and I just might be able to set things right with Mother. In any case, please, don't worry and, again, don't try to fight my battles for me. Mother will come to accept what I have done—or not. It is hers to decide."

Lucy dried her tears and, hand-in-hand, the two young women descended the staircase to the first floor. Everyone had gathered in the entrance hall. Martin stood by the open door, dressed in country tweeds. Impatient, he reached for Irene's hand and pulled her to his side. "As soon as the servants have stored your luggage in the car, we're off."

A moment later, Werner walked up the stone steps to the entrance. "We're ready to go, Sir."

Under a shower of confetti and paper snakes, the newlyweds made their way to the waiting automobile, climbed in, and, through the open car window, waved wildly, throwing kisses as the car slowly moved away from Schloss Warteburg.

Happy ending. Happy beginning. Next stop, married life.

Toni, with Ana Marieke at her side, stepped out of the sheltering warmth of the Lubitz Depot and onto the wintry platform as the train from Breslau clanked and screeched to a halt, letting go a sky-climbing column of steam. Lucy waved from the open window of her first-class compartment, disappeared from view, bounced down the few steps to the platform a moment later, and rushed towards the two women. As soon as Toni realized Irene was not on the train, her eyes opened wide, thunderclouds gathered on her face and froze her features into a mask of bitter disappointment.

"Both my daughters have betrayed me," she managed to hiss between a sob and strangled breathing as she turned her wrath on her youngest. On the three-hour long train ride Lucy had prepared herself for the anticipated onslaught of her mother's fury she knew would greet her. Lucy let the barrage of boiling anger wash over her, kept her eyes pleadingly on Toni, and finally interrupted her in mid-sentence.

"Please, Mother," she said in a consoling tone that had an edge of impatience to it, "nothing you or I could have done or said would have changed this outcome. Irene didn't get married to spite you or disrespect you. She got married because she met the man she loves."

Without a reply, Toni tossed her head in a defiant manner, turned sharply on her heels and headed for Arthur and the waiting car. During the short ride to the house, she remained silent, her features set in stiff lines of dour disappointment. Back upstairs in the family's quarters, she addressed Ana Marieke and Lucy in a toneless, dry voice. "I want to be left alone; I do not wish to be disturbed." She dropped her hat and coat on a chair in the small vestibule, walked into the guest room under the eaves, slammed the door shut, and turned the key in the lock.

Lucy buried her face in her hands and let out a deep groan. When her hands came down again, tears flowed freely as she looked at Ana Marieke with wounded eyes. Before she could say anything, Ana Marieke grabbed the weeping young woman by her shoulders. "Listen to me," she said, shaking her gently, "I am going to say it one more time. Leave her alone; go about your life. Neither you nor your sister are responsible for your mother's happiness. She is going to be all right. Just leave it alone."

When Herman discovered his wife's latest act of revolt, he decided not to interfere in what he called her crisis tantrum. He would give her time to come to her senses.

On the morning of the second day of Toni's withdrawal from the household, Ana Marieke pounded on the guest room door until Toni finally let her in. The two women spent more than an hour together, and when they finally emerged from Toni's sanctuary they acted as though nothing out of the ordinary had happened. Neither woman talked about what had gone on between them in that hour-long confrontation. Ana Marieke wore a tiny, secret smile of satisfaction for the longest time and Toni appeared cheerful. When Herman welcomed her back from her self-imposed isolation, she mumbled something about "having had to take time to sort out womanly things," closed the incident by saying that all's well that ends well and hid the rest of the story behind a silly, little, apologetic grin.

Time would do the rest.

PART TWO

THE HARSH SOUNDS of steel-heeled boots cracking sharply against the pavement were coming closer to the city square, heralding the immediate arrival of columns of marching men. Like undulating snakes, throngs of people lined the sidewalks of the street, eyes searching the distance—waiting. Soon, long lines of marching Brown Shirts in full voice, goose-stepping in time to the *Horst Wessel Lied* (Germany's new national anthem) came into view. The men strutting smartly at the head of the parade carried flashy standards, each topped prominently by a shimmering, silver eagle. Others were carrying huge, wind-whipped red-and-white flags with Hitler's black swastika emblazoned in their centers. Automobiles stopped and hugged the curb on both sides of the broad street to make room for the SA's (*Sturmabteilung* storm troopers or Brown Shirts) swaggering display of brute power.

". . . *Today . . . Germany . . . Tomorrow the World* . . ." Male voices roared their obscene message and the wind carried it down the street, up through the air, and into the open windows of the tall apartment buildings that lined the avenue.

His face closed against the world, a slight man of medium height, his shoulders hunched inward, his head tucked down, and his eyes frozen to the ground, was trying to be invisible. Hastily making his way to the nearest doorway, he was trapped by the excited masses who viewed the impromptu parade with glowing pride. Their arms were raised high in the Nazi salute as they frantically shouted a string of *Sieg Heils* at the parading Nazis. The quiet man tried in vain to leave the scene unnoticed. But in his silent haste, the metal latch of his briefcase caught in the coarse netting of a housewife's shopping bag and accidentally yanked it from its owner's hand. Surprised, the stout, ruddy-faced woman looked up and, taking one quick look at the offender's gray face, she shrieked, "Jew . . . Jew . . . Thief . . . Goddamned Jew pig. He tried to steal from me . . . Jew pig!"

In the flash of a second, the frightened man's briefcase pulled free and the furious woman hauled off, aiming her heavy bag at the offender's head. No sooner had the housewife's weapon connected with her target, than a policeman rushed to her side. His heavy club came crashing down on the man's head and shoulders in a relentless series of cruel blows. The innocent pedestrian raised his hands, in a futile gesture to ward off the descent of the wooden club as the crowd pushed in against the two men, fists raised, yelling "*Jude, Jude . . . Juden-Schwein!*"

The man's knees folded under him in an almost comical way, and the slight figure silently crumpled, unprotestingly, into a motionless heap onto the sidewalk.

Less than a minute had passed since the first blow fell on the mute bystander, when a broad-shouldered SA man broke away from the marching column and forcefully pushed his way through the onlookers. "Pig! Jew-pig," the newcomer yelled in tune with the crowd, his handsome face contorted in an ugly mask of hate and disgust. He raised his foot, and his shiny boot gave the gray-suited heap of misery a swift kick to the groin, followed by several well-aimed, vicious, bone-crushing blows to the head. A thin line of blood appeared on the man's caved-in forehead and slowly trickled down his pale face—all signs of life, spent.

The crowd fell silent, turned its back on the lifeless figure, and watched the uniformed column smartly straighten its ranks as the men resumed their high-stepping march. The song rang out again . . . *"When the Jew blood runs from our knives . . . Today Germany . . . Tomorrow the world."* Slowly, as the parade disappeared down the street, the people dispersed. Some older boys left the sidewalk and joined the tail end of the offensive procession to march along with the fast-moving columns. Kicking their legs high, they attempted to keep pace while blending their young voices with those of their goose-stepping heroes.

The strident words of the Nazi songs still hung in the air but were no longer offensive to the lonely, lifeless figure of the quiet man on the sidewalk—a piece of human refuse; garbage; a discard hardly worth noticing.

Sieg Heil!

Tomorrow . . . the world!

Chapter Twelve

LESS THAN AN hour's drive from Breslau, and in total contrast to the noise and hustle of the big city, Marienhall dozed quietly—peaceful in the hot summer sun. The air was fragrant with a blending of the sweet scent of summer roses and freshly cut clover. Huge chestnut trees lined the golden-gravel driveway that started at the tall iron gates, led past the stately old manor house, and eventually disappeared into the sun-dappled denseness of a small forest. A lazy quiet hovered over the well-tended lawns, the wide ribbons of flower beds, and the rose garden. Winding in and out of the shade, several narrow paths led away from the house to the formal gardens and the boxwood maze. One path circled the big pond—where Tristan and Isolde, a pair of regal, white swans made their home.

At the back of the manor house, below the west terrace, rose bushes edged the gravel walk that led to the gazebo and meandered all the way to the banks of the sparkling, narrow stream that rambled through the land. Large stone urns planted with an abundance of bright red geraniums sat among the wicker furniture on the west terrace—Irene's favorite spot for tea, talk, and dreaming, since that first summer day when she and Martin moved into Marienhall.

Irene's dark head nestled against the pillows of her wicker lounge. Her hands, with fingers spread wide apart, rested on the small mound of her belly, patiently waiting to feel signs of the new life she was carrying. She and Martin had waited a long time for this baby: almost nine years.

Irene closed her eyes and let her mind roam back to the events that brought her to this time. She could recall every detail of their wedding day: the generosity of Martin's family, the fragrance of the flowers, and the love in Martin's eyes as he slipped the precious ring on her finger. In their first night together their commitment to each other came full circle—a marriage made in heaven.

The romance of their honeymoon trip remained a vivid memory. How could she ever forget those heavenly days exploring Italy—Rome, Florence, Venice, Naples. The pages of her father's atlas had come to life in a whirlwind of colors, antiquity, glorious music, and art. Martin was a thoughtful and lively companion but, at the end, he confessed sheepishly that he was not wild about traipsing around the world on long, extended tours. He preferred short trips. He was, basically, a homebody.

Irene and Martin started married life in his comfortable bachelor flat. During their absence, Antonia had brought in some potted greenery and, celebrating their arrival, she filled the place with fresh flowers. She left a note for Irene, saying she would be delighted to take her around town and help her get acquainted with her new milieu. Frau Holland, Martin's housekeeper of many years, had fussed and scrubbed and polished the place to a shine.

Marriage fit the couple like a glove—it was made for them. Intuitive, thoughtful, and respectful of each other's feelings, they acted as though they had already spent a lifetime together. Martin, Irene reaffirmed, was a gentle and simple man with simple needs and a big heart. He was not impressed by wealth or social standing, and was as much at home sharing lunch with his workers, as he was dining in the stately halls of Warteburg. He loved people, had a small circle of good friends, and soon, to the delight of her proud husband, Irene hosted her own dinner parties. He loved everything about her, and she could find no fault with him.

No sooner had they returned from their honeymoon, when the Old Baron whisked them away to Marienhall in his magnificent new automobile—all chrome and shine and leather. After heading west out of the city on a narrow country road for about thirty-five kilometers, the chauffeur tuned into a half-open, ornate iron gate, followed the tree-lined gravel path, and stopped the car in front of an unpretentious-looking, three-story structure.

"Welcome to Marienhall, your new home!" The Old Baron looked expectantly at his son and his bride, waiting for their reaction to his gift. "What do you say?"

"Father, I don't know what to say," Martin mumbled, overwhelmed. "It's . . . it's . . . beautiful . . . actually . . . quite wonderful. Let me catch my breath."

More than 150 years old, and void of any fancy or artistic trimmings, Marienhall made no pretense of being anything other than a sturdy, spacious old manor house that promised shelter, comfort, and continuity to its masters.

Irene took in the gray stone building with its tall, narrow windows, French doors, and its surprisingly flat roof. Her moment of awe quickly gave way to a small fit of the giggles when her eyes fell on the short, turret-like structure that squatted importantly, smack in the middle of the roof. Encircled by a filigreed, knee-high iron fence, the "tower" looked more like a misplaced gazebo.

"Somebody," she laughed, pointing at the roof, "wanted to make a castle out of a manor house; somebody with a sense of humor. I like it. It makes me feel at home."

Martin chuckled as he took Irene's hand and playfully skipped up the broad stone steps that spilled onto a wide terrace. As if on cue, both wings of the weathered-oak front door flew open, and eight handsome people with smiling faces stepped onto the terrace, lining up four by four on each side of the entrance.

Beaming with pride, the Old Baron reached for the older couple's hands and pulled them forward. "Martin, Irene, I want you to meet the heart and soul of Marienhall: Lothar and Trude Burdach. These two, and their wonderful family, are the true keepers of the land."

Irene took one look at Trude Burdach's deep blue eyes and her kind, finely lined face. On impulse, she embraced the older woman with a deep knowing that another Ana Marieke had come into her life. She then shook hands with Maria, the older Burdach daughter and Liesel, the younger one. Tall and handsome, Otto and Fritz Burdach introduced their respective wives, Heidi and Margarete. Little could Irene and Martin know just how much they would come to depend on the Burdachs, and what an unwavering source of strength and loyalty they would be.

"When we've finished our tour of the house," the Old Baron announced, "we are going to have tea with the Burdachs in Lothar's cottage. You can get better acquainted and find out what everyone does. Just wait, you'll be impressed."

After admiring the spacious hall with its softly glowing, silver-gray marble floor, they entered the library. Handcrafted bookshelves, waiting to be filled, lined the walls of the big room and heavy, carved, masculine furniture rested on burgundy-red Persian carpets. A large dining room, a huge formal "main" room, as well as a good-sized drawing room completed the main floor.

The second floor was less formal and had been designed for family living. There were two bedrooms with adjoining dressing rooms, a bright and sunny breakfast-sitting room, and a nursery wing with a schoolroom and nanny quarters. The third floor consisted of several guest suites and ample storage areas for linens, china, crystal, and household goods. One of the attic rooms was filled with rolls of Oriental carpets, paintings, bronzes, and odd pieces of antique furniture, all waiting to be placed.

On the way to the cellar, the Old Baron proudly explained that the antiquated kitchen had been remodeled and refurbished with white cabinetry and the most modern equipment available. Irene immediately compared the "new look" to the old tavern kitchen where she and Lucy had prepared countless meals. It certainly was a "world-away" improvement over Lubitz.

"This kitchen," the Old Baron boasted, "is better than the finest restaurant kitchens in Europe. It has everything, and everything is brand new."

"Just so Irene is happy here," Martin exclaimed, "I love her cooking and I want her to have whatever she needs to prepare her wonderful meals."

"Oh," she retorted, tongue-in-cheek, "don't ever worry for a minute. I love this kitchen and I am certain it will fill my needs, perfectly." She smiled to herself, with designs of her own as to how the kitchen would function.

The rest of the big basement was taken up by a not-so-modern laundry facility, food storage space, and a well-stocked wine cellar.

"Father," Martin put his hands on his broad shoulders, "whatever made you find this place is nothing short of a miracle. I am so grateful. Thank you . . . "

The Old Baron winked wickedly at his son. "I'm glad you approve."

On their way to the Burdach cottage, Martin and Irene admired the sprawling lawns, the pond, the groomed gardens, and the well-tended orchard. Spring had arrived early that year, and the fruit trees were resplendent in their pink and white tutus of blossoms. With each compliment, with each joyful exclamation about their new home, the Old Baron's chest puffed out a bit more.

"I have grown very fond of Marienhall. I can't wait to see you and Martin settled in. And, I might add," he beamed, "Marienhall is a good place to raise my grandchildren—all in good time, of course," he added hastily. "All in good time."

"I have always wanted to travel and to see the world," Irene mused, "but I think that now I will have a hard time tearing myself away from this place. Paris and London may just have to wait a while."

The air in Lothar and Trude's cottage was humming with animated conversation as everyone settled around the big round table. A bowl of lilies of the valley, blue-and-white dishes, small platters piled high with tiny sandwiches, tempting pastries, and a basket of fresh strawberries from Lothar's greenhouse, graced the table.

One thing became clear to Irene at once. There was no "master-servant" tone at this gathering. If anything, the Burdachs were more reserved than the Blombergs. The Burdachs belonged to the land and made the newcomers feel welcome. With a blend of graceful respect, camaraderie, and unassuming pride, Lothar explained the workings of Marienhall.

"You can look at Trude and me," Lothar began with a chuckle in his voice, "as the faithful old retainers. We see to it that Marienhall is well run, but we make our offspring and their spouses do all the work. And their service makes us look very good."

Teasing, Otto let out a theatrical groan, matched by a painful grimace explaining that he and Fritz, along with the villagers, managed the land, the dairy, and the livestock. "Heidi and Margarete take care of our two boys and Fritz's twin girls. And, I have to brag a bit, our wives are fine cooks; they bake and baste their way into everyone's heart."

"Maria is my head housekeeper," Trude spoke up, patting her daughter's hand. "She bosses her sister Liesel around and, Liesel,"

Trude paused, looking at her youngest child with just the slightest hint of a frown, "is getting married in the fall. Her young man will be working with our sons."

"I am the black sheep of the family," Maria interjected with humor, "I have no intentions of getting married. I quite like it this way." Trude shook her head in disagreement, but kept a twinkle in her wise, blue eyes.

While Martin and Irene learned about the workings of Marienhall and its tiny village of fifteen families, they fell in love with the Burdachs. Later, they confessed to each other that it felt like they had found a long-lost family of relatives. Irene was especially aware of Trude and Maria, whose faces seemed to light up each time their eyes met hers. An unspoken bond was immediately formed between the new owners of Marienhall, and the Burdachs.

With the Old Baron in the lead, they left Marienhall reluc-tantly, and on the way back to the city—excited and euphoric—they made plans to finish the manor house and move in by summer. One look at his father, and Martin knew how pleased and content he was. The Old Baron confirmed his feelings once more before they parted. With his arms around Martin and Irene's shoulders, pulling them close against his big frame, he cleared his throat, "I have to say it again: you've given this old man another reason to be happy."

———————

Irene held her breath for a second and smiled contently when she felt a soft poking movement under the hands that hugged her belly. "Hello, child of mine," she whispered into the summer breeze and, for a brief moment, wondered if the first grandchild in the Blomberg family could be the key to open the iron door to Henrietta's iron heart.

She had a vivid memory of the day Helene had taken her to Breslau to meet her mother-in-law. A heavy layer of furniture polish mixed with a good dose of chlorine clogged the air in the grand foyer and followed them into the kitchen. Henrietta motioned her guests to be seated at the bare, wooden table. She ignored the basket of bright spring flowers Irene attempted to hand to her. The older woman, attired in a dark gray cotton dress of Victorian vintage, sat down and, with fidgeting fingers, arranged the folds of the full, floor-length skirt. She had not said a word.

"Mother," Helene broke the uncomfortable silence, "this is Irene, your new daughter-in-law. I am sorry you missed the wedding."

"I know," Henrietta replied with neither a glance at Irene nor a sign of emotion. "She married Martin. I knew you would come. Didn't you tell her," she charged at Helene in a cranky, raspy voice, forcing the words through clenched teeth as though in pain, "that I don't go out and I don't have time for visitors? Young woman," she turned to Irene, "I hope Martin doesn't turn out like his father—all blow and bluster and mischief. And," she added, eyes turned down, searching for an offensive spot on the scrubbed-to-death wooden table, "I don't meddle in my children's lives. I'm very busy with my own."

She got up, rubbing her hands together nervously with a rotating motion. Turning away from her guests, she announced coldly, to no one in particular, "I've got things to do. Maybe we'll have tea the next time." Irene took a deep breath of relief when the poor woman disappeared through a door at the end of the antiseptic room.

"Well," Helene exclaimed, as she draped one arm protectively around Irene's shoulders, "I hope you're not too shocked. We predicted this kind of welcome, but still, I kept wishing for more . . . but," her voice trailed off into a low sigh, "life is what it is."

On their way out, Helene turned on the light in the dark foyer. The magnificent chandelier sparkled to life, mirroring its image on the black marble floor. Ornate, white doors with shiny brass handles came into view. Helene tried one of the doors, but it was locked.

"This is what she does," she groaned. "She locks every door. I can't even remember what these rooms look like." Helene sighed. "My mother is truly a prisoner of her own doing. But, enough said," she added with an attempt at cheerfulness. "Let's go to Hutmachers, check out the crowd, and have champagne with our lunch."

Irene, who had said nothing except good day and goodbye during this dismal encounter, had not been offended by Henrietta's impersonal and vague manner; she only felt a deep sadness for that forlorn and empty woman. What had gone wrong with Henrietta's soul? Why this separation from life, she wondered?

Back on the street, she had tossed the unanswered questions into the crisp, clear air and, like balloons released from their string, they sailed away. Helene was right, *life is what it is.*

In contrast to the fiasco of meeting Henrietta, a letter from Toni a few days later brought Irene's satisfaction with her new life to full circle. In a warm and genuinely cheerful tone, Toni Burger, waving the white flag of parental surrender, belatedly conveyed her good wishes and a promise to visit soon. She confessed how much she missed her eldest daughter and how much she meant to her.

Being the original peacemaker, Irene glowed with gratitude and contentment from head to foot. And when she came face to face with her mother in Lubitz, at Lucy's wedding in late May, Irene flew into Toni's arms. Between sobs and tears and laughter, all wounds healed and there were no scars remaining. With a graceful motion, Toni then reached for Martin's hands with both of hers and welcomed her son-in-law with wordless acceptance. Martin, who had remained at Irene's side, raised her hand to his lips and, encouraged by Toni's warm and pleasant demeanor, bent down and kissed her on both cheeks.

From behind a shadow, pleased and smiling, Ana Marieke appeared, embraced Irene, and whispered, "See, I told you she would come around. She just needed some time."

Watching the happy proceedings, Herman stood grinning in the background. Satisfied, he said to himself, "All's well that ends well." He was content that his family was no longer divided.

Lucy's wedding had been a simple family affair. She was married in the synagogue she grew up in, but had insisted on a less ritual-burdened, shorter ceremony. She was pleasantly surprised when Toni accepted her wishes without the slightest opposition. And Lucy was elated when, after telling Toni that she and Max would be making their home in Breslau, her mother replied with a smile, "Well, this is good news. Now I have a double reason to come to the big city. It will be an adventure for me; I have never been to Breslau, you know."

Content and happy, Irene left Lubitz the day after the wedding. On the train ride home, she couldn't stop wondering how the town could have become so small, and shrunk so much in just a short four months.

"You wait until we settle in Marienhall," Martin had teased. "The town of Lubitz will take on more worldly proportions."

"Marienhall is not a town, it is our home and only a skip and a jump away from Breslau. It is really almost part of the city," Irene laughed.

On August 21, 1919 under a clear blue sky, with the gardens in full bloom and the fields waiting to be harvested, Martin and

Irene Blomberg moved into Marienhall. At the front door, in the company of eight loudly applauding Burdachs, Martin carried his wife over the threshold of the manor house.

"May God bless the master and his wife, and may God bless this house." With these words and a bouquet of fragrant blooms which he handed to Irene with a deep bow, Lothar greeted the new tenants with gladness in his eyes.

And the sun kept shining.

But the sun didn't shine on Germany—a beaten nation trying to heal the wounds of war. A crippling inflation raced across the country and ineffective leadership added fuel to the fires of national misery. It was the Old Baron's prophetic vision and shrewd business tactics that kept his whole family, and anyone who had listened to him, unaffected by the financial turmoil that brought hardship to the life of millions of Germans. He had protected himself against inflation by keeping his holdings in Swiss banks and dealing in foreign currencies. His children followed his advice and reaped the benefits of their father's counsel. If only his father had a hand in politics, Martin insisted half-seriously, Germany would be in better shape. But as much as the old man liked the game of tricky wheelings and dealings, he considered politics a gamble on shaky grounds with dubious, unreliable characters as players.

When Irene, with Antonia's help, finished the manor house, soothing shades of French blues, spring greens, ivory, and old rose warmed the large rooms. Antiques, paintings by the old masters, etchings, age-faded tapestries, stunning bronzes, sculptures, and pieces of crystal spoke of the owners' love for the arts.

The Burdachs were as proud of Marienhall's revival as Martin and Irene, not to mention the Old Baron. The latter visited often, but never appeared announced or empty-handed. He seemed to have unlimited access to the hidden treasures of Europe's antique dealers and collectors. His latest gift to Irene was a nine-piece cluster of precious snuff boxes dating back to Louis XIV.

"Don't overdo, please," Irene pleaded with him. "I don't want to live in a museum. If you bring any more treasures," she joked, "the house itself will rebel."

Although the old man melted in her presence, he respected her quick mind, admired her sense of humor and her unobtrusive nature. He also knew that behind that seemingly innocent smile, there lived a woman of purpose, steel-edged determination, and boundless strength.

He realized quickly that Irene's dark, pool-like eyes saw right through him, yet the young woman never sat in judgment of his interesting acquisition methods. Every once in a while, he swore that a quirky, almost conspiratory smile played on her face when some of his escapades came to light. His son Martin, he concluded, was one lucky man.

As much as he loved Marienhall, Martin didn't care where he lived as long as Irene was at his side. When his work or bad road conditions threatened to keep him in town, Irene would accompany him to the city and they would spend a few days at the apartment. Since, in the winter season, the theatre, operas, and concerts were in full swing, Irene was more than happy with the arrangement.

No sooner had the newlyweds settled in the old manor house, when Antonia and Helene introduced Martin and Irene to their sets of "country" friends and small dinner parties grew into big, festive occasions. Soon, it was time to reciprocate and Marienhall became the host to midnight dances, harvest balls, spring musicales, and summer gaiety around the small, lantern-lit lake. Chandeliers glittered, urns with Irene's favorite tea roses nestled in green, lacy ferns and slender candles in tall glass chimneys, all set the mood for enchantment.

Sleigh bells jingled gaily on starry winter nights, when guests were whisked away on big sleighs to Neukirch's Lake, where they skated to the lilting sounds of a waltz. Returning to Marienhall with red cheeks and cold noses, the merrymakers shed their furs, danced till the wee hours of the morning, and dove head first into Maria's scrumptious breakfast buffet before returning home.

The Old Baron was in his glory. He had finally found a splendid setting in which to entertain his friends and associates. Both Martin and Irene were delighted to share Marienhall with him, and Irene grew into a formidable hostess. The Old Baron reigned over a masked ball each March, a hunt ball in October, and hosted a winter gala in early December. At each occasion, he outdid his son and daughter-in-law and spared no expenses. These extravagant nights started at the dinner table with champagne, caviar, and sumptuous food, and ended with a performance by tumblers and acrobats, clever magicians, sketches from favorite classic ballets, or whole acts of a lively opera. Versatile musicians accompanied the performers in their renditions, switched beat, and played for the tireless guests who danced until dawn.

After Lucy and Max had been in Breslau for a year, Herman and Toni came to visit their daughters.

As usual, Henrietta remained unavailable, while the rest of the Blombergs couldn't do enough to entertain their visitors and celebrate the new family ties. And it worked. Kosher or not, Toni was a good sport and went along with the crowd. Later she confessed to Irene that she had taken the time to examine her ways and attitudes, and was seeing things in a different light.

"It's not healthy to be so wrapped up in one's ways and views as to dismiss the rest of the world. Look at me," she added, cupping her hands over her mouth to hide a smile, "may God forgive me. I haven't eaten kosher for two weeks and I'm still a good Jew." The Burgers' visits to Breslau became an annual event that tightened and strengthened the bond between the two families who not so long ago had been worlds apart. Little did they know then just how much they had in common.

Protected by financial freedom, and adopting a laissez-faire attitude about Germany's political future, Martin and Irene, like so many others, buried their heads in the sand and enjoyed the good life. Her dream of visiting Europe's capitols, of cruising the Mediterranean and Aegean waters, exploring the Canary Islands and Africa's north coast, had come true. But Marienhall was her anchor, the home she became more and more reluctant to leave. When her husband surprised her with a beautiful set of honey-rich, handmade luggage on their eighth wedding anniversary, she stored it away in the attic. Three years later, the suitcases still hadn't been used. Martin called her his Marienhall homebody.

From the beginning, he had taken an interest in the land, the livestock, and the small family dairy. He learned about farming and, with a good sense for business, encouraged Otto and Fritz to expand and modernize the farming activities to make them more profitable. Some of the extra monies went straight into Irene's waiting hands. She had taken it upon herself to see to the welfare of the village families. These poor people had been shamefully neglected by the previous owners, and responded with undying gratitude to the changes.

Trude Burdach often accompanied Irene on the visits to the homes of the villagers and, between the two of them, the life of Marienhall's small population improved tremendously. Hardwood replaced the dirt floors of every cottage. The installation of indoor plumbing and the addition of gleaming tile ovens moved these hardworking women to tears. They called Irene the patron saint of Marienhall.

Irene arranged and paid for proper medical care for the village families. She brought new ideas and modern methods for more sanitary housekeeping to them. And, finally, she saw to it that all the children—well fed and appropriately dressed—regularly attended school in the next village, twenty-six kilometers away. Leaving nothing to chance, she talked Martin into buying a truck for the farm, which also would serve to transport the youngsters to school and back.

Over the years, Martin had filled the empty library shelves with leather-bound classics, current literature, and an impressive number of first and second editions. With his passion for printing, he reveled in the feel and smell of aged paper and inks, and handled the books with gentle, caressing hands. Irene, equally fascinated with old volumes, accompanied him on many of his searches for printed treasures.

Life was good. Irene called it her fairy-tale life . . . *And they lived happily ever after.*

But there has never been a fairy tale without a villain.

From within Austria, shortly after the war, there rose an obscure nobody whose strident voice would soon be heard all over Germany. As early as 1920, Adolf Hitler founded the German National Socialist Party which boasted a rapidly growing membership. Hitler was on his way to becoming the villain of the twentieth century—a villain beyond evil.

Adolf Hitler delivered passionate promises of not only returning Germany to her proper place among Europe's leading nations, but to create a super state, a master race of pure Aryans that would eventually take over the world. He blamed losing the war, as well as Germany's post-war financial fiasco on the blood-sucking Jews whom he declared to be "the plague of the world."

When in 1923 an attempted *putsch* by his brown-shirted, swastika-toting followers failed, Adolf Hitler was incarcerated at the Landsberg prison. During his imprisonment, he wrote the book *Mein Kampf*, the blueprint for his reign over Germany which, of course, included his tirades against the Jews. His followers made *Mein Kampf* their Bible, while thousands of other good Germans—the Blombergs among them—dismissed Hitler's message as the rubbish ramblings of a crazy man. "Nobody in his right mind would let an upstart, an uneducated, hysterical rabble-rouser like Hitler run our country. Just you wait," they said, "he will return to the obscurity from whence he came."

But he didn't return from whence he came. In the fall of 1927 more than 20,000 Nazis flooded into Nuremberg to celebrate Third Party Day. In rapture, they listened to the *Führer's* incendiary speeches and shouted *Heil Hitler* into the night. By 1929, his brown-shirted storm troopers had grown to a powerful force of 60,000, and Hitler's voice became the insidious harangue that echoed through the country. His persistent message of national recovery and making real the myth of Parsifal and the Holy Grail appealed to the Teutonic mind of the masses.

Like an uncontrolled cancer, the evil tentacles of Nazism spread and invaded Germany. Even the confines of a peaceful, idyllic Marienhall would not be able to keep them out.

Chapter Thirteen
1930–1933

IT WAS A misty September day when the Old Baron's car pulled to a stop in front of Horst von Brunnen's baroque villa in Scheitnig, a quiet residential suburb of Breslau. Horst had called him in the morning and, with an urgency-laden voice, asked his friend to see him. No, he had insisted, not at the *Stammtisch*. He wanted to talk to him behind closed doors in the privacy of his home. He had been secretive and persistent.

Krueger, the butler, escorted the Old Baron to the library where Horst was waiting for him in front of a crackling fire. The two friends greeted each other warmly and Friedrich Wilhelm settled himself in the big chair facing his host. He placed his unlit cigar in a crystal ashtray on a table at his side and looked around himself. He loved this room with its deep red walls, fine paintings in ornate gold frames, and floor-to-ceiling bookshelves. Cheerful chintz prints covered comfortable down chairs and tall French doors made the room light and summery, even on the gloomiest days.

"So," the Old Baron asked a bit impatiently, "what is so important, Why this secrecy?"

"Let's wait for Krueger to bring us our coffee before I get started. I want to be sure all ears are far away from this room."

After Krueger served the men and left, Horst stood up. He put his forefinger against his lips and walked slowly to the tall double door which the butler had closed softly behind him a moment before. He waited for a few seconds, cautiously opened the door a crack, and peeked into the big hall. Satisfied that no one was in sight, he closed the door and returned to his chair by the fire.

The Old Baron's bushy eyebrows climbed up his forehead and a frown, like a question mark, appeared between his eyebrows. "What is going on? Is someone after you? Or what?"

His slender frame bent, Horst leaned forward in his chair and looked at his friend with troubled eyes. "Friedrich," he let out a deep breath, "I must have your word of honor that you will not talk about what I am going to tell you."

Serious now, the Old Baron reached for his friend's hand and shook it. "That goes without saying. You have my word."

"Let me ramble a bit and set the scene," Horst started slowly. "I need to make myself perfectly clear. Please bear with me, this is going to take a while.

"We've known each other for more than thirty-five years. We're friends, we're partners in business ventures, and adventures; we're closer than brothers. We've pulled our share of mischief, but we've never hurt anybody and we've always paid our debts. I trust you with my life, and I know that you have that same trust in me. What I am about to tell you will shock you, but you'll soon see the reason for my action, and do your part."

He took a sip of his coffee and, before his friend could interrupt him, continued breathlessly, "I have become a full-fledged member of NSDAP, swastika, armband, flag, and all. In other words, I am a registered Nazi now."

The Old Baron's mouth dropped open and, for a moment, he couldn't catch his breath "You what . . . ?" he whispered hoarsely, half rising out of his chair. "You did what?" he plopped back down again.

Horst grinned, sardonically, and raised both hands in a pleading gesture. "I knew you would come apart. But, please listen; please hear me out. It is going to make sense in the end, I promise."

There was a moment of heavy silence in the room before Horst continued.

"You know that I am a seeker, a searcher, a nosy, detail-oriented individual. You're the one who flies with the wind—the one with the ideas, the wild schemes. You found the deals, and I checked and researched and planned. We are both visionaries, but in different ways. Together, we have made a fortune or two.

"The same thoroughness of searching and questioning and planning with which I have handled our business affairs—and successfully so, I might add—I have devoted to Adolf Hitler for the past three years. I have watched the frightening rise to popularity of his Nazi party. I have looked beyond the man and the message and I have searched the minds of the masses. Here is what I see: Adolf Hitler is *not* going to be stopped. Adolf Hitler *will* eventually be elected to power, and he *will* deliver what he promised. And that translates into one very ominous fact: the Jews are his whipping boys, and may God help them." Horst von Brunnen stopped talking and looked at his old friend who sat, shaking his head in disbelief.

In a low and trembling voice, the Old Baron replied, "You are very convincing, Horst, and you have rarely been wrong with your assessment of any given situation. On the other hand, I haven't been exactly blind to what is going on around us. Stresemann's untimely death may well be the end of the 'good-times' of the Weimar Republic. Chancellors—as unpredictable as the weather—come and go at the Reichstag, not lending any stability to government. And I don't believe that Hindenburg has any idea what he is doing. So what is next?"

"Next," Horst sighed deeply, "is something I never thought I would have to mention. But it has to be said, dear friend, and I am going to say it with the deep affection I have for you, with respect and some humor. Soon after we met, I discovered that you had a Jewish mother and a half-Jew for a father. You are a Jew. Baron Friedrich Wilhelm von Blomberg, Protestant, doesn't exist. He is simply a role you assigned to yourself—a role you have played to perfection. In all those years, no one, but no one, has ever questioned the authenticity of your background. And I, for one," Horst mused, letting a smile wash around his mouth, "I didn't care. I never judge a man by his ancestry, I look at him for what he is, for what I see. And in you, Old Baron, I have always seen the best."

Flustered and visibly shaken, Friedrich Wilhelm cleared his throat. "I don't know what to say, except that I am embarrassed, and that it never occurred to me that I deceived you— my best friend. You are right. When I married Henrietta in 1882 and left that pitiful dung heap of a village, I left the past and the original me behind. Baron Friedrich Wilhelm von Blomberg, Protestant, arrived in Breslau. The new me felt good. It fit me so well, that I became real, and life was a magic kaleidoscope of new shapes and forms that I could create and control. I've never looked back. I should have told you," he stammered a bit, "but it never came to me that I wasn't who I believed I was. I hope that makes sense."

Horst waved away his friend's concern with both of his slender hands. "Come, come. Forget it!" he soothed, "I just said that it never bothered me, nor did I ever give it any thought. If anything, it convinced me that we can be anything we choose to be. You have grown into being the Old Baron rather nicely. The only reason I bring it up now, is to make you aware of the dangerous threat that is heading your way. If your children don't know that they are Jews, you had better tell them now. It may come as a shock to them, but you know the old saying, forewarned is forearmed. I know for certain that the Nazis already employ an army of zealous researchers who are developing a registry of all Germany's Jews, including people of Jewish background as far back as grandparents. These Nazis are relentless and methodical in their search; no one will be overlooked."

Friedrich cupped his chin in his hands, hiding his eyes. Finally, he looked up. "I am glad you know. You may call it playing a role. but when it comes right down to it, I live a lie. I shall have to find out what my children know. I don't remember if the subject of our religion ever came up in our house. You know Henrietta; I doubt she ever said anything. On Easter Sunday we went to church and hunted Easter eggs. At Christmas we had a tree, presents, and apple-stuffed goose. We sang the songs of the season and we went to church. I don't know what else to say. This make-believe person is the only one I know. I don't know that other one . . . I . . . I can't . . . " He was at a loss for words and at the edge of tears.

"Come, Friedrich," Horst intervened firmly, "don't make a tragedy out of a well-done comedy. You are who you are: you are the Old Baron. I had no intention of making you feel bad, I just wanted you to get a grip on reality and help you make plans to keep you and your family safe in the future. And that is the reason why I joined the Party."

He stopped, walked over to an ornate Chinese cabinet, and retrieved a bottle and two snifters from its red-lacquered interior. He splashed a generous amount of the golden brown cognac in each glass, and handed one to his friend. Raising his glass and with a smile in his voice, he made a toast.

"Here's to us and our foolish ways. Let us drink to the goodness of life and to the things that make us laugh. *Prosit!*"

The Old Baron tossed down his cognac, straightened his shoulders, got back his voice, and said huskily, "Thank you, Horst. I won't ever let you down."

Horst nodded, "I know, I know.

"Quickly now," he said, "let me finish what I started out to say and then we'll change the subject. In order to get to know one's enemy, one has to get close. And the only way I could do that was to join the enemy. I now have a seat at the round table of the evil knights. In order to become privy to inside information that could save our lives, I shall continue to attend meetings regularly, and shout a few *Heil Hitlers*. I am not telling anyone but you what I am doing, not even my dear wife. After all, I don't want to be shunned by my family and lose my friends. I'll wait until it becomes an absolute necessity, and deal with the consequences then. When Hitler becomes Chancellor, and he will, I will have the advantage of having been an early party member."

He paused for a moment, his eyes still serious. "I am not a merchant of doom, but I think we should both keep a low profile and stay out of the public eye. We do not need to make any more deals; we do not need any more money. And, if it is all right with you, I would like to liquidate the properties we own jointly. That way we have no visible ties to each other."

"Great idea," the Old Baron came back to life. "Go ahead and do it, and hold on to the proceeds of my share. Who knows, I might need quick getaway money."

"One more thing, Friedrich. I don't want to be indiscreet but," Horst sighed, "be careful with those three young protégés, of yours, all of whom you have set up in business. If I were you, I would slowly sever all relations with them. If they still owe you money against your loans or investments, make them a present of the amount, wish them well, and kiss them goodbye. Tell them you are planning to move to a warmer climate; tell them anything, but remove yourself from the scene. I'm afraid that goes for Fraülein Charlotte as well. Remember, keep a low profile."

The Old Baron nodded in agreement, "All right, I'll do what I can. Next you'll tell me to take up needlepoint," he joked feebly.

"Not a bad idea," Horst bantered, "if it keeps you out of trouble."

For the next hour the two men schemed, planned, and plotted how to protect themselves and outwit the lurking enemy who was determined to abolish the way of life which they cherished.

Disturbed and deeply troubled, the Old Baron left his friend's house. He had never felt so naked, so vulnerable, so helpless. Not for the last fifty years had he ever thought of himself as being a Jew. Anti-Semitism had existed in Germany for two hundred years, at some times with worse results than at others. Growing up in a no-name village, the oldest of seven children of a poor Jewish family, he learned early that being a Jew was an inconvenience, a heavy yoke. Due to his tall frame and powerful figure, his gray eyes and light-brown hair, he had rarely been the target of Jew baiting. But during those growing-up years, he had witnessed enough hateful acts against the Jews and heard more than enough cruel and brutal comments directed at them, all of which convinced him that Fritz Blumberg, Jew, would have to stop existing. He had no spiritual connection with Judaism, the teachings, its rituals, and its age-old traditions, nor did he remember his parents living by the laws of the Talmud. Their daily concern had not included being on good terms with their God. They worried more about getting food on the table for their growing family, wood for the stove in their two-room dirt-floor hovel and, in the winter, shoes for the children. Friedrich associated Judaism with poverty and prejudice, and he would have neither.

Fritz Blumberg was fifteen years old when he left home and walked sixty-five kilometers to Witten, the nearest small town. He was lucky. He found work in a general store, whose owner also dealt in commodities. In between sweeping the premises, loading and unloading goods, and waiting on customers, he watched his boss dealing in everything from beets to butter. Fritz immediately liked the game of buying low and selling high. It made good sense.

Sleeping in the boss' barn, and scrounging leftovers from the man's friendly kitchen maid, enabled Fritz to save every penny he earned. The day came when he had enough money to do a little buying and selling of his own. Shrewd in business dealings from the start, and blessed with an unerring sense of timing— not to mention a hay load of charm and sweet talk—his pockets soon jingled with gold pieces. He needed a bigger arena. It was time to move on.

Baron Friedrich Wilhelm von Blomberg, Protestant, was all of eighteen years old when he arrived in Breslau to establish himself as a dealer of goods and properties. Within three years he accomplished what he had set out to do. He was a man of means, admired and well liked. The poor Jew from a no-name village had died at a young age.

The day turned darker and it had started to rain as Herr Schmidt drove the Old Baron home. Friedrich rested his body against the backseat and closed his eyes. His mind raced in all directions. He wanted to doubt and argue with Horst's view of the world. He wanted to prove him wrong. But deep down inside he felt a stirring of doom. His friend could be so right.

Perhaps he should take his money and run. Maybe they should all go to America and watch the Nazis from afar. He had always dreamt of America. He admired that big country where a man was free to stretch, to be anything, to reinvent himself.

I would fit right in, he thought to himself, amused for a moment, at the thought. But then, his eyes fell on the copy of *Mein Kampf* that Horst had insisted he take and read.

"Please," his friend had urged, "read it. It will open your eyes to what is coming our way. If Herr Hitler only makes good on half of the threats and promises under his regime, he is a terror to be recognized."

He picked up the book, riffled through a few pages, not reading a word. Then, holding the book between two fingers as if it were a piece of filthy trash, he dropped it on the floor of the car.

"Herr Schmidt," he addressed his chauffeur, "I've changed my mind. I don't want to go home. Please turn around and take me to Fraülein Charlotte. I'm ready for a good laugh."

He had a lot on his mind.

Chapter Fourteen

MARTIN AND IRENE desperately wanted to have children, but the nursery had remained as empty as Irene's womb. There were several false alarms, as well as two heartbreaking miscarriages. And no amount of tears could wash away the hurt and disappointment Irene had stored away. Sensitive and attuned to his wife's innermost feelings, Martin never brought up the subject, hiding his own pain and disappointment behind his cheerful attitude.

So, as time passed by, it was not surprising that Irene dismissed the first sign of being with child. She wasn't going to get excited. But within a few weeks other changes in her body took place, all of which pointed to a pregnancy. Again she waited. Not until her doctor confirmed that she was indeed pregnant and in her fourth month, did Irene tell Martin. He was beside himself with joy, reached for the telephone, and promptly told the whole world. Delighted, the world responded with gifts and advice and good wishes. This baby would be the first Blomberg grandchild and would, most probably, take the happy grandfather's gift-giving practices to new heights.

Trude and Maria Burdach appointed themselves guardians of the baby and took to pampering the expectant mother. Trude counseled Irene with advice from her bottomless source of old wives' tales.

"Only look at beautiful things so that you have a beautiful baby. Don't ever look at a hunchback," Trude warned. "Eat three apples every day, and your baby will have perfect skin. Drink two cups of *Lindenblueten* tea at night and your baby will not suffer from colic."

There was no end to Trude's tidbits of folklore superstitions and, when Hedwig Muller made her entrance at Marienhall, she brought with her a whole new set of baby lore. Hedwig, a seasoned midwife and baby nurse, was an old friend of Trude's and had delivered babies all over the countryside. In some cases, she stayed on for several weeks and helped take care of the newborn infants.

In late summer, over a cup of coffee with Irene, in the second-floor morning room—so named for its sunny eastern exposure and yellow-and-blue decor—Trude brought up the subject of hiring Hedwig, praising her work and her experience with delivering babies.

"I know you plan to be in the city to have your baby," Trude chatted, "but just in case you won't make it in time, let's have Hedwig here soon."

Trude went on to say that the woman could stay with her and Lothar until the baby came and then move into the nanny quarters next to the nursery.

"Hedwig is a good, old soul; she is a hard worker, competent and trustworthy," Trude explained. "She was only eight years old when her mother died in childbirth and her father, a no-good drunk, took off never to be heard from again. There she was with two younger sisters, a newborn set of boy twins and not two pennies to rub together. No one knew of any relatives to raise the children, so an older, childless couple took Hedwig to live with them. The two little girls and the newborn twins were placed in an orphanage in Breslau."

Trude paused, looking expectantly at Irene. "Right now," Trude sighed, "she is staying with a family on a small farm in

Mokbern where she delivered a baby two weeks ago, and is now looking for her next job. She has never had a place of her own and I worry that she'll end up in a poorhouse. I would very much like to see you and the baby in her care."

"Well, Trude," Irene smiled at the older woman, "I always listen to you. Of course, have her come now. There is certainly enough room to put her up, and she can help out around here until the baby comes."

Pleased, Trude nodded. "I'll get in touch with her. I told her that you were expecting a baby and that I would recommend her to you. She'll be so happy."

It was the last week of September when Hedwig Muller walked through the gates of Marienhall, carrying a worn-out canvas bag in each hand. A floppy, age-defying straw hat sat crookedly on top of her steel-gray braids and the hem of a gaily flowered dress fluttered at the top of her sturdy shoes. By the time Trude brought her to the manor house to meet Irene, she had changed into a light-blue cotton frock that peeked out beneath a wrap-around white apron. She was every bit the picture of a nursemaid: crisp, clean, and cheerful.

After Hedwig duly admired the nursery and her quarters, she approached Irene shyly. "Madame," she asked softly, "may I touch you, please? I can tell if a baby is coming early or not."

Here comes more folklore, Irene thought to herself, slightly amused as she offered her round belly to Hedwig's inspection.

With her head bent back and her eyes closed, Hedwig's hands slowly probed the extended firmness of Irene's body. Over and over, the midwife's strong hands, with their blunt fingers, roamed and pressed, almost caressing the expectant mother's roundness.

Satisfied, Hedwig dropped her hands, stepped back, and with a beatific expression on her face—as though just having had a peek at heaven—announced excitedly, "The little one is coming early, much earlier than the doctor told you. Maybe in two weeks already."

"Oh, Hedwig," Irene giggled, "that would be great. But from all the arithmetic my doctor and I have done, the baby is not due until November 4th."

Hedwig shrugged her shoulders, "We'll see who is right—doctor or midwife. But, just in case, come October one, I will move into the nanny room, if I may?"

"Yes, of course, you may," Irene replied, "but you'll get awfully lonely."

Hedwig smiled a secretive smile, reached deep into the pocket of her apron and retrieved a golden chunk of clear amber, dangling from a fine golden chain, which she handed to Irene.

"Madame, please keep the amber on your person from now on. It does good things for you and for the baby."

Irene looked at the magic amber in her hand, slipped the chain around her neck, and, with a serious face, thanked Hedwig.

"I shall wear it day and night," she promised.

"Good," Hedwig beamed, "Madame will have an easy birth. We shall have a healthy baby and healthy mother and," she added with a grin, "this baby will come early."

Trude winked slyly at Irene as she ushered the midwife-nanny out of the nursery, and out of the house, "I'll see you in the morning."

From one of the tall windows in the stillness of the nursery, Irene watched the gangly midwife walk down the gravel path. As the two women headed toward the Burdach cottage at the edge of the woods, Irene's hand fondled the piece of amber. Just then, the baby executed a round of strong, swift kicks. "That child is turning somersaults," she mused. Surprised and delighted, she rubbed each little knob as it poked out against her skin. Maybe Hedwig did know something no one else knew.

Martin was unusually quiet at dinner that night. Not even the story of Hedwig's arrival and her straight-from-the stars prediction about an early birth elicited more than a polite and superficial reply from him. What strange and unusual behavior for him, Irene thought. On most evenings, he could never hear enough about her pregnancy. Full of wonder and awe, it was almost as though he wished he could be the one to carry the child.

When he refused a serving of his favorite dessert, Irene waited for Liesel to leave the room and then turned to her husband, placing her hand on top of his to keep him from getting up.

"I won't leave you alone, my dear, until you tell me what is bothering you. You might as well get it over with, because I'll stay on your trail, I promise. And," she added, putting a playful note in her voice, "as you well know, I do keep my promises."

Martin shook his head, sighed deeply, and topped her hand with his. "Well," he started, "I really didn't want to burden you with my concerns. But if you really must know, it's that Nazi trash, this Adolf Hitler—that is beginning to bother me. I worry how serious all of this could get."

He took a sip of his tea, and told her that an advertising company owned by a man named Oscar Helbig, had moved into the ground floor offices of the building next to his printing shop. Haltingly, Martin continued, "I went next door with a bottle of champagne and a bouquet of flowers. After I introduced myself to Mr. Helbig, I handed him my welcome-neighbor gift. But that man kept his arms stiffly at his sides, and in deep growl like a mad dog, he stuck out his chin and barked, 'I don't have any use for Jews. Don't come around here again.' With that, his arm shot out straight into the air, he yelled *Heil Hitler,* and spat at me. That's when I saw his swastika armband, and on my way out, I noticed Hitler's picture on the wall and a huge swastika flag unfurled in a corner. Next day, the word *Jude* was scrawled across our front door in white paint.

"How does he know that I am a Jew? How does anyone know that I am a Jew, for that matter," Martin's voice rose. "I wasn't raised a Jew and I don't attend services in a synagogue. I don't close my business on Saturdays or on Jewish holidays. We don't discuss our religious preferences at work. I don't understand. I am going to have a talk with Father and get a few things straightened out in our family," he stopped for a moment.

Before Irene could comment, he continued in a lower voice. "Now you know what bothers me, *Liebchen*. I am not an isolated case. I have seen storefronts decorated in the same disgusting fashion as ours . . . and worse. And that's not all. There are more and more Brown Shirts strutting around in the city every day and even boys, just kids really, wear that damn swastika armband that's bigger than their arms."

Irene nodded, "I have been so busy being pregnant and preparing for the baby, that I paid little attention to anything else. On top of that I spend most of my time right here in the peace and tranquility of the gardens—removed from the real world. But I do read the newspaper and I listen to the radio occasionally; I don't like the news. Mother wrote in a recent letter that Joseph in Neustadt had some ugly confrontations with a handful of loudmouth Brown Shirts. She is also disturbed at the sight of a small band of local Nazis who regularly march around the Ring in Lubitz, waving big swastika flags and yelling a lot of *Heil Hitler*s."

Irene's right hand kept moving over the damask tablecloth, making tiny piles of forgotten bread crumbs and scattering them with a flip of a finger, only to round them up once again.

Haltingly and thoughtful, she continued. "Last week when I went to the city, I met briefly with Max and Lucy at Hutmachers. Max brought up the subject of Hitler and his threats against the Jews. He remarked on how, throughout history, Jews have been cursed to suffer at the hands of one fanatic or another and right now, Hitler is the latest on the list of tyrants. We came to the conclusion that this man has come out of the Dark Ages. But we live in modern times and the German people won't stand for the senseless killing of their friends and neighbors."

"Maybe Max is right," Martin mused. "Maybe we are paying interest on a loan that isn't due. German Jews are good Germans first, and Jews second. They fought in the war, they were decorated heroes, and they love their country. Anti-Semitism isn't anything new, and the Jews have always lived with it and survived."

Martin rose from his chair, reached for Irene's hand, and pulled her up onto her feet. "We're not going to solve this problem tonight, and you need your rest. Why don't you stretch out, *Liebchen*. Maria told me that a package of books came today. I'll have a quick look and then I'll join you."

The windows in their bedroom were wide open. A fragrant breeze danced with the filmy curtains and Irene went to bed by the light of a huge harvest moon. She was fast sleep by the time Martin slipped quietly into bed beside her. She was breathing softly and her face was bathed in the mellow glow of the moonlight. He brushed his lips against her cheek and said good night to the moon.

———————

Promptly, on the morning of October 1st, Hedwig Muller moved into the nanny quarters, straw hat, canvas bags, and all. After she had inspected the nursery and the small bathroom, and found things to her satisfaction, she appeared in the morning room where Irene had curled up with a book.

"Madame, I've come to stay in the nursery," Hedwig announced to a smiling Irene. "I am bringing you this bell. Please put it on your nightstand and use it when your time comes. I can hear it in my sleep."

She handed Irene a brass bell; the kind teachers use to ring in the beginning of classes.

"Thank you, Hedwig," Irene took the bell by its smooth wooden handle and gave it a playful shake. The sound was loud and clear, and seemed to echo through the entire upper floor.

"No doubt you can hear that," Irene laughed. "It'll wake the dead."

Pleased, Hedwig placed the bell next to Irene. "This bell has announced the birth of more babies than I can remember. It has a lot better sound than one of those newfangled telephones. And," she ended on a mysterious note, as she turned to leave, "I can hear my bell before you ring it. It won't be long now, Madame."

When Trude arrived with her lunch tray, Irene asked her to stay. "There is more than enough food for two, Trude; please join me. Tell me more about Hedwig, she is a rare one. She seems to have a connection with that unseen, untouchable something in which we all have our being. Maybe she is a witch, a good witch? Or maybe an angel?" Irene puzzled.

"After all the years I've known her and have seen her predictions come true, I still don't know what to call her," Trude chuckled. "But she knows things I don't know, and she sees things I can't see. She is a rare one. A long time ago, I asked her how come she knows the unknown. She looked at me as though I wasn't all together, and gave me a reply I'll never forget," Trude shook her head, "nor do I understand it. She said that she goes to a place where all the answers are."

"Strange," Irene replied, deep in thought. "But I believe it. Sometimes I think we live on the surface of life and only experience what we can see and touch. So much of our folklore comes from the country people, the peasants who work with the earth, who can smell rain on the wind, who learn from the animals, and who read the clouds in the sky. They are connected to nature and her secrets. Hedwig is one of them; she knows."

Trude pointed over at the bell. "Hedwig told me it was time to move in and give you the bell. It's like a trophy, and her confirmation that the baby is coming soon. She also told me, in confidence, that you are carrying a girl."

Irene perked up, grabbed her belly with a hug, "Oh, hurray! I'm not going to argue with her. You know that I want a girl."

Irene rolled up her napkin, slipped it through the wide silver band with her initial around it, and laid it next to her plate. "One more thing, Trude. When Hedwig's baby-nursing days are done here, and she has no other place to go, or for that matter, may not want to go anywhere, Martin and I want her to stay on. We'll make room for her here at Marienhall. She should have a safe place for growing old. We all should have that."

Trude grabbed Irene's hands, pulled the young woman's ungainly body against her, and planted a noisy kiss on each of her cheeks. "Oh, that is wonderful. Thank you, Irene . . . and thank your husband. Hedwig will be overjoyed. She loves it here and, besides that, she is a great extra pair of hands. She polishes silver brighter and faster than anybody."

"That is good to know," Irene giggled, "she probably talks to the Silver Polish Fairy."

Comfortable with each other, the two women chatted for a while longer. They talked about the small chapel the Old Baron was having built in the village as a gift to Marienhall's families. He had hired a talented young apprentice architect whom he met on a recent trip to Florence, to design and build the chapel. The Old Baron had taken an immediate liking to the young man and, no doubt had serious plans for him. Roberto Pellegrini, a first-year draftsman, had jumped at the chance and brought along a gifted helper to work on the stained-glass windows and the interior of the building. If all went well, the chapel would be ready for the Christmas celebration. It was up to Trude to find a priest and get him settled in; the Old Baron would take care of expenses.

Not only had Marienhall's land and buildings been restored, but the tiny community of people had been made to feel part of a caring family. Trude insisted that Marienhall was magic, and the Old Baron was the magician.

Three days later, the pleasant, clear-blue October skies turned dark and murky, its clouds swollen with unshed raindrops. On the fourth day, the heavens opened and let go with sheets of torrential, wind-driven rain. Martin called from the office in the afternoon, saying that he would spend the night in the city, rather than risk getting stuck on the muddy dirt roads to Marienhall.

Irene stayed by the fire in the morning room and went to bed early. Around midnight a sharp pain brought her out of her sleep, and a gush of warm fluid ran between her legs, soaking the clean sheet. Her water had broken; her baby was on its way. She would summon Hedwig when the next pain came.

"Well, Hedwig, old girl," she said out loud, "you were right. This baby is early."

Irene turned on the lamp at her bedside table and watched the clock. The next pain came fifteen minutes later and took her breath away. She reached for the bell and rang it. She had barely put it down, when Hedwig appeared at her bedside, dressed in her blue-and-white nursemaid attire, wearing a satisfied I-told-you-so expression on her broad face.

"Don't worry, Madame. Relax and we'll have a baby in no time. Trude and Maria are on their way." Hedwig was all business, shifting the bedding around and making Irene as comfortable as possible.

In between contractions, Trude made Irene drink a dark and pungent brew that Hedwig had prepared from her storehouse of herbs.

"It tastes as awful as it smells," Irene objected feebly. "What does it do?"

"Just drink it; it helps with the bleeding," Hedwig shot back. "Relax and push . . . relax . . . push."

After four hours of pain and pushing and potions, and with the expert help of Hedwig's guiding hands, Irene gave birth to a beautiful little girl. Quickly, Maria and Trude changed the bedding, dressed Irene in a fresh gown, washed her face, brushed her hair, and propped the new mother up against a small mountain of pillows.

Cleaned, diapered, and wrapped in a piece of soft flannel, the baby was gently handed into Irene's waiting arms.

"Congratulations, Madame," Hedwig grinned, "may I present the new princess of Marienhall—a perfect and healthy baby. May God bless her, and may God bless this house."

Irene snuggled the baby against her body and through tears of joy, looked at a tiny, wrinkled face with light eyes and a hush of no-color fuzz on her head. She raised the warm bundle to her face and kissed the baby's cheek. "Welcome, little one. Your name is Ursula."

Trude, Maria, and even Hedwig, who had gathered around the bed, wiped away a few tears. After counting every pearly toe and holding hands no bigger than the top of her thumb, Irene reluctantly let Hedwig place the baby in the padded basket next to the bed and closed her eyes.

Irene had asked Trude not to call Martin until after eight o'clock in the morning, with the news of his daughter's birth. Even though it had stopped raining, the roads would still be a hazard to drive in the dark. "Three hours won't make a difference," Irene said, "and then he will be traveling in daylight."

"Enough now, Madame. Go to sleep. You've worked hard. I'll take care of little Ursula. I can hear a baby cry before she opens her mouth." There was no doubt about that in Irene's mind.

Martin arrived mid-morning, barely able to hold on to a huge bouquet of red roses and a velvet jeweler's case. He raced upstairs, dumped his gifts on the chaise longue in the bedroom, and gathered Irene in his arms. "Are you alright, *Liebchen*? How do you feel? Oh, this is wonderful." Words tumbled out of his mouth and tears ran down his face as he kissed her hands and her face over and over again.

Hedwig, who had heard him coming, held his child out to him. "Sir," she announced formally, "Please meet your daughter."

Martin reached out with gentle hands to hold the newcomer. Her little face had smoothed out, the blotches had disappeared, and her eyes seemed to be a light shade of green. As he held her in the crook of his arm, the warmth of her small body went straight to his heart.

"She is beautiful," he stammered, "and she is ours."

I will keep you safe, he promised in silence from the very depth of his being. No harm would ever come to her; he would see to that.

————————

When the baby was a week old, Friedrich Wilhelm arrived at Marienhall with a carload of toys, a trunk full of little-girl clothes from France, and a large envelope prominently secured with a red ribbon and a hefty chunk of red sealing wax. Scrawled across the front were the words: *For Ursula Blomberg—To Be Opened Upon My Death.*

He handed the envelope to Martin, "Don't misplace the envelope; put it in your safe. Horst von Brunnen has a copy of the contents, and so has our attorney, young Hoffman. Now, may I hold my granddaughter, please?" He almost jumped out of his skin with excitement.

When Hedwig placed the small bundle in his arms, the Old Baron's face lit up the room like sunshine. He scrutinized the little face and touched one of her tiny fists, his eyes riveted to her light-green eyes.

"Why," he exclaimed, his voice laced with wonder, "she is beautiful; just beautiful! Who do you think she looks like?"

Hedwig was quick to reply. "Well," she drawled impishly, "from the front she looks like her mother, and from the back she looks like the rest of the family."

When the laughter died down, and after Hedwig had returned to the nursery with her charge, Friedrich Wilhelm reached in among the many packages he had brought into the nursery, and retrieved a dark blue velvet case which he handed to Irene.

"And this, my dear, is for you. Again, I say, you continue to bring me joy, and this is your most crowning effort yet. Now," he urged, "go ahead, open it."

Irene gasped when she turned the lid back on its hinges to reveal a stunning sapphire and diamond necklace. For a moment she said nothing and just stared at the treasure in her hands. She looked up, shook her head, and said, "I'm left with a similar problem. Again, I too have to repeat myself. *Thank you*. Thank you a million times. This is so beautiful, so extravagant . . . so . . . so . . . *you*." She reached out and hugged her grinning father-in-law.

"The next time we come to town to go out, I shall wear my sapphires and you must come along to celebrate the occasion."

"Agreed," Friedrich Wilhelm nodded. "Why don't we attend a performance of *Tosca* next month? I'll ask Helene and Antonia and their husbands to come along. That's one way to get the family together."

Irene followed Hedwig into the nursery and told the men she would join them for tea in the library, where a cheerful fire was waiting.

Martin and the Old Baron settled themselves into comfortable man-sized chairs in front of the roaring fire. Martin had turned on several table lamps whose light filtered through silk shades and added warmth to the big room. Father and son discussed the new addition to the family and the old man commented how pleased he was to see Irene looking so well.

"Before Irene gets here," Martin said abruptly, "Father, I have to talk to you about something we have never discussed before. I'll come right to the point. We are Jews, aren't we? We've just ignored it and lived a non-Jewish life, haven't we?"

Dead silence. Once again the Old Baron experienced that raw
and naked feeling that had overcome him at his visit with Horst.
The truth had come to haunt him. He raised his shoulders,
shrugged, and in a hoarse voice rasped, "I'll get to the point too.
Yes! We are Jews." And so he began to tell his story, ending it with
a part of his conversation with Horst von Brunnen. He left out that
his friend had joined the NSDAP; that would remain his secret.

With pleading eyes he looked at Martin. "Please try to understand. I buried the truth so deep and so long ago, that I had truly
forgotten it—never would have gone looking for it either. I was
young and ambitious. I wanted to be somebody. And I wanted to
be somebody right there and then. So I gave myself a title, became
a Protestant, and played the part. Nobody ever questioned."

"Oh, my dear Papa," Martin laughed, "you don't have to be
embarrassed. All your children have known about your shaky
family tree for years. We chuckled about it—agreed that the shoe
fit, and filed it away along with all your other acts of harmless
mischief. I'm not concerned about that. What worries me is Herr
Hitler. I worry about his growing popularity, his threats against
the Jews, and that we can't hide our Jewishness behind a
Protestant façade—titled or not. If, as according to Horst, the
Nazis are indeed researching everyone's background and developing a Jewish register, they'll turn over every rock and they'll
discover who is who."

Martin then described the ugly encounter with his new
neighbor in the city, and how the word *Jew* had been scrawled in
huge letters across the front door of his business, the day after
the incident.

The Old Baron admitted that he had seen storefronts and
windows smeared with insults and walls plastered with hate-
oozing posters, all of which he considered to be the handiwork of
trashy Nazi youth. He expressed his surprise that it happened
with something that carried his name.

"Well," Martin, replied, "if the Nazis have been at it for a while they may have already discovered who we are."

"Now," Friedrich Wilhelm interrupted, gesticulating with his hand to emphasize his words, "do you see why, even fifty years ago—without a Hitler or a bunch of Nazis on the horizon—I didn't want to be a Jew any longer? I hated the smallness of the *stedtl* atmosphere, the clannishness of the Jewish people, the narrow-mindedness of the gentiles, and the poverty. Dear God, the poverty! Every penny was turned three times before it was spent. I wanted something better and I knew it wasn't going to happen in Pankow . . . or in Witten. And I didn't believe it would happen to me as a Jew. End of story."

"This is all well and good," Martin took a deep breath. "You made it work for you. But it may not work any longer. On the other hand, Hitler is not in power and, as the saying goes, *There's many a slip, between the cup and the lip*. At least we are aware of it. Let's just wait and see."

And it was the wait-and-see policy that would eventually be responsible for the senseless deaths of six million Jews.

Chapter Fifteen

WITH THE BIRTH of Ursula, the pace of life at Marienhall picked up considerably. Like a magnet, the infant became the catalyst for attracting friends and villagers alike to the old manor house. They came and went, bearing gifts and good wishes, oohing and aahing over the baby and taking turns at holding her, under the watchful eyes of the ever-present Hedwig. The visitors gathered in the morning room where they chatted, drank cups of hot, black tea from the handsome silver samovar, and munched on tiny pastries and bite-sized tea sandwiches. Lucy, who was pregnant with her first child, often spent several days at Marienhall. It was like old times for the two sisters.

Whenever possible, Martin hurried home from work early, just to see his daughter. He rarely spent a night in the city any more, saying he didn't want to miss a day watching her grow and change. The Burdach family, including the four grandchildren traipsed through the nursery regularly to see the baby.

Antonia, Helene, and the Old Baron made their weekly pilgrimages to Marienhall bringing more gifts and taking turns fussing over the little girl. Irene stood by amused as she listened to the Blomberg clan planning, envisioning, and predicting the little girl's future. Ursula had become everyone's child.

Hedwig was in her glory watching over her charge. She clucked around the infant like a mother hen, and sent visitors on their way when she thought enough was enough. She reigned over the nursery in her noisy and yet gentle ways. If she wasn't singing to the baby, she was talking to her. Her raspy voice commanded a rich repertoire of nursery rhymes and children's songs, some of which had their beginnings in ancient lore. The aging nanny kept the nursery spotless and shared the baby with Irene—sometimes grudgingly.

Ursula was three months old when Irene returned the chunk of amber to Hedwig, and thanked her for the use of it. "The amber's magic must have worked, Hedwig," Irene commented. "Mother and baby are well and healthy."

Hedwig looked thoughtfully at the golden piece of petrified tree sap, walked over to the baby's crib, and tucked it away under the mattress. "I won't be using it any more," she announced, looking lovingly at the sleeping infant. "I have delivered my last baby. This one isn't going to have a sister or a brother. I want her to have it to keep her safe."

Touched by the gesture, Irene hugged the older woman and told her that she was welcome to stay at Marienhall for as long as she wanted. Her eyes filled with tears when she thanked Irene, and the sudden glow on her face seemed to wash away old worry lines. "I've known for the longest time," Hedwig, blew her nose noisily, "that this was going to be my home one day. And when I met you, Madame, I saw nothing but goodness and kindness in your being. I knew the amber would work its magic. Now its power is with the child."

Hedwig also gave the amber credit for Ursula's content and happy disposition. The child rarely cried or complained. Her green eyes looked at people with great curiosity, her tiny hands curled trustingly around the fingers of her admirers. She was a friendly little thing who loved company but was just as content entertaining herself.

By the time she was four years old, the three slim birch saplings that Lothar had planted at the time of her birth had grown into fine young trees, sheltering the child-size table and benches he had built in his workshop. He planted a hedge to hold back the chilly blow of the north wind and, when he added a sandbox and a sturdy wooden chest to store the collection of toys, the children's garden was complete.

Several events took place around the time of the child's fourth birthday. Antonia had volunteered to search for a governess to move into Marienhall. For almost a year, she interviewed a parade of eager applicants, but to no avail. But the moment Fraülein Amanda Schubert sat down, and no more than ten minutes into the interview, Antonia knew she had found the right person. Everything clicked about the thirty-five-year-old woman—from her background and her bearing to her personality and academic qualifications. Antonia wasted no time. Without further ado, she packed Fraülein Amanda into the car and brought her to meet Irene. Chatting with the young woman on the ride to Marienhall, listening and discovering more about her, Antonia's insides never stopped grinning: Fraülein Amanda was a rare find.

One month later, a teary Hedwig moved out of the nanny quarters and into the cheerful back room of Maria's cottage. She left Fraülein Amanda with a list of instructions, threats, and promises for the care of Ursula. Deep down Hedwig as well as Irene had, at their first meeting, immediately recognized the governess' qualities; they liked what they saw. But it would have been out of character for Hedwig not to quarrel and fuss and nag upon giving up her territory and handing *her* child into the care of a stranger. Hedwig made it very clear that she would keep an eye on the nursery as she left with a canvas bag in each hand and her floppy, age-defying straw hat teetering dangerously on top of her gray braids. An era had come to an end.

Beyond the walls of Marienhall, the era of political struggle for the control of Germany was raging. The wait-and-see policy of Germany's idealistic hopefuls was energized by the election in 1932 when Adolf Hitler ran for President of Germany against Field Marshal von Hindenburg. When Hitler lost, they cheered and patted themselves on the shoulders. He was reported as being suicidal after admitting not being able to accept defeat, and the hopefuls cheered again. But Hitler's popularity had mushroomed since 1930. He was the masses' Parsifal who would bring them the Holy Grail.

On New Year's Day 1932 a famous seer, Erik Jan Hanussen, cast Hitler's horoscope and predicted that he would come into power within thirty days. Whatever happened backstage of the political theatre is not certain, but the incredible happened: recently repudiated by the German electorate, Adolf Hitler was made Chancellor of the Reich on January 30th, 1933. His measure to outlaw all other political parties passed in July of that year and Germany, like the Soviet Union, was now controlled by a single party and by a single man.

It was a quiet evening in late February when Martin and Irene entertained Antonia, Erich, and their neighbors, Renate and Albert Seidenberg for dinner. The Seidenbergs, and their two young boys, lived only a few kilometers from Marienhall. Their home was in an old mill they had lovingly restored and remodeled over the last sixteen years until it oozed charm and authenticity. Albert operated a textile factory he had inherited from his father and had a passion for history and for growing exotic orchids in his greenhouse. Irene and Renate, who were the same age, had become close friends and the two couples saw each other often.

As soon as dessert and coffee were served and Liesel had left the dining room, the pleasant and lively dinner conversation turned at once to the latest political development. With voices lowered, the upstart Hitler and his Nazi party were up for discussion. Back and forth they tossed their concerns, their fears, and their hopes, leaving unanswered questions hanging in the air and worry lines on their faces. The main question was: what is going to happen to the Jews of Germany?

Finally, Erich spoke up, "You know that old saying," he started out slowly, "'Nothing is eaten as hot as it comes off the stove.' The man has been making a great deal of noise about eliminating the Jews. Well, that is biting off more than the rest of us Germans can chew. To win the race, he needed a whipping boy for his campaign. Well, he won the race and got what he wanted. I'm certain he is going to relax now.

"The first thing he is going to have to do," Erich took a deep breath, "is to get Germany out of the Versailles Peace Treaty. He is just gutsy enough to get back the lands we lost in the west, and he is going to stop paying those enormous, crippling war reparations. All of that takes time and energy. He will be too busy to do anything about the Jews."

Albert raised his hands, "May I throw out another old saying by which I have learned to live? 'Hope is no substitute for judgement.' Hope and good feelings aren't going to make these threats go away. Hitler is a fanatic and totally convinced that the Jews of the world are the flaw of the world. He is handing the masses a sacrificial lamb, and they love it. Furthermore," he stopped and reached for Renate's hand, "I, for one, am not going to sit and wait around.

"Renate and I have decided to go to America and have applied for our visas. I am about to close the sale of the factory, and our home is next."

Irene's voice cracked with emotion. "Albert," she shook her head. "No! Aren't you being a bit hasty? . . . Renate . . . ?" Irene stopped, eyes filling with tears.

Then everyone spoke all at once, tossing questions at Albert. He waited and heard everyone out. "Look," he said, "we don't want to leave, but I am not going to worry and stew as to if or when the Nazi ax is going to fall. This Jew here," pointing his fingers to his chest, "is not waiting around to be thrown out of his own country. He is leaving in his own time and on his own terms."

"Albert," it was Martin's turn to be heard, "I have never known you to be a doomsayer. Why is this getting to you and making you run? To give up without a fight?"

"Martin, my good friend," Albert was searching for words. "I read *Mein Kampf*, I've listened to Hitler's speeches, and I've watched his popularity grow. Frankly, I am scared. This man is not making empty promises. Hitler is walking, talking evil. And just look at the history of the Jews. We've been the target of so many tyrants over the centuries, since time began—and this is no different. I have never had such a compelling nagging, nor such an inner urging, to do something. It won't leave me alone." He shrugged his shoulders. "That's all I can say, except," and he turned to Martin pleadingly, "I wish you would go too."

The evening broke up in a pensive mood. As the Seidenbergs, and Erich and Antonia wrapped warm scarves around their necks and slipped on their coats, they lingered in the hall for quite a while—reluctant to say goodbye. This time, it seemed, parting had a finality about it.

When the weathered old front door closed behind their dinner guests, Martin and Irene walked upstairs hand in hand. Halfway up the stairs, Martin stopped. "I'm not going to panic like Albert has done." He looked at Irene. "Do you think I am wrong?"

"I don't think you are wrong, my dear, but I do believe we need to be watchful and stay on the alert. Maybe," Irene mused in an attempt to take the dark out of the night, "I should consult with Hedwig and her amber and ask what she sees."

Martin immediately responded to her effort to lighten the load. "By all means," he grinned, "and don't forget to check in with Lothar and Trude, they see and hear more than you and I—and they do that without a piece of amber."

Irene laughed softly as she turned out the lights in their bedroom. "Don't make fun of these mysteries. There's more to life than what we see and touch and hear." He kissed her and held her close. "Good night, my dear, take good thoughts to sleep with you."

The house fell silent as a bright winter moon shed its cold glow on Marienhall.

A few weeks later, Liesel was pouring a cup of breakfast coffee for Irene when the right sleeve of her blouse rose up to her elbow, exposing an ugly, black-and-blue bruise. Quick to notice, Irene grabbed Liesel's wrist, looked into her face, and saw a smaller, but equally dark bruise on her left cheek.

"What happened to you? How did you get hurt?"

Liesel turned bright red, hastily pulled down the sleeve over the offending arm, and mumbled something to the effect of having tripped over the hem of her long skirt on the back hall stairs.

"You must have had quite a fall," Irene challenged her. "You are bruised on your right arm and left cheek. That doesn't come from any ordinary fall."

Liesel protested feebly, and excused herself saying she was needed in the kitchen. Hurriedly, she left the morning room.

As soon as Irene finished breakfast and looked in on Ursula and Fraülein Amanda, she threw a knee-length Loden cape over her shoulders and headed for the Burdach cottage. Lothar and Trude sat in front of a cozy fire with cups of hot chocolate. Delighted to see her, they rose from their chairs to greet her.

Irene always marveled at these two favorite people of hers. Lothar didn't seem to have aged at all. There was no slouch in his broad shoulders and his sturdy frame carried no extra weight. His walk was brisk and purposeful and his steel-gray hair and matching eyes only added to his distinguished look. Trude's hair had turned silver, but her lively, twinkling blue eyes, and the way she acted and carried herself, belied her age.

After Irene greeted them warmly, she urged them to sit down. "Please, no formalities. I want to feel like family." She draped her cape over the corner hat rack, pulled up a low stool, and sat down between them. She lost no time voicing her concerns about Liesel.

Lothar and Trude looked at each other for a long moment. Lothar sighed deeply, "This is not the first time Liesel had bruises on her face and arms. But she claims that she is clumsy, that she walks into doors and trips on stairs. I don't believe that for a second. She is as clumsy as a squirrel running up and down a tree." Lothar put down his cup.

Trude steepled her hands in front of her face and said slowly, "I just know that Oscar beats her. Liesel isn't that good at lying. I didn't like Mr. tall, blond, and handsome from the day I met him. Outwardly, I saw a charming, friendly individual. But deep-down, behind the mask, I sensed an arrogant, cruel, and ambitious man. As you know, Marienhall was too small for him and, for the last seven years he has been managing the Hartlieb estate. He is doing well, has his own car, and spends a lot of evenings in the city," Trude paused. "But I don't know what to do about Liesel . . . she's so . . . so . . . reserved, so . . . ." Words failed her.

"Well," Lothar added, "I have never been comfortable with him, but what disturbs me even more is that I have noticed changes in Liesel. She is often quite subdued. Her sunny, happy disposition and her sense of humor rarely come into play anymore. She is quiet, serious, and removed from all of us. There is something very wrong. Now here's another thing I haven't even told Trude. Oscar is a full-blown Nazi. I am sure of it. I saw him leave for the city the other day. When he climbed in his car I got a glimpse of the Nazi uniform he wore under his raincoat and those spit-polished boots on his feet." Looking at Irene, he went on. "He knows that the Blomberg family are Jews and I wouldn't put it past him to use that information to gain recognition with the Nazis. I don't trust him.

"I questioned Liesel about him, about the uniform and his trips into the city. But she claimed to know nothing about any of it. However, I know my daughter. She was nervous and fidgety, and I am certain it was because she was lying to me." Lothar stopped, thought for a moment, and then added, "You know, I am going to have a casual talk with him. I'll be diplomatic and cautious and find out where he stands. I don't think it will be difficult because he is so full of himself. He will be only too glad to share his views and opinions."

As the conversation continued, both Lothar and Trude confirmed the fact that they belonged to the "I-can't-believe-this-is-happening" segment of the German population. Unfortunately, that segment's numbers were dwindling as fast as a spendthrift's money.

"I've lived for quite a few years," Lothar pondered, "and I have always believed in the goodness and the integrity of people. I also believe that any actions, any dealings—be it by an individual, a group, or by a government—based on hate and prejudice will bear no fruit. And," he continued, shaking his head, "if our German people condone Hitler's promise of elimination of the Jews in a rush of Teutonic madness, I shall die in shame."

"That's all fine and good," Trude interrupted, "but before it's over, they will leave a trail of blood and misery. And as far as Liesel is concerned, I shall get to the bottom of this. I won't have our daughter beaten and abused. She ought to have more sense and self-esteem than to allow such behavior."

Irene embraced the two people who had become not only her friends, but her family. Next to Martin, they were the rock in her life. She remembered the Old Baron's words, "The Burdachs are true gold, they *are* Marienhall."

Deep in thought and disturbed, Irene left the Burdachs and walked on the grounds for almost an hour. Just as she rounded the path that cradled the pond and led back to the house, she came across Hedwig who had cleaned out the swans' dock house and was now feeding the graceful birds.

Hedwig, bundled up against the chilly air, looked up at Irene with a serious face. "Good morning, Madame. Spring is late this year," she announced, "and these creatures don't have enough to eat."

"How do you know that spring is late?" Irene inquired, putting an arm around the old nanny's shoulder.

"Look at the buds on the trees and bushes. Why, they're less than half the size they should be this time of the year. The tulips and all the rest of the bulbs we planted have not yet poked their shoots up through the earth. And," she added woefully, "there's not a frog in sight."

"Let's get out of the cold," Irene took Hedwig's arm, "and go to the kitchen for something hot to drink and sample some of Heidi's baking."

The two women walked in comfortable silence to the side of the house where a door led to the cellar steps and down to the kitchen. Welcomed by the surprised smile on Heidi's face and the tempting aroma of freshly baked bread and yeast cakes, they sat down at the kitchen table. Setting down cups of hot tea and a basket of little surprise-filled pastries, Heidi joined her visitors. Hedwig kept silent while the two women chatted on about food and children and Marienhall.

Noticing Hedwig's unusually quiet mood, Irene finished her tea, put down the cup, and asked, "Why so quiet? Is something troubling you, my dear?"

Hedwig raised her head, a puzzled look on her face. "I don't know," she said hoarsely, "I just don't know what it is. All I know and all I see is . . . bad times are coming. I keep having the same bad dream," she stopped and burst into tears. "I know bad times are coming," she repeated over and over again, wiping away at her tears.

Heidi consoled the old nanny until she had quieted down. Irene got up, patted Hedwig lovingly on her back, and slipped away—her mind in turmoil.

Hedwig knew. Bad times were coming.

Chapter Sixteen

1935–1936

FROM HER FIRST day at Marienhall, Fraülein Amanda felt at home. After Hedwig departed from the nanny quarters, Irene had completely redone the large sitting room. The walls were painted a soft sunny apricot, and flowery chintz covered the three chairs and a sofa. Matching drapery dressed the tall windows and the alcove which hid a bed and washstand. The warm wood tones of the antique tables and chests dignified the room; and the fireplace, flanked by mahagony bookcases, gave it the final touch of comfort.

Fraülein Amanda rearranged the pleasant schoolroom to fit her needs and purchased schoolbooks, supplies, charts, and maps for her teaching curriculum. Irene, in the meantime, raided the attic storage for furniture and carpets, turning the nursery into a room more suited to a growing girl. Rosy silk fabric dropped from the ceiling where a friendly cherub, whom Ursula had named Sisha, gathered it in his arms and let it drape on each side of her big bed.

Early on, Fraülein Amanda realized that Ursula's patience with dolls and toys was short-lived. Thanks to Hedwig, who had taught the little girl to read by the time she was four, books held her attention for hours. Ursula thrived under her governess' tutelage. Fraülein Amanda had established a fairly demanding regimen which included daily lessons in French and English. A stickler for good manners and behavior, Fraülein Amanda never let up and raised a well-mannered, respectful, and responsible little girl. Growing up with adults, and rarely in the company of children her own age, Ursula was referred to by Fraülein Amanda fondly as "the oldest child" she'd ever known.

After breakfast with her mother, Ursula was always eager to start classes which ended at two o'clock in the afternoon, interrupted only by a light lunch. A hard taskmaster, Fraülein Amanda added another hour and a half of assignments each day for her student. When the weather was fair, Ursula had riding lessons. In the company of Otto Burdach, she rode her horse, Princessa, on the bridle path that edged the forest. Neither Martin nor Irene displayed any great passion for horses and were perfectly happy to watch their daughter enjoy the sport.

Sometimes the child joined her parents for supper, but most of the time she had high tea with Irene and Fraülein Amanda, and visited with her father before bedtime. After Fraülein Amanda tucked her charge into bed, she retired to her own quarters where a stack of books was waiting for her. She seldom took a day off and the only time she went to the city was in the company of Irene and the child.

On the surface, life flowed easily and harmoniously at Marienhall. Liesel insisted that she was happily married and her husband, Oscar, confided to Lothar he was just *playing* at being SA to be accepted in the new world. And, no, he wasn't taken in by Nazi politics, and considered the meetings he attended to be a male social affair, nothing more. Neither Trude nor Lothar were convinced they had heard the truth. They dropped the matter, but kept a close eye on the couple.

Martin went to work everyday, but found little pleasure in Breslau, the city he so loved. From government and office buildings, from apartment complexes and storefronts, a sea of red flags with the huge black swastika in their white centers fluttered in the wind and changed the face of the city. Ugly posters with caricatures of hook-nosed, bearded, evil-eyed Jews and offensive headlines, glared from the walls of buildings, store windows and kiosks. Groups of thirty to fifty storm troopers goose-stepped their way daily through the streets of the city, carrying huge Nazi flags and eagle-topped standards. They sang their *Horst Wessel Lied*, shouted obscenities against the Jews—and reassured themselves that "Today Germany, Tomorrow the World" was their truth. Crowds gathered on the sidewalks. With arms raised high, they yelled *Heil Hitler, Sieg Heil* and joined the Brown Shirts in their songs. Boys from age twelve on now wore the uniform of the Hitler Youth organization, looking like short Storm Troopers and acting just like them. The poison of the Nazi doctrine was seeping across the country and settling deeply into the blood of the German people.

Like waiting for the weather to change, the great majority of the Jews did not lose faith in their fellow Germans. Rather, they sedated themselves with useless hope and naive expectations, dreamt and wished for the evil to go away. They held on to a fantasy that sanity and right would overcome the evil and people would come to their senses. Surely they would not continue to follow a madman bent on destroying their countrymen.

And so the Jews waited.

The Blomberg and the Burger families were no different from the rest of the hopeful dreamers. They ignored the official boycott of Jewish shops, the ousting of Jews from government positions, and the 1935 Nuremberg Law forbidding Jews to marry Aryans. Herman Burger announced he had not lost one customer in his tavern, and his sons Joseph and Arthur reported business as usual. If anyone was apprehensive and more realistic than the rest of the family, it was

Toni Burger, whose grandparents and parents had fled from Russian and Polish pogroms. She insisted that history repeated itself, expressing great fear of the future.

The Old Baron had taken Horst von Brunnen's advice. He liquidated his holdings, took his money out of the country, and severed the relationship with his protégés, and with Fraülein Charlotte. He simply claimed failing health and his intention to eventually live in Switzerland. His home life had not changed: it was as barren as the Sahara Desert. Henrietta continued to live in her own world where there was no room for anyone else. Fortunately, he was always welcome in the homes of his friends and his children. Both Helene and Antonia and their respective husbands had laughed off his confession about his shady past, assuring him that he was born to the personality he had invented for himself. They all had known about it for years. Friedrich Wilhelm was who he was, and his children accepted him. He was a good man.

He visited his granddaughter every week, and from the time she was five years old, he would pick her up in his shiny automobile, with Herr Schmidt at the wheel, for a visit to the city. The day always included tea and cakes at Hutmachers. The void of business activities had robbed him of the joy he got from the game of wheeling, dealing, and getting away with mischief. But every once in a while, he pulled something harmless just to prove he hadn't lost his touch.

His latest escapade took place when he escorted Fraülein Amanda and Ursula to the circus in town. Announcing that he wanted to walk a bit, he asked Herr Schmidt to drop them off a block away from the circus tent. He walked up to the ticket booth, after cautioning his guests not to utter a word. Pointing to Fraülein Amanda and Ursula, who stood a few steps behind him, he informed the ticket vendor that he and his family had lost all their belongings in a fire the day before. "All we have left," he managed a theatrical sob, "are the clothes on our backs. Could you find it in your heart to give us three free tickets to the circus? God will bless you, I am certain."

The man in the booth hesitated only a second and handed the Old Baron the three requested tickets.

Fraülein Amanda's mouth dropped open as she watched the old man's game. Friedrich Wilhelm thanked the man profusely and assured him of his place in heaven. Then, once inside the tent, he pulled the same act on the candy vendor and received three sticks of candied grapes.

The Old Baron grinned wickedly and winked at Fraülein Amanda, who had barely closed her mouth. "Just wait," he whispered, "I'm not done yet. But now, let's enjoy the circus."

All this was lost on Ursula who sat, wide-eyed, watching the dancing elephants, the tumblers, and the high-wire acts. She laughed at the clowns and reached for Fraülein Amanda's hand, holding her breath, when a young girl in a pink-and-glitter gown danced and played with two big snakes. Applause and whistles greeted the grand finale—the traditional parade of animals and performers around the ring.

On the way out, the Old Baron stopped the candy vendor, handed him a fistful of money, and said, "You have a big heart, young man; life will be good to you." Next, he walked over to the man in the ticket booth, bought 100 tickets, paid for 103, and left a hefty tip. "You're a good man." Friedrich Wilhelm shook his hand and, with great glee, watched the surprised look on his face as he once again evoked God's blessings upon the him. Back in the car, the Old Baron asked Herr Schmidt to stop at St. Mary's Orphanage to drop off the circus tickets. He turned to Fraülein Amanda and said, "Forgive an old man his pranks. Life can be awfully dull without them. And," he added, "you must agree, this one had a happy ending."

Back in Marienhall, after having tucked Ursula into bed, Fraülein Amanda gave a lively rendition of the circus story. Martin just shook his head and laughed. "That old rascal is at it again. This is one of his favorite tricks when he has nothing else to do."

To the delight of Irene, who loved her father-in-law dearly, Martin told the story how the Old Baron had talked the woman at a street corner flower stall out of a bouquet of roses. He used the ruse of having a sick wife who had a birthday, and he had no money to buy her flowers. He thanked the woman profusely and disappeared around the corner. One hour later, to the great surprise of the flower vendor, he showed up again, bought every bouquet she had, and overpaid her handsomely. He then handed the flowers to equally surprised women passers-by, wishing them a happy birthday—happy day—whatever.

"That's just one of many of my father's practical jokes," Martin mused. "How he gets away with these pranks is a puzzle to me. If I were to attempt to do the things he pulls, I would probably get beaten up or land in jail. I need to talk to him. It's time to stop that nonsense. With all the Nazis around, and as outspoken as he is, he could get into serious trouble."

The conversation turned to Carl, Helene's husband whose heart condition had confined him to complete bedrest. In order to be near doctors and a hospital, they closed their house in the country and rented a small villa in the city. Martin stopped by, almost daily, to see Carl. Erich and Antonia were regular visitors, as well.

Irene confessed she had not visited Carl recently. "I have a hard time with the changes in Breslau. Those hateful flags and those strutting Nazis are everywhere. And the SS, Hitler's elite in their black uniforms and their arrogant ways, frighten me. Being Jewish has made me a bit insecure lately," she confessed. "I am just as content to stay at home. Here I feel out of the way and safe."

Fraülein Amanda's reply was short and terse. "Ruffians and hoodlums is what they all are. Arrogant, puffed up with self-importance, believing they are better than the rest of us, they'll drop like flies when the tide turns. A government that doesn't serve humanity defeats itself, eventually."

Irene walked over to her, placed a hand on Amanda's shoulder, and said, "It's the *eventually* that worries me. What if we Jews run out of time?"

Martin broke the silence by saying that he wasn't going to pay that much attention to the bullies and he certainly wasn't going to pull up stakes like his friends, the Seidenbergs. He closed the subject with the usual, *let's-just wait-and-see* remark.

Year after year, when the fields were harvested and the trees were changing color, a small caravan of fifteen or so gypsies came to camp at the outer edge of the forest of Marienhall. They gleaned the fields, hunted rabbits in the forest—shot a deer or two—and helped themselves to anything available, when backs were turned. But nobody could deny that they brought color and excitement from another world to the quiet village. To everyone's delight, the night wind carried their music and their laughter beyond the forest. Over the years, Lothar Burdach developed a special relationship with Woyczek, the "king" of the caravan—a handsome, husky fellow whose sixty years had barely left their mark. Dark hair topped a lively, unlined face and curious dark-brown eyes sparkled with mischief. His body was as tough and muscled as that of a man thirty years younger. He moved like a cat, nimble and quick on his feet, and danced as though he had quicksilver in his veins.

Lothar liked these exotic, roaming folks and had become their benefactor. In order to cut down on their stealing, that might cause unpleasant feelings among the villagers, he brought them eggs and butter from the dairy and sausages and hams from the butcher. He even talked Heidi out of a few pounds of sugar and flour here and there. Many an early autumn night, he sat around their fire, shared a meal with them, and watched the men and women abandon themselves, dancing to the strains of their gypsy fiddlers. When January came around, the caravan left as quietly as they had come, and the night wind fell silent once more.

It was about the same time the gypsies pulled up stakes, that a strange thing happened. Oscar, Liesel's husband, disappeared. At first, Liesel speculated that he stayed in the city. She had called his friend with whom he usually spent the night, but no, Herr Vollmer had not seen him for several days. But when a phone call from his Hartlieb employer inquired why Oscar hadn't shown up at work for five days, Liesel went to her parents' cottage, to tell them about his absence.

Lothar and Trude had just finished their breakfast, when Liesel walked in, looking disturbed and worried. One look at her daughter's face, and Trude reached for her hands.

"What is wrong, child? Come, let's talk by the fire."

"Oscar has been gone for five days," Liesel started out. "I have no idea where he is, not that he ever tells me what he is doing or where he is going. The last time I saw him was last Sunday morning before I went to help Maria in the big house. I came back in the afternoon and he was gone. I haven't heard from him since."

Trude wasted no time looking for answers. "Liesel, we've talked about this before," she started, watching her daughter's face closely, "and I know you have not been truthful with me. But this time I insist you tell me what has been going on in your married life. I'm your mother. I know you are unhappy and you have been hiding things from me and I know your husband is arrogant and cruel and that he beats you."

Liesel, between sobs and wiping away tears, swallowed her pride and told her parents everything. Yes, she was miserable in her marriage. Yes, Oscar did beat her. Yes, they fought a lot. She had never been able to please him. He blamed her for the marriage and for remaining childless. He called her a stupid country girl who was satisfied cleaning up after a bunch of filthy Jews. And, yes, he was going to get rid of her; let her go back to her Jew-loving parents. The only reason he stayed around at all, was the fact that one day soon, he would own Marienhall. And yes, he had been a member of the Nazi Party for seven years, had been attending meetings regularly, and was fast moving up the Party ladder to an important position. He was waiting for his appointment.

Trude could barely catch her breath and her eyes reflected her anger. "Why in the world did you wait so long to tell us? He's worse than I thought. With such evil around us, we are all in harm's way. I just hope he got his big position and that he never comes back."

"Would he go away and leave all his clothes, his toiletries, and his personal treasures behind?" Liesel interrupted her mother. "That's not like him. If he wanted out, I would have let him go. You were right from the beginning, Mother, and I should have listened to you. He is not a good man and I am afraid of him."

"My dear," Lothar, his face void of any expression, spoke up for the first time, "I have no intention of being rude or unfeeling, but perhaps we should say good riddance to a man who has caused you so much pain and unhappiness?"

Liesel shook her head, and in a puzzled voice said, "You know, Father, even though I wonder where he is, I have to confess that I had the most peaceful five days in a long time. And I discovered that I liked my own company. It's just so strange that he left without a word. I feel I should do something, but I don't know what."

"Don't do anything," Trude advised. "He is the one who left. In the meantime, I want you to stay with us. He'll know where to find you, if he shows up."

They talked for a while longer, and except for reassuring Liesel of their love and support, nothing was solved. After she had gone, Lothar went to his greenhouse. He loved to grow things and when he was troubled, he found peace working in the rich dark soil of his indoor flower beds. Watching seeds come to life, pruning and nurturing them, was like an elixir for him.

He pulled a high stool up to the table where he had earlier placed his strawberry cuttings. He put his hands on the dark earth and closed his eyes, letting the warm topsoil trickle through his fingers. Over and over again his mind replayed the events of the previous week.

He had been sitting in the same spot a week ago, on Friday morning, when Oscar walked in with a request to borrow one of Lothar's rifles. He wanted to get a couple of rabbits, boasting that he made the best Provence rabbit stew. He told Lothar that he had his rifle repaired, but left it in his car which was in the city being serviced. He was going to stay at home the following Sunday and wanted to go hunting. His handsome face was flushed and his speech was loud and slurred. He had been drinking.

Standing in front of Lothar, hands tucked into his pants, he rocked slightly on his feet, and there was a sudden undisguised arrogance in his voice. "I knew you'd be by yourself. I've been wanting to talk to you without the women around. It's time you know about reality. I'll make this short." With his voice as cold as his eyes, he charged ahead. "I am through playing your game, and living in a make-believe world. I am a Nazi and I am proud of it. Things are happening, and they are happening fast. I have moved up in the NSDAP and have been given an important position among the higher echelon.

"Let me just tell you this, Herr Burdach, for your own good," he continued loudly, "I have been a faithful Party member for seven years. I am well connected, and I am now in a place where I make Party decisions and act on them. The Nuremberg Laws are in force and the boycott against the Jews is going into high gear. I am leaving Hartlieb and as of next week I will be in charge of the registration process of Jewish properties, and their confiscation. Jewish wealth will be returned to the German citizens from whom the Jews stole it to begin with. I'm also turning in the gypsies to be picked up by the Gestapo. They are unclean, filthy like the Jews, and our Führer is getting rid of them. I'll get an honor badge for that," he concluded smugly.

Lothar hadn't said a word. Barely able to breathe, he only nodded his head while a low boil was rising on his insides, rushing through his veins like a fire, as his son-in-law kept talking.

"Furthermore," Oscar hissed, spit flying from his mouth, "you would be wise to join the Party, display our flag, and hang Hitler's portrait on your wall. And, you had better listen to Hitler's weekly speeches; it's a must, you know. People get reported for not doing it."

Listening to this tirade, Lothar began to breathe deeply, forcing himself not to react, keeping his temper under control. He wanted to hear it all.

Oscar pulled up another stool and sat next to Lothar. When he continued speaking, his foul beer breath assaulted his father-in-law's face. "I'm going to let you in on a little secret," he sneered, "Burdach, you're looking at the new owner of Marienhall—it goes with the job. Marienhall will be confiscated, lock, stock, and barrel, the Jews will be gone, and I am giving you back your useless Liesel. I'll get a wife who will give me children. Hitler offers handsome rewards to large Aryan families." With a voice sharp as a razor, he added, "And unless you and your sons join the Party and follow our Führer, you better find another place to live before I report you." Oscar's arrogant features had turned mean and ugly.

Hardly containing himself, Lothar got to his feet. Controlling the shudder inside of himself and steadying his voice, he gave Oscar a friendly slap on the shoulder. "Well, that was quite a speech. I'm impressed with your success. I had no idea. I'm sorry about Liesel, but I can understand your position. You are right. We had better keep in step with the new world. Maybe you can help us join the Party and get us a flag and Hitler's picture for the living room. I might as well get started."

Oscar got off his stool, squared his shoulders, puffed out his chest, shot out his right arm, and yelled a hearty *Sieg Heil!* And, for good measure, he threw in another *Heil Hitler!* Lothar, his face a frozen mask of emptiness, returned the greeting.

"Let's walk over to the barn and get you a gun," Lothar suggested. "Come to think of it, I'll join you for a little rabbit hunting myself. I know a spot in the forest where the big ones are. Let's meet at the small clearing at the far north end—you know, the one we call the Wild Berry Clearing."

Oscar's mood had changed to jovial and he settled on a time to meet Lothar on Sunday morning. After throwing another *Heil Hitler!* at his father-in-law, Oscar swaggered off with Lothar's gun shouldered, whistling the *Horst Wessel Lied*.

Still in the barn, Lothar sat down heavily on a bale of hay, held his face in his hands, trying to regulate his shallow breathing and stop the pounding of his heart. He was still shaking. He knew what he had to do, which was against everything he believed, but he took an old work jacket off the hook by the barn door, slipped it on over his sweater, and headed straight for the gypsy camp. It was a good two-mile walk, and it gave him time to clear his raging mind and rehearse his plan.

Woyczek greeted Lothar with an exuberant bear hug, called him brother, and brought out a bottle of wine and two beautiful crystal goblets which must have followed him home from one his scavenger hunts.

The two men sat at the far end of the gypsy king's colorful wagon and talked for quite a while in low voices, their heads close together. When they were done, Woyczek got up, refilled their wine glasses, raised his in a toast, and let go with a string of words in his native Hungarian. Reverting back to German, he touched his glass to Lothar's. "To you, my friend. Rest easy. It is done. It won't be my first time. *Prosit!*" The gypsy drained his glass, put it down, shook hands with Lothar, and followed up with another one of his enormous bear hugs.

On his way home, Lothar stopped off at the empty chapel. In the quiet half-dark, and by the light of the candles that flickered in their glass cups near the altar, Lothar slipped into a pew and sank to his knees. With his forehead resting against the wooden bench in front of him, his heart in turmoil and tears slowly flowing down his cheeks, he spoke to his God. He spoke to Him for a long time.

By Sunday morning, a thin layer of snow covered the ground and frosted the trees with a soft padding of white. A leaden, gray sky promised more of the same. After breakfast, Lothar told Trude that he had some chores that needed doing and that he would be back for the family's Sunday meal. He put on a heavy coat, a pair of sturdy boots, pulled a thick, knitted cap down over his ears, and headed out into the cold winter morning. Every step brought him closer to the nightmare he would have to live with for the rest of his life. By the time he reached the far side of the clearing, he stopped and leaned against a large fir tree, puffing his breath in and out, attempting to still the harsh pounding of his heart and control the nagging, inner shaking. This would never do, he thought. He had to get hold of himself.

He had just slipped his rifle off of his shoulder when he heard the sound of whistling coming from across the clearing. Dressed in a heavy Loden cape, a hunting cap trimmed with the traditional pheasant feather and a stubby goat's beard, Oscar came into view, stepped away from the trees, and looked around.

And then it happened. It happened so fast, that it would remain a blur in Lothar's memory forever—like a little illustrated book where one had to flip the pages to give action to the pictures.

One shot rang out, and then another. Oscar's knees folded under him and he pitched silently forward on his face. Blood seeped from his head and chest, stained the pristine white of the snow, and puddled in the hollows of animal paw prints.

Silence.

Woyczek appeared from behind the thick trunk of an ancient, long-needle pine and walked over to the fallen man. At the same time, Lothar entered the clearing and, catching himself from falling, stumbled over to where the gypsy had placed his foot on his prey, leaning on his rifle.

Lothar had lost his voice; words would not come across his tongue. The gypsy king let go of his rifle and held out both arms to steady his friend.

"I know what you are thinking, Lothar," Woyczek spoke quietly. "But I could not let you do it. I don't believe you could have lived with it. Just being a witness to it is more than you can bear. I know." He walked Lothar to a fallen log, brushed off the snow, and sat him down, with his back to the dead man.

"Let me finish what I came to do. I was here yesterday and dug a deep pit, just a few feet into the forest. Nobody will ever find him."

Lothar nodded his head helplessly and managed a hoarse, "Thank you. I'm in your debt forever."

Woyczek patted him on the shoulder. "Say no more, old friend. Rest easy; say no more." With that, he walked off. Effortlessly he picked up the dead man in his arms like a rag doll and disappeared into the dense darkness of the woods.

Time stood still for Lothar as he sat on the weathered, downed log, the two shots still ringing in his ears and echoing back from the forest. He had no idea how long the gypsy had been gone, when he suddenly stood by his side again. Woyczek reached inside his jacket, produced a slim, silver flask, unscrewed the top, and handed it to Lothar. "Here, let's toast to wine, women, and song, and let evil destroy itself. *Prosit!*"

Lothar took a big sip, and let the brandy burn his throat and warm his blood. He got to his feet and, wordlessly, embraced the man, holding him so close that he could feel the steady beat of his friend's gypsy heart. Snow was beginning to fall again, placing a blanket of innocence on the clearing and on the forest floor. All passion spent; the present evil gone.

"You better get home before you turn into a snowman," Woyczek advised, his face crinkling with laughter, his white teeth gleaming behind his dark mustache. "Go in peace, my friend and bury the past." Woyczek adjusted his colorful head scarf, shouldered his rifle, waved a final goodbye to Lothar, and was swallowed up by the trees.

When Lothar returned home, the house was filled with the tempting smell of roasting ducks and baking bread. He quietly slipped into the bedroom, took off his working clothes, and went into the bathroom. With hot water and a big bar of fragrant soap, he scrubbed himself raw, from head to toe for the longest time. Dressed in a clean shirt, pants, and a warm sweater, he joined his family in the living room. As always, a cheerful fire was crackling in the stone fireplace where his two sons and their wives, along with Maria, had gathered. Liesel, Maria reported, was still at the big house.

"Knowing my Liesel," Trude remarked, "she'll make it in time for dessert."

Otto asked if Oscar was at home, but no one knew. No one had seen him. Having been an enigma to the family, and not particularly well-liked, no further talk was spent on him. Lothar felt like a hollow tree, all leaves and branches and nothing inside. He spoke, but the words held no meaning. He listened to the conversation around him, heard nothing but the two rifle shots which were still ringing in his ears, blocking out the world around him.

At the dinner table, Trude asked him to say the blessing. With his eyes closed, Lothar rested his chin on his folded hands and, in a low voice, recited the familiar blessing. To the surprise of his family, he added words he had never spoken before. With his head bowed, he whispered, "And may God forgive my sins. Amen." He wondered if anyone at the table had heard his heart breaking.

The next day the gypsies were gone.

Chapter Seventeen

1937

IT SNOWED FOR several days and when the sun finally made a noble attempt to come out, it was a mere white glow behind a bank of silvery clouds. Marienhall was a Christmas card of white, shimmering crystals; winter perfect.

In spite of Fräulein Amanda's feeble protests, Lothar rescued Ursula from the schoolroom for a short while. Together, they built a snowman on the north lawn, complete with the traditional carrot nose and black-coal eyes. Placing a vintage English bowler at a tipsy angle on the icy bald head, the old man and the girl agreed that their snowman was quite handsome. They named him Herr Winter and advised him to stay out of the sun.

Lothar had the same deep affection for Ursula as he had for his own grandchildren. He was drawn into her green, curious eyes which always held his glance in a most trusting and loving way. Lothar's heart went out to her. What lay in store for the young child? He had been a partner in a black deed which he believed may have halted the immediate danger for the occupants of Marienhall. But in the very bottom of his being, he had a sinking feeling that he had only cut off one of the snakes on Medusa's head. Not only would the snake grow back, but was destined to multiply—and there was nothing he could do about that.

When he returned Ursula to the care of Fraülein Amanda, Irene walked into the room, carrying their mid-morning treat—a platter of sliced apples and oranges. The four of them settled themselves around the school table, chatted, and munched on the fruit. Growing up in the company of adults, the eight-year-old Ursula had no trouble keeping up with the conversation, as well as contributing to it. The talk turned to the missing Oscar whose disappearance was discussed in an impersonal, curiosity-filled way. No one had ever been close to Liesel's husband, nor did they care for his know-it-all, arrogant behavior. That being the case, the conversation quickly turned to Liesel's well-being.

"Other than being shocked that she hasn't heard from him," Lothar said, "she seems almost relieved. She admitted that for the first time since their wedding and the move into the cottage, she felt at home; as though the little house finally belonged to her."

Lothar went on to say that she had discovered all of his Nazi paraphernalia—a Brown Shirt outfit, a complete SS uniform with matching boots, Nazi propaganda material, swastika armbands, a flag, and two portraits of Hitler. She found it all in a small wardrobe in the attic that he had always kept locked. Earlier, when she jokingly asked him what secrets he kept hidden, the simple question had made his blood boil. He started to scream at her and she ended up with a beating.

"I don't know why she would keep quiet for so long and never complain or—for that matter, why she didn't leave him. Perhaps she was ashamed?" No one had an answer, but everyone agreed that it would be just fine if he stayed away. No more was said; the room fell silent.

Breaking the silence and lightening the mood, Lothar invited Fraülein Amanda and Ursula to join him on a sleigh ride. He was going on his weekly run to the Neukirch Post Office to pick up the mail for the families of Marienhall.

"What is better than a sleigh ride after a new snowfall under sunny skies?" he asked the disciplined tutor. "Hold your lessons for tomorrow; it is time for a little fun," he coaxed.

"Please, please, Fraülein Amanda," Ursula begged. "I'll do my lessons later. Please?"

Convinced, Fraülein Amanda wrapped herself in her warm cape, and bundled up her young charge to ward off the sting of the icy wind. In the meantime, Lothar went to the stables to hitch his two favorite mares, Schneewitchen and Rotkäppchen, to the big, ornate sleigh with its furry lap robes. He rang the big brass bell, announcing his arrival at the front terrace, and his two passengers appeared immediately. They climbed into the back seat, pulled the blankets up to their chins, and off they went with the ringing and jingling of the horses' bells. Swiftly, the obedient team whisked them through the village, pristine in its coat of snow. Ursula waved and shouted greetings at the children they saw pulling their sleds up a nearby slope, only to come swooping back down again with shrieks of delight. Fraülein Amanda promised an eager Ursula that they would join the children on their sleds the following day. "Don't worry, my child," she soothed her fears, "the snow will still be here tomorrow. It is so deep, it cannot melt overnight."

One hour later, rosy cheeked and red nosed, Lothar dropped his elated passengers off at their front door, handed Fraülein Amanda the mail for herself and for the family, and was off to make deliveries to the villagers.

"Thank you, Fraülein. Two letters from Mother and one from Lucy," Irene exclaimed with pleasure. "Mother is such a reliable correspondent." She snuggled deep into her fireside chair, opened the letter from her mother with the earliest postmark, looking forward to the news from home.

Her face took on a worried look as she let the pages, filled with her mother's spidery handwriting, drop into her lap. Hurriedly, she tore open the envelope of the second letter, hoping against hope for something—anything, more pleasant.

"Hitler and his henchmen came through Lubitz," Toni wrote. "A huge motorcade of SS and SA—with the Führer in the lead car—roared into town early last Sunday. A sea of swastikas blocked out the sky and the cacophony of their singing still echoes in our ears. For the rest of the day, Brown Shirts and Black Shirts took over the square, filling the air with their hysterical speeches, their screams of *Heil Hitler*, and the vile words of their songs: 'When Jew blood drops from our knives . . . Today Germany . . . Tomorrow the World!'

"Before they left, every Jewish business, including our tavern, was painted with JEW in big, white letters. Offensive posters of anti-Semitic messages were pasted to windows, walls, and doors. I told your father it is time to sell the tavern and find a quiet apartment, maybe even an old folks' home in Breslau. I'm wondering—can we hide in the big city?"

Toni concluded her letter by reminiscing about her family and the cruel pogroms which made them flee home and hearth in Russia and Poland decades ago, to settle in Germany. "It's happening all over again," she wrote. "Poor Jews; there is no home for us. We are, and have always been, eternal strangers."

Disturbed and overwhelmed by her mother's news, she tore into Lucy's letter, only to find more of the same. Lucy wrote that her eight-year-old Inge, along with the other Jewish children at school, had to sit in the last row of the classroom. Rumor had it that soon, all Jewish students would be banished from attending Germany's private and public schools, as well as universities. Next, Lucy mentioned that they had to move from the apartment they had occupied for more than ten years because the landlord no longer wished to have Jewish tenants. And, that wasn't all. Several of Max's clients had moved their business to a non-Jewish accounting firm. And worse than that, two of Max's Freemason friends had been picked up by the Gestapo in their respective homes three weeks ago. No one had heard from them since. The words concentration camp took on a threatening meaning.

"I don't know where all of this is heading," Lucy wrote. "I am scared. But my husband, like yours, keeps insisting that if Hitler is not going to ease up on his boycott against the Jews, our good German people will get rid of him. I wish I could be that optimistic. I think this madman has the German people exactly where he wants them. He has given the masses a scapegoat—a reason for any ill, any misfortune from which they suffer, real or imagined—and they love it." Lucy ended her letter with a fervent wish to get the family together. "We need to look at the future realistically and make plans to protect ourselves."

Trance-like, Irene returned the letters to their envelopes. Turmoil raged in her heart. What was reality? Marienhall was an island in an ocean of fear. Removed from the big city which daily witnessed brutal acts against the Jews, the serenity of the gardens, the shelter of the tall trees and the silent fields, made up the fortress that protected its inhabitants from the invasion of terror.

But how much longer could they depend on such protection? How long before the enemy would intrude?

An overwhelming wave of fear washed over her. She realized there were no barriers, real or imagined, strong enough to hold back the evil that was sweeping across the country. Whipped by the frenzied winds of hate, it was seeping into the very soul of the German people, who were demonstrating their willingness to follow the ways of the New Reich.

Rising from her chair, she walked over to the window facing the west lawn under its blanket of snow. A few birds hopped about their feeders on the terrace, a lively squirrel scrambled up one of the tall trees, and a gray rabbit raced toward the thicket at the edge of the stream. The land was at peace.

But the silence was broken by the pounding of her heart. How blind, she wondered, are we? Why do we refuse to see what is going on around us? Politics have always been "Man's Business." Emperors and kings, tyrants and generals held the power of nations in their hands. Women had children; they produced and raised sons to be future kings and tyrants and they birthed and nurtured daughters to bear the heirs. Men made war—and women picked up the pieces.

The temperature rose the next day, the snow began to melt, and Martin was able to make it home. Appearing in the late afternoon, Irene met him in the hall. She embraced him and clung to him for the longest time. Martin kissed her and took both of her hands in his. "If I can expect this kind of welcome home when I've been away for a night or two, I'll stay in town more often," his eyes sparkled with pleasure.

"I need to talk with you," she replied quickly, pulling him toward the stairway.

Seated in the morning room, Martin smiled at her and said, "What is this urgency? Can't we have tea while we talk? I am hungry." Irene rang for tea and returned to her chair, facing him. "Now, my *Liebchen*, what great news have you?" he asked.

"Unfortunately, I have no happy news, but I will tell you what is bothering me. But I do not want anyone to overhear our conversation, so I will stop when Maria comes into the room." Without giving him a chance to question, she read him Toni's letters, and then the one from Lucy.

Just as she finished reading, Maria appeared with a tray of appetizing tidbits, poured tea for them, and left. Martin sat in silence, his worried eyes fastened on his wife's face.

"Of course, this is disturbing," Martin finally managed to say, "and I am aware of a lot of it. This brings it close to home. Yes, it is very disturbing and . . . terrible . . . "

"Yes, terrible!" Irene interrupted him. "But what are we going to do? We just can't sit here and hope that Hitler will go away." Martin looked at her for a moment, surprised at his wife's passion and anxiety. Irene went on, the words tumbling out like hailstones, "The Seidenbergs have left, so have the Rosenthals and Berthold and Rachel Levin. Anna and Robert Rothbart are leaving for Canada next week with the Landsbergs. The Villa Hochstein is empty—Maude and Klaus—gone! All around us, people are fleeing from Hitler, and we are doing nothing."

Irene stopped to catch her breath and fight back the tears threatening to flood her eyes. "We don't talk about those who have left—gone for good. We act as though they are just away on holiday." Then, in a theatrical falsetto voice, she mimicked, "'The Rosen's are on a divine cruise to New Zealand, and the Cohens are exploring exotic Brazil; isn't it marvelous?'" Sobbing, she went on, "We won't admit to ourselves that they are all running for their lives."

"Shh, shh, *Liebchen*," Martin rose and went around to the back of her chair. He rested his cheek on her silky, soft hair, his arms around her shoulders. "Hush, dear one, hush. I promise you, I will begin looking into emigrating to America—just in case. I am also going to talk to my father and Horst von Brunnen. But we are not going to just run away—we will handle this situation with clarity and with good sense. I do not get alarmed easily. I know that tyrants come and tyrants go and that dictators die of their own poison—a fact proven throughout history. If people were to pick up and run at the first sign of trouble, everyone on the Continent would be constantly on the move and we could never expect to establish stability."

He had chosen not to tell her that every morning, he scrubbed the word JEW from his front door. He had chosen not to tell her that two of his workers quit their jobs; they no longer wanted to work for a Jew. He conveniently forgot to tell her about witnessing

the beatings of innocent "Jewish"-looking people on the streets
by strutting, obscenities-shouting SA members. He had closed his
eyed to the threats around him, nor did he listen to the pitiful
cries of the beaten. "Sit still; wait it out," his faithful master
printer advised him, "this too, shall pass." He was waiting.

Reassured by the calm in his voice, and the reasoning in his
words, Irene relaxed a little and made an effort to put the current
news out of her mind—at least for the time being. When it was
time for high tea, they sat down with Ursula and Fraülein
Amanda in the dining room.

The governess gave a glowing account of her pupil's
progress and reported what a bookworm she had turned out
to be. Throughout all of the conversation, Ursula remained
unusually quiet and, finally, Martin asked if something was
troubling her.

She seemed reluctant to speak, at first; frowned and bit her
lip. Puzzled, and with sadness in her voice, she said, "It's
Grandfather. He's so quiet when he comes to see us now. He
doesn't joke, he doesn't tell stories, and he doesn't laugh much
anymore. Is he ill?"

Martin reached over and smoothed a strand of blond hair out
of her face. Taking her chin in his hand, he replied, "Well, my
child, you are right. I have noticed a change in him, as well." He
didn't want to upset her with the whole truth, but neither would
he tell her a lie. "Your grandfather decided not to work anymore.
He sold his holdings and stopped all of the wheeling and dealing
which he enjoyed so much. He misses the challenges of the
business world and the friends he left behind. He is bored. But
perhaps now he will spend more time with us and you, young
lady, can help to make him laugh again. "

In simple terms, Martin explained to his daughter, who
listened intently to every word, that life in Germany was difficult
at the moment for many people, due to a ruthless and arrogant

government. Adolf Hitler, a dictator and tyrant, was the undisputed leader of the nation, he went on to say, but many believed that a better government with a fair leader, was on the horizon.

"Just like in a fairy tale," Ursula commented, "bad people always want to ruin something, but in the end they never win." With a hug and a kiss Ursula said good night to her parents and followed Fraülein Amanda to their rooms.

Martin and Irene sat in worried silence for a while longer, until Irene spoke up. "I'm willing to wait too, but when I see the first swastika in the village . . . " her voice trailed off and she shook her head, "I'll be a lot more scared."

Before Martin went to bed, he called Horst von Brunnen and the two men agreed to meet at the print shop after everyone had left for the day. He also called his father's house several times, but there was no answer.

———————————

The next morning, Martin rose long before dawn and left the house without waking his sleeping wife. He wanted to be at the plant before anyone else arrived; he knew what his first chore would be. The pleasure of accomplishment and success he had experienced each day as he walked into his shop was slowly giving way to a hollow feeling and a nagging anticipation of dread. He used to love the smell of paper and ink, the hum and clatter of the presses, and the rows of neatly stacked cartons of completed jobs waiting to be delivered. Now he looked for problems and trouble, going listlessly about his day. His master printer, who had been with Martin for twenty-five years, had made noises about acquiring the business. Should he throw in the towel, sell his business, and, like a thief, sneak out of the country? "No! Not yet, not yet," his thoughts tried to chase away the gloom. He would know what to do when the time came. Surely, he could wait a little while longer?

When he arrived at the plant, a new hand—in glaring white paint and huge letters—had scrawled the words "You Can't Wash Away the JEW in You" across the heavy glass panels of the main entrance. He sighed deeply, retrieved a bucket and rag from the storage room, and like a machine void of emotions, washed away the offensive message with automatic thoroughness. Martin's spirits rose considerably when he received a large print order from an old customer—programs for an international soccer match to be held in Berlin in the spring. The elation did not last long. A visibly agitated Horst von Brunnen appeared shortly after the midday break. One look at his face and Martin knew something was wrong; very wrong.

"Sit down, Martin. Brace yourself, I am not the bearer of good news. I don't know how else to say it, but your father is dead. He must have died in his sleep sometime during the night. I called the appropriate authorities, and I will help you with all further arrangements. There are a lot of things you will need to know about your father's investments, but we'll talk later." Horst placed a consoling arm around his friend's shoulders. Rubbing furiously at streaks of tears on his cheeks with a handkerchief, he let a deep breath escape his mouth, "I just can't believe that he's gone. He was always bigger than life—my best friend."

Horst went on to say that he had become concerned when he was unable to reach him by telephone, and decided to drop in on the Old Baron. Henrietta informed him vaguely, that she had no idea if there was anything wrong with him. "I don't go into his room," she snapped coldly, and headed for the kitchen, leaving Horst standing in the middle of the foyer. He described to Martin how he went down the hall of the huge apartment, trying out doors until he finally found his friend's bedroom.

"And, there he was, in his bed with the quilt tucked under his chin. Dead!" Horst kept shaking his head in disbelief. "For a man who made a lot of noise in his lifetime," and, in an attempt to sound lighthearted, Horst managed a moist chuckle, "he certainly left this Earth quietly."

Martin, who was hiding his face behind his hands, waiting for the shock waves in his heart to stop, finally dropped his hands revealing rivulets of tears, running freely. "It'll take a while for it to sink in that he is gone. But he is so much a part of all our lives, that I believe he will always be around. Let's do what we have to do now. I'll cry some more later."

"Always remember this, my friend," Horst looked at Martin's tear-streaked face, "Death does not diminish him; he left all his gifts behind."

Martin clasped both of Horst's hands in a firm grip, "Thank you, Horst, what a good friend you have been all these years. And thank you for being here, now."

With a vague, but loving gesture, Horst dismissed the compliment and suggested the funeral be a family affair only. "Let's not draw any attention to the Old Baron's passing. The less is made public about Jewish affairs these days, the better," he said thoughtfully. "Your father has been away from the business world for a while now. Eventually people will find out, but not for some time. And that's all right."

The two men decided to have the body transported to Marienhall and bury him at the place he so loved, but was too restless to make his home during his lifetime. Martin then made the necessary calls to the immediate family, and left to see his mother.

Henrietta never ceased to amaze him. She refused a comforting hug from her son and before he could utter a word, informed him in her customary cold and stoic way that she had already found a small apartment to her liking in the same building. She would be settled into her new quarters the following day. Pointing to an old leather valise on the kitchen table, she announced, "I shall not be needing money from any one of you. I have scrimped and saved from the household allowance your father gave me every month. And," she managed a frozen half-smile, "I now have a goodly sum. It'll last me till I die."

"One more thing," she said handing him a bundle of keys, "you will have to close the apartment after I'm moved. I'll take a few pieces of furniture and some household things. I don't want anything else. And," in a voice void of emotions said coldly, "I'm not coming to the funeral." Henrietta dismissed her son by leaving him standing in the middle of her kitchen. Unceremoniously turning her back on him, she went into her room, closing the door firmly behind her.

Speechless, stunned and empty, Martin walked slowly down the hallway to the Old Baron's room. He knew he would never have an answer to the puzzle that was his mother. Had there ever been any affection between these two so very different people, he wondered, or did Henrietta simply perform her expected duties?

Opening the door to his father's room, he found, not unexpectedly, that the bed had been made and everything was neat and orderly. Later, he and Antonia would go through his personal things. Later. At this moment, he was in a hurry to get home to Irene—home—where love and comfort were waiting for him. His home, a haven for laughter and a safe place for crying.

With Otto's help, Lothar cleared a path that led from the main house to the willow grove by the stream. It was in this hidden grove that the early owners of Marienhall, as well as the Burdach families, had buried their loved ones. Three days later, the Old Baron's five children with their spouses, all the Burdachs, and Hedwig, holding Ursula by the hand, stood at the stark, wintry graveside, in the early afternoon. Fraülein Amanda remained at the house nursing a sore throat and a bad cold. When the news of the Old Baron's death reached the schoolroom, the task of telling the child fell on her shoulders. She had a long and loving talk with the sad girl—all about life and death, trying to console her.

"Most importantly," Fraülein Amanda had said softly, "keep your grandfather alive in your heart. You were his only grandchild, and the love of his life. He'll never be far away from you."

"I shall always be looking for him," was Ursula's reply.

Father Paulus, the young priest who served the spiritual needs of the people of Marienhall and three neighboring villages, who always considered that, next to God, Baron Friedrich Wilhelm von Blomberg was his employer, delivered a warm and at times humorous farewell to a beloved old man. "His spirit now soars free of earthly bonds. The love he had for you in his lifetime shall demonstrate itself when blessings upon blessings come your way. Let us not mourn his death, let us celebrate his life." He closed the service with a short prayer, threw the first shovel of Marienhall earth on the open, rose-filled grave, and stood aside as everyone followed his example saying their own farewells.

Suddenly, Ursula yanked hard on Hedwig's arm. "Hedwig," she whispered into the old nursemaid's ear, "Grandfather is here. He knocked me on my head three times, like he always does and then he said something strange."

"What did he say?" Hedwig whispered back, her eyes glowing with excitement.

"He said, *Don't look for me among the dead; look for me among the living.* He said it twice." She sounded puzzled, "Is Grandfather a ghost now?"

"Heavens no! He is the same spirit he always was, but he is in a different body now." Hedwig held on to her, promised to talk more about it later, and led her away from the graveside. "Let's get to the house, I'm about to turn into an icicle."

When everyone was seated at the long table in the formal dining room, the mood turned festive. Dozens of yellow roses and some of the gorgeous silver, crystal, and Venetian glass pieces the Old Baron had brought to Marienhall graced the table. Antonia and Helene were passing platters of cold meats, smoked salmon, cheeses, and baskets of crisp rolls. Everybody seemed to be talking. The conversation was all about the Old Baron . . . "Remember? . . . Remember when? . . . Remember how?" All around the table, people reminisced as they told anecdotes about him, and among theatrical groans, chuckles, and bursts of laughter, the richness of his character unfolded in a rousing celebration of his life.

Martin rose to his feet, reaching for Irene's hand. He pulled her up beside him and held her close. He gently tapped his champagne glass with a fork and the chatter stopped. He raised his glass, "A toast to my father, a man who knew how to live and how to give. He is as big today as he was yesterday. Here's to the Old Baron—a man who stood by his heart."

Just then, the sun unexpectedly broke through the thick, gray clouds, poured into the dining room, danced over the table, and made brilliant rainbow glitters in the crystal glasses.

"Oh, well," Irene chuckled, "perfect timing. The Old Baron always did have the last word."

Chapter Eighteen
1938

T HE SUN WAS setting on a blue day in late June, when
Horst von Brunnen drove through the gates of Marienhall.
He had recently learned to drive to avoid having anyone know
where he went and whom he saw. Any kind of association with
Jewish people, when reported, was looked upon as treason to
the Hitler doctrine, and resulted in severe punishment for the
offenders.

After the Old Baron's death, more than a year ago, Horst had let
Martin and his siblings know that he was the guardian of his father's
estate. He would make the monies available to his old friend's heirs,
upon request, any time. The transactions would have to be done in
great secrecy. Antonia had thanked him and remarked to the rest
of the group, "Anyone who has Horst for a friend, doesn't need
another one." The bonds of friendship between the Blomberg
family and Horst ran strong and deep and true.

Martin and Irene greeted their old friend with open arms,
and the three settled down in the library where the last rays of
the sun brightened the room, bringing the rich colors of the
Persian carpets to life. It was a comfortable place, books, art, and
all. Martin offered Horst a snifter of brandy, and poured glasses
of lemonade for himself and Irene; neither of them had developed
a liking for the taste of liqueur.

"I always seem to be on a mission when I come to Marienhall," Horst sighed. "And today is no different. Our world has gone crazy," he shook his head. "Let me tell you what is on my mind, and with your permission, I will go back and briefly review the last three years. I won't go into the inner conflicts and turmoil that constantly plague the Nazi Party, or comment on Hitler's relationship with the other European nations. I just want to talk about what has been happening to the Jewish people, and what we need to do."

Slowly and methodically, he took his friends, step by step, decree by decree, through the exacerbating pressures that not only had severely limited normal activities for the German Jews, but had become life threatening, leaving no hope for the future. First came the verbal abuse and ridicule of Jews, followed by daily boycotts against all Jewish businesses. Vile posters of hook-nosed, swarthy people—representing Jews—accompanied by ugly slogans painted on Jewish storefronts followed. Soon books, beautiful literature by Jewish authors were burned. Jewish professors were no longer allowed to teach at universities, and Jewish students could not attend the halls of higher learning. Marriages between Aryans and Jews were forbidden; people were jailed and severely punished for "Racial Offenses." Since late 1937, Jewish establishments had been confiscated without legal justification. Male Jews were no longer permitted to employ Aryan women under the age of fifty in their homes.

Without opposition, Hitler walked into Austria (the infamous *Anschluss*), added it to his Reich, and imposed the same anti-Semitic laws on Austria's Jews. General opinion had it that Czechoslovakia would soon succumb to the same fate.

With calculated regularity, never letting up, new anti-Semitic laws went into effect. All Jewish wealth had to be registered; Jewish children were banished from public schools. Late afternoon shopping hours were established for Jewish citizens, and public transportation within the city was no longer available to them. The Munich synagogue was destroyed. Jews were not permitted at theatres, concert halls, operas, and ballet performances. Jewish artists and musicians were dropped and the music of Jewish composers could not be performed. The humiliation and brutalization of Jews on the fine streets of Germany's cities and in the newly built Concentration Camps were no rumors; they were a fact. A heavy tax on the earlier declaration of the wealth of Jewish citizens was levied, and had to be paid in cash—immediately.

People spying on people and turning them in for making unflattering remarks about Hitler or the Nazis (true or imagined), or disregarding one of the new laws, were rewarded for their betrayals. Fanatic members of the Hitler Youth even reported family members for the same reason—some real, some fabricated. Friend became foe, and trust ran low.

Horst drained his glass of brandy and looked at his friends who had listened to him intently. "Not a pretty picture, is it? I have never been a pessimist, but l don't believe it will change for the better. I know that many things are keeping you here. Your parents and Ana Marieke," he turned to Irene, "are now living in the city, as well as your brother, Arthur. At the risk of sounding harsh, that is no reason to stay in Germany. You must think of yourselves and Ursula first; you are still young and have a life to live, and you cannot live it here any more," he urged.

"In order to save Marienhall from being confiscated by the government," Horst suggested, "sign everything over to the Burdachs, either as a gift or as a sale. I don't know how long you'll be left alone, Martin, but your little prank of paying your taxes in bags of coins could not have gone over very well. I bet you are on their list."

Horst was referring to Martin and his friend, the banker, Phillip Morgenstern, who each had delivered bags of silver coins as their share of the newly imposed wealth tax for Jews. The money had been returned to them the next day in exchange for a bank draft. The SS who handled the transaction had been less than pleasant. Eight days later, Phillip Morgenstern's bank was confiscated.

Martin reacted to Horst's words with something between a forced grin and embarrassment. "I know. I know," he groaned, "it was a stupid and foolish thing to do. I don't know what possessed me to go along with Phillip, except it sounded so carefree, so silly, and like so much fun. I have regretted it ever since. But on the positive side, let me tell you, that I have feelers out to sell the shop, and I have registered us at the American Consulate. Carl Schreiber's nephew, Albert, who, as you know, is an American citizen and lives in New York City, is providing us with an affidavit. As soon as it arrives, I'll take it to the American Consulate in Berlin and apply for visas."

"Don't forget to check on other countries as well. I've been told that American visas are few and far between in coming. America is working on a quota system, and the German quota is filling up fast." Horst, who had arrived with a bulging briefcase, now reached for it and handed it to Martin.

"Since there is no telling if or when your bank accounts and your business may be confiscated, I brought you a good amount of money for a quick getaway or whatever you may need. There is more where this came from. I gave Antonia and Helene the same amount to keep the disbursements even."

"Thank you for thinking of everything," Martin said, his voice full of emotion.

Irene spoke up in a quiet, faraway tone. "My brother Joseph and his family are finally leaving for America next week. It took him seven months to get his visa. Arthur thinks that Joseph's decision to emigrate is premature. He bought himself a small car, learned to drive, and is now selling brushes to house painters.

"My father is devastated by his oldest son's leaving and he misses Lubitz and his business. He left a lifetime behind and seems to have lost all interest in the present one. Sometimes, when I look at him, I just see a ghost," Irene stopped for a minute to regain her composure before she continued.

"Mother is quiet and withdrawn. Retirement is not what they expected, especially under the present political circumstances. The other day, Mother had that forlorn look on her face and said to me that one should never pray for old age or for a new king. She is right," she sighed, "we always want things to remain the same, and refuse to accept change until our very lives are threatened."

Before Horst left Marienhall that evening, he reminded his friends that the time had come for him to put on the despised swastika armband. "I have warned my closest friends and told them my reasons. I hope I can accomplish what I have in mind."

Wrapped in the silence of a clear summer night, Martin and Irene took their worries to bed with them, all of which grew into nightmares invading their troubled sleep. Only the land was at peace.

At the end of June, the affidavit from Albert Schreiber arrived and Irene and Martin celebrated the event. Fortified with bundles of money from Horst's briefcase and full of hope, he took off for Berlin the following day to present the papers to the American Consulate. He was unprepared for what was awaiting him there. As he approached the American Consulate, a double line of people a block long waited in the sweet June sunshine for a destiny over which they knew they had no control.

A middle-aged woman sat behind a small table halfway inside the front entrance to the Consulate, handing out numbers to newcomers, which placed the applicants in the

American visa quota system. Number 1532 was waiting for
Martin, who figured that at best, it would take weeks before he
would make it through the front door. Up and down he paced
the line, looking for what, he didn't know, when a young man
with a hard face and icy gray eyes approached him and
motioned him aside.

When the two reached the curb of the broad sidewalk, the
man whispered hoarsely in a strong Berlin dialect, "You want to
buy a low number for ten thousand marks?"

Martin didn't flinch at the high price. "How low?" he shot back.

"Number fifty-two."

"Let me see. Is it real?"

"Don't insult me, Jew, or the price goes up," the man snarled.
"Take it, or leave it."

"I'll take it," Martin snapped.

"Follow me to the Café Schuster across the street. We'll do our
business there."

Ignoring the outdoor tables of the pleasant sidewalk café, the
man casually strolled inside and picked a table against the far back
wall. When Martin joined him, the stranger showed him ticket
number fifty-two with one hand and held out the other for the
payoff. From the inside pocket of his suit jacket Martin brought out
a bundle of bills and placed it in the man's empty hand.

"Nice doing business with you," the man sneered, "and," he
added, "don't forget to pay for the coffee and the cake."

Without a word, Martin placed several marks on the table and
left the café. Back across the street, he approached the lady giving
out numbers and asked her when she thought number fifty-two
would be called. The friendly woman consulted a sheet, suggested
he return in the next afternoon, and wished him good luck.

Returning to the American Consulate at the suggested time,
Martin waited only an hour when his number was called. A few
minutes later he found himself seated in front of a big mahogany

desk looking at the kind face of a member of the American Consulate. The man introduced himself as Jason Manning, and quickly, with a trained eye, examined the sponsor's credentials and the affidavit that guaranteed financial responsibility for the needs of the emigrants for the first five years in the United States. The sponsor's obligations ended at the time the emigrants became United States citizens.

"The affidavit is sufficient; everything is in order," Mr. Manning declared with a smile. He retrieved a big stamp from a desk drawer and stamped the front page of Martin's papers with a long number.

"Please refer to this number when contacting us. However, do not call us about the status of your visa. We'll let you know ahead of time when to expect it, so that you can book passage to America."

When Martin politely asked if Mr. Manning had a wild guess how long that could be, the nice man's face took on a woeful look. "A year or more, perhaps. I wish I could be of more help. But all I can tell you, is that the quota for 1938 is filled. It takes a special act of Congress to change immigration laws to increase the quotas." His voice ended in a sigh. He got up, shook hands with him, and wished him the best of luck.

For the next two days, Martin canvassed Central and South American Embassies. He visited the Canadian, New Zealand, and Australian Consulates; all to no avail. Some consulates posted signs stating "Emigration Department Closed," or "We do not accept applications for emigration." Disheartened, he boarded the train back to Breslau. Waiting had become not only uncomfortable, but downright dangerous.

Upon his return, Irene greeted him with open arms and listened to his story with great concern. But true to her nature, her own fears and worries receded into the depth of her consciousness, as she took on her husband's concerns. She did not commiserate with him and instead, she put on a big smile and with a strong voice said, "Let's not get discouraged, dear. Something will turn up; I just know it. I believe that we are two lucky individuals, and that our luck will hold."

Martin hugged her and replied softly, "I hope so too, but coming home on the train, alone with my thoughts, I couldn't help but feel that the *clock of waiting*, as I call it, has turned into a trigger mechanism for a time bomb: ticking . . . ticking . . . ticking. *Boom!*" his arms flew out, "ready to explode and bury us."

Before Irene could reply, Ursula walked into the morning room to see her father and to tell her parents about the bird which had flown into the school room and refused to leave. "I think it is a sparrow," she said. "Every once in a while, he comes flying down from the top of my bed, lands on the table, and listens to my lessons." Her eyes sparkled with excitement, when she told her parents that the little fellow sat on her head twice. "His tiny feet scratch and tickle," she giggled with delight.

"Smart bird," Irene laughed. "You'll know how much he learned when he starts chirping in French." The mood changed and, for a moment, the ugly world out there dropped away as the small family took refuge in the safety of the love they had for each other.

Martin didn't stand still. He had the papers drawn up by his attorney, gifting Marienhall with its contents and all its holdings to Lothar and Trude Burdach. Irene wrapped the thick document in tissue paper, rolled up the deed, and tied a huge red silk bow around both. She invited Lothar and Trude for tea, as she often did, and placed the gaily wrapped packages at Lothar's place at the table.

Protesting that it wasn't his birthday, or any kind of gift-giving day, Lothar slipped the ribbon off of the roll and straightened the heavy parchment paper with both hands. His facial expression went from shock to disbelief and back to shock. Puzzled, he finally stammered, "What does this mean? Is this a joke?"

"No! No! This is no joke. This is a legitimate gift deed, prepared by smart attorneys who swear that it will uphold in any court. You two are now the legal owners of Marienhall and we are your tenants." Martin explained that he had been forewarned that the confiscation of Jewish properties and wealth had only just begun, and he didn't want Marienhall to fall into the hands of the Nazis.

"No use fooling ourselves any more," Irene spoke up, "as long as Hitler is in power, there's no future for the Jews of Germany. We must leave, and the sooner the better. We have not mentioned any of this to Ursula. We don't want to burden her with our daily uncertainties and worries. When we know where we're going and when, that's the time to tell her. I think that children adjust a lot easier to change than adults. Instead of making a tragedy out of emigration, we'll make it an adventure. We hope to make it to America, and," she smiled, "we want you to have Marienhall."

Lothar rose to his feet, facing Martin and Irene. "Marienhall will always be yours," he said, unashamed tears streaking down his face. "We will guard it with our hearts and our souls and pray for the day when you return to claim it again."

The four friends talked way past midnight. They talked about everything under the sun, trusting each other with their hopes and with their dreams. They laughed and they cried and when they finally parted, each took away the deep knowing that life was not about events, life was about people.

The month of August brought the news of the destruction of the Nuremberg Synagogue. A new decree required male Jews to carry the middle name of Israel and females were assigned the name of Sarah. Jews had to report to passport offices to make the name change official, and at the same time, had a huge, red "J" stamped next to their picture. The Nazi government did not want to leave a doubt in the mind of any good German who the enemy was. The stranglehold tightened.

But that was not all. August turned out to be a month of mourning for the Blombergs. Frail and failing, Carl Schreiber died in the middle of the month. On the heels of his death, came the news that Ida's husband, Werner Bohne, had been killed in a freak accident on location somewhere in East Africa. The burden of bringing the family together fell on Irene and Martin, whose own problems and worries took a backseat to the loss of the two men, and the broken hearts of their widows. Ida returned to her home in Berlin, having made no decision about her future. Time would tell her what to do, she said.

Helene journeyed to Wiesbaden to spend some time with an old friend who had lost her husband the year before. She, too, hoped that time would bring her an answer about how and where to live her life. Vulnerable, without the protection of their non-Jewish husbands, both Helene and Ida now faced the same fate of every German Jew. What would they decide to do?

Being told about the deaths in her family, Henrietta reacted in her usual uncaring way and remained behind the stone walls of the prison of her own making—wanting to be left alone. Finally, her children gave up on her and accepted the fact that nothing would change her; she was who she was. They would leave her alone.

Harvest time came to Marienhall and after a year's absence, one lonely gypsy wagon pulled into the back field and edged its way into the forest. When Lothar ventured out to see who his guests were, a tired, worried-looking Woyczek clambered down from the wagon and wrapped one of his bear hugs around Lothar. "It is so good to see you, old friend," Woyczek managed to say in a low voice, heavy with unshed tears.

The two men sat down on a sun-warmed log, and Woyczek began to talk, slowly at first. He told Lothar how his caravan had been stopped and searched by a handful of SA, and how they had taken the men away and burned three wagons. "I was so lucky," Woyczek sobbed, "I was looking for work in the village of Teschen in Upper Silesia, when this happened. There are only four of us left. Ever since then, we travel by night and hide in forests or with friendly farmers during the day. Our songs have gone still. We no longer dance. Just like the Jews, gypsies are another racial impurity Hitler wants to destroy. We are running for our lives, and we don't know where we can go."

Lothar assured his gypsy friend that his people were welcome and safe at Marienhall. He was quiet and thoughtful for a moment. Then a light flashed on in his eyes and a wide grin spread across his face. "I know what we are going to do. I know!" Lothar almost shouted. "We'll strip your wagon of your personal belongings and store them in a hidden spot in the small barn. We'll take the wagon into the big barn, fill it with bundles of hay and top it off with one of our famous scarecrows—sort of country-picturesque. You and your family can move into the empty cottage, and we'll get you some farmers' clothes and a haircut. You'll be regular hired help. You can stop running. What do you say?"

It took Woyczek less than a split second to match Lothar's grin. "Done!" he shouted. He bounced off of the log like a jack rabbit, and, dropping years off his face, he did a little gypsy jig when his feet met the ground "We'll stay out of everybody's way. We'll work hard; there's nothing we won't do for you and for Marienhall." Lothar already knew that.

At the evening meal, Lothar told his wife about the plight of the gypsies and his decision to give them a place to rest and work for as long as they needed it. He was pleased when Trude agreed with him without hesitation. "I'm so glad you did that," she reached for his hand across the table. "I am always happy when we can do something for others. We are so fortunate. We have had such a life of plenty. It is good to give back. I'll help them get settled. I'll shop for clothes for them, and," she added with a chuckle, "as you know, I give a wicked haircut." Lothar's heart was at peace.

By late October, more of Martin and Irene's friends had fled the country, and three of Martin's Jewish business acquaintances had been picked up by the Gestapo. They were shipped to Concentration Camps for no other reason than being Jews. Martin had not heard a word from the American Consulate, nor did his further inquiries for entry permission to other countries, including European nations, bring any results. The waiting continued.

And then all hell broke loose.

In Paris—in protest against the deportation of his parents to Poland along with ten thousand other Jews—a German Jewish refugee, by the name of Herschel Grynszpan, intending to murder the German Ambassador to France, instead shot and killed harmless Ernst Vom Rath, a German official. Goebbels advised his top Party member that *spontaneous* anti-Jewish riots were in order. Swiftly, Heydrich, chief of the Reich Security head office, organized the Night of Nazi Pogrom throughout much of Germany. During the night of the ninth of November, he sent urgent guidelines for spontaneous riots—to all police headquarters:

1. Surrounding buildings must not be damaged when burning synagogues.

2. As many Jews as possible are to be arrested.

3. Jewish business storefronts are to be destroyed.

4. There would not be any interference by police with the demonstrations.

November 9, 1938, *Crystal Nacht*, as it would be called, became the night of unbridled terror, as hordes of demonstrators swinging axes and hammers shattered glass and display windows of Jewish stores. The night sky over towns and cities turned red from the flames of burning synagogues. When morning came, seventy-four Jews had been killed, 20,000 arrested, 818 stores destroyed, 191 synagogues and 171 Jewish homes were burned or destroyed. The terrible irony of it all was that in order to pay for this state-sanctioned destruction, Germany's Jews were fined one billion marks, and countless Jewish businesses were acquired by the Reich in forced sales maneuvers.

If it had not been clear before, *Crystal Nacht* was more than an indication of Nazi confidence (in terms of international sanctions) to act against German Jews with impunity. That night of horror marked the transition of anti-Semitism from planned but isolated attacks to the national policy which was to end in the Final Solution. No one came to the rescue of the German Jews. Quotas were not raised, entry permits even to the doors of hell were unavailable. Waiting for things to change had become a death sentence.

Breslau's beautiful old synagogue was burned to rubble; the city's streets were littered with glass. Under the supervision of SA men shouting obscenities, Jews could be seen scrubbing a sidewalk with toothbrushes.

Horst called Marienhall early the morning after *Crystal Nacht* and advised a shaken Martin not to venture to the city until the following day. Rowdy bands of Hitler Youth were roaming the streets, he said, assaulting Jews and looking for trouble. Disregarding his own safety, Martin's loyal old friend, Hugo, the master printer, cleared away the shattered glass, and must have pulled some strings to have the windows and doors replaced that same day. Both Hugo and Martin decided not to paint the business name on the front door; the house number would have to do.

Like the shards and bits of shattered glass that were swept away after *Crystal Nacht*, the lives of thousands of innocent people were broken into pieces and discarded. There was no doubt that a future of pain and terror was waiting for the remaining Jews of Germany, Austria, and Czechoslovakia. Where could they go? Who would open a door to safety? And not just who, but when?

The days of November dwindled away as a frightened people mourned the death and destruction around them, and tried to make sense out of their lives. With Christmas approaching, Irene turned the first floor of Marienhall over to Trude and Lothar so that the Burdachs could carry on with the traditional and beloved holy day celebrations for themselves and for the villagers.

The little family and Fraülein Amanda stayed in their second-floor quarters where Irene observed Chanukah with its seven-day-gift-giving and storytelling ritual. But nothing was the same. The black cloud of worry and uncertainty hovered over everything and took the color out of the days that in the past had been a time of joyful celebration.

On Christmas Eve, when the first notes of *Silent Night* and the sound of visiting people reached the second floor, Fraülein Amanda took Ursula downstairs to join the festivities for a little while. The big hall was festive with its tall tree, trimmed with glittering decorations and flickering white wax candles in silver clip-on holders. As always, big urns of red roses and greens filled nooks and corners and a table heaped with gifts was waiting in a corner. Several small tables offered trays of Christmas pastries, and tiny cucumber-and-lox sandwiches. From a huge silver punch bowl rose the spicy aroma of mulled wine, and bowls of special candy waited for eager little hands.

Ursula headed straight for the cluster of village children who were waiting for that long anticipated visit from Santa Claus. Soon, the sound of sleighbells drew nearer, announcing the arrival of jolly, old Nick. Stomping snow from his boots, Saint Nicholas, huffing and puffing, entered the hall with a big Ho! Ho! Ho! and immediately became the focus of young and old as he distributed gifts from his sack. When it was empty, he walked over to the corner table and, carefully reading the names on the green stickers, handed out the rest of the presents. With a big belly laugh and lots of Ho Ho Hos, the ancient elf got back into his waiting sleigh, and, accompanied by jingling bells and children shouting "Merry Christmas!" off he went into the star-filled winter night. Undisturbed by the ugliness of the outside world, Marienhall celebrated its own peace on earth.

After the villagers had left, Lothar brought Woyczek's family to see the tree and to give them their presents. Martin and Irene had joined the little group, and Lothar filled crystal glasses with a pale golden wine from Erich and Antonia's vineyards on the Mosel. No longer chased by Hitler's henchmen—at least not for a while—Woyczek had regained his playful spirit, looked healthy, and his heart overflowed with gratitude for the people of Marienhall.

In his full-sleeved white shirt and black velvet toreador pants—straight out of *Carmen*—he raised his glass with a flourish: "*Prosit!* and *Santé!*" his rich voice echoed through the house as he asked God for His blessings on all assembled. Moved to tears, he shook Martin's hand and with a graceful motion raised Irene's to his lips. It was a perfect ending.

On New Year's Eve, Martin and Irene sat across from each other in front of the fireplace in the lovely, second-floor sitting room. Irene, in a favorite burgundy velvet gown and Martin, resplendent in white tie and tails were not only saying goodbye to a year, they were bidding farewell to an era of grace, tradition, and elegance.

"I'm grateful for what we have had," Irene mused, slowly twirling the slender stem of her champagne glass between her fingers, watching the parade of bubbles rise to the top, "and I am grateful for having each other. As long as we have that, we have everything."

She raised her glass to touch her husband's, "Here's to us and to the future. May we find shelter from hate and destruction—somewhere, anywhere in this world."

"And here's to you, my dear, to us and *le chaim!*" Martin's voice choked on the emotions that rose in his throat.

The year 1938 had passed, leaving a trail of blood on the pages of the history books, only to be outdone by the events of the next seven years.

Chapter Nineteen
1939

THE BITTER JANUARY winds that swept across Silesia that January came straight from the frozen heart of Siberia, took one's breath away, and turned tears into icicles of fear. An uncharted panic played havoc among the Jews of Germany, who finally realized that this man, this Hitler, this terror, wasn't going to go away. Instead, he had made the country of Goethe, Schiller, and Beethoven into a slaughterhouse of infamy.

Although Lothar was not really surprised, he was quite disturbed and angry when he saw the first swastika armbands adorning the overcoats of two sons of one of the village elders. When he confronted the father, the man just shrugged his shoulders and came to the defense of his boys. "They had to do it," he muttered. "They were pressured by their employers to join the Party in order to demonstrate unity within the company, and express their loyalty to the Führer. I don't believe that my sons are too serious about all that—it's just going along with the times, that's all. Just going along."

Just going along with the times, Lothar mused. How many thousand good German citizens had said that, and by doing so, turned their backs on all that was decent and humane?

In his mid-January trip for the mail in Neukirch, wind-whipped Nazi flags cracked loudly from several buildings. Instead of the usual, friendly good-morning-how-are-you? greeting, the post-master snapped a crisp *Heil Hitler* at Lothar, who, to his own surprise, limply raised his right arm and mumbled the offensive words back at the man. There! He had done it! *Just going along with the times?* Dear God! Lothar grabbed the mail and fled the post office, certain that his face was as red as the Nazi flag.

After he handed Irene her letters, he wrapped his ice-cold hands around the hot cup of chocolate he was offered, and sat down. He told her about his shock at returning the postmaster's unexpected *Heil Hitler* salute. He also mentioned his surprise at seeing several large Nazi flags in Neukirch—just a village . . . ?

"Just think, Irene," he said agitated, "Neukirch, a little village, a *no-place* of a handful of people who work the land, go to church, and live in peace. Why would they get involved with hoodlums? Why?"

Irene's helpless shrug of her shoulders matched his. "Six years ago Hitler got into power. Before that, in his ten-year struggle to get there, he announced loud and clear what he was going to do, namely, get rid of the Jews. *Today Germany, Tomorrow the World!* And we didn't believe . . . " Irene paused, "I could go on and on," she shook her head, "but here we are still looking for a country to take us in, but there's no place to go, no place to hide."

For the next hour, they tossed the subject of the Nazis around and around, and solved nothing. Nothing. Soon, there would be new decrees.

During the second week of January, Martin and Irene were informed that they had three days to surrender all jewelry into the hands of the Finance Bureau in Breslau. Attempts to keep a precious item would result in severe punishment. Bitter bile rose into Irene's throat when she entered the stone and marble foyer of the Finance Building, carrying her jewelry in a black leather bag. She didn't care about the value of the pieces, but she treasured the memories of the occasions upon which they had been given to her. Martin's engagement and wedding gifts, the beautiful pearls he fastened around her neck upon her arrival in Breslau; the rings and trinkets that marked a holiday, an anniversary, or a special moment, and the just-because-I-love-you presents at different times. Then there were the fabulous necklaces of sapphires, emeralds, and diamonds the Old Baron had lavished on her with such joy throughout the years.

Stiff as a bone and with her heart iced over, Irene handed her belongings to the Nazi official who sat behind a desk surrounded by an extravagant display of Nazi propaganda. Since there were no chairs by the desk, and none were offered, Martin and Irene had to remain standing. The man drooled as he checked off one beautiful piece after another from his own copy of the insurance policy. When he was satisfied that every-thing was in order, he tossed the receipt at Irene, and with an ugly, hog-like, snorting chuckle said, "Well, Jew whore, the next piece of jewelry you are going to wear will have to come from Woolworth." His offensive, braying laughter followed her all the way down the long hallway of the Finance Building and would echo in her head for the longest time.

A few days later, Max's accounting firm was confiscated and he, with Lucy and Inge were forced to move into a single room (with kitchen privileges) in a "Jewish" house. Herman and Toni Burger, and the ever faithful Ana Marieke already lived in such a "Jewish" house and were left alone—for how long no one knew.

Without notice, leaving a bank draft for the next three months' rent, the three Burdach men moved Irene and Martin's belongings quietly out of the bachelor apartment, and into a three-room flat on the second floor above the plant that had never been rented. Since Jews had to report their changes of residence to the Gestapo, Martin registered the new living quarters as their main address, hoping to draw attention away from Marienhall. Even though the latter now officially belonged to the Burdachs, the Gestapo with its total power, could twist anything around to make it come out in their favor.

With Maria and Liesel in tow, Irene made the small flat into a cozy and pleasant home away from home. Liesel, who had retrieved Oscar's car from the repair shop after his mysterious disappearance, had learned to drive the small *Opel*, and often took Irene on errands and to visits with the Burger family. Liesel's self-assurance and strength had blossomed in Oscar's absence. Her sense of humor returned full force, she rediscovered her love for books, and took up painting in watercolors. She was a whole person of her own, no longer an appendix to someone else's views and rules.

Before returning to Marienhall the next day, Irene asked Liesel to drive through the city she had loved from the day Antonia and Helene had introduced her to its imposing buildings, broad streets, and some of their favorite hangouts. The buildings were still imposing, but now the structures' handsome façades were hidden behind the ominous black swastika. The streets were still broad and well kept, but now they were crowded with men and boys in Nazi uniforms, and men and women wearing swastika armbands. The Ring, the center of Old Town, with its picturesque city hall had become the assembly point for goose-stepping SA troops who paraded through the city, proclaiming their superiority by singing their songs of hate and blood. Irene felt a sharp jab in her heart when they passed the State Opera House and the Breslau Symphony Hall where a young woman's dream had come true. Now, their doors were closed to her. She was a Jew.

"Liesel," she tugged on her friend's arm, "let's go home, please. I have had enough. This is no longer my world." No sooner had those words escaped Irene, she wondered out loud, "Just what and where is my world, Liesel? What do you think it is?"

Tearing up immediately, Liesel shook her head, reached for Irene's hand, and gave it big squeeze. "I don't know. I wish I did. All I know is that you deserve the best, the most beautiful world . . . " her voice ended in a sob. Holding hands, the two women sat in silence all the way home to Marienhall.

By the middle of February, Herman Burger, like the Old Baron, didn't wake up one morning. His broken heart had stopped during the night. Once again the family gathered to say goodbye to a loved one. The load of the losses grew heavier and added its weight to the burden of worries that everyone carried already.

Irene and Lucy were touched and they breathed easier, when Ana Marieke announced she would give up her little place and move in with Toni. The two women had been friends and family for four decades and took a great deal of comfort from each other's presence.

Toni was composed and serene, as she chatted about her husband, telling anecdotes about him, bringing rays of sunshine to the somber occasion.

Holding a photo of him in her hands which was taken in front of the Lubitz Tavern before they moved to Breslau, she ran her fingers lovingly over his face. "He was one lucky man," she mused. "He always wished for death to meet him in his sleep; no lingering illness, no fuss. He was a fine man and God must have heard him."

In full control of her emotions, consoling her children as she kissed them goodbye upon leaving her apartment, Irene realized her enormous strength and her ability to make the best of the worst.

"God grant me her strength, I'll need it," she said to herself.

By March 18th there was still no word from the American Consulate, nor was there a glimmer of hope that something else, somewhere else, would open up. The efforts of a couple of the

Blomberg's old friends to get them admitted to Mexico, where they owned a small sunglasses factory, had failed. Where to go?

Irene had just finished her breakfast when the phone rang. It was a call from Horst von Brunnen.

"Irene, guess what?" he shouted into the phone, his voice at a high pitch. "Good news! I just discovered that Shanghai, China accepts emigrants, actually they accept anybody, without visas, without landing fees or guarantees. Shanghai is an open port. All you have to do is book passage for the three of you and when you arrive in Shanghai, you just walk off the gangplank. There are absolutely no landing requirements, no restrictions. Please, go to the office of the Nord Deutsche Lloyd and buy your tickets. Bribe them, if you have to. This shipping company owns three luxury liners that travel all the way to Japan and back—the *Gneisenau,* the *Potsdam,* and the *Scharnhorst.* They also represent several Italian liners. I'm sure the news is out and passage to the Orient will sell out. So, don't wait; start packing."

Horst finally came up for breath, and Irene got a word in. "Horst!" she exclaimed, "China is on the other side of the world. Marco Polo went there and he came back," she laughed with nervous excitement while being carried away by a wave of relief.

"Don't be funny with me," Horst chuckled, "just tell Martin and call me back. In the meantime, I will check around some more."

Irene dialed Martin's number at the plant and was surprised that no one answered. Strange, she thought, it was past ten o'clock. She would wait a while and try again.

What she didn't know was that at the precise moment she was talking to Horst, Martin was in his office checking print proofs. He was so absorbed in his task, that he didn't hear the door open. When he finally sensed the presence of someone in his room, he looked up and stared straight into the cold, no-color eyes behind the steel-rimmed glasses of a man dressed in a long black leather overcoat, a swastika wrapped around the left sleeve. Pointing to the man on his right, the intruder hissed, "Gestapo. This is Stoeffler, I'm Ehrlich. We are here to do some business with you."

With one swift motion, he placed a sheet of paper, a fountain pen, and a handgun in front of Martin and explained, "This document in duplicate represents the sales agreement for your business and all its assets, which include your bank accounts, between you and the German Reich. You have a choice: you may use the pen or the gun. We will give you five minutes."

"No! No! That won't be necessary," Martin protested quietly. He reached for the pen, signed his name at the indicated lines, returned the pages to the man, who gave Martin his copy.

"You may leave now," Ehrlich announced coldly, "but don't come back. That goes for your apartment, too. Nothing here belongs to you any more: not the building, not the contents. Just walk, Jew, walk!"

Martin rose from his chair, took his hat and coat in hand, and wordlessly, without a backward glance, he walked out of his office, past the clanking presses, past the men, and stepped out into the unfriendly streets of his hometown. Unaware of the icy wind that bit his face, he kept walking and finally ducked into the shelter of the entrance to an apartment building. He breathed deeply to still the pounding of his heart and to gather his thoughts.

"Done," he said to himself. The inevitable, for which he had tried to prepare himself for some time, had happened. Prepared or not, the calculated and so casually executed theft of his business shook him badly; he felt an unaccustomed surge of boiling anger rise to the surface from within.

"Quiet! Back off!" he instructed himself. "Think! Find a way to get to Marienhall." He had intended to spend another day in the city, and had sent Otto and the car home. To return to the plant was out of the question. Where could he make a telephone call?

Think! Get oriented! He looked around for a moment as though he had landed in a strange city and didn't know his way around. Stop! His mind raced. Then the idea came to him.

"Of course! My barber!"

He crossed the busy intersection with a purposeful stride and two blocks later arrived at the door of the barbershop. The place was crowded with people waiting their turn for a shave or haircut. Johannes Bader, the man who had cut Martin's hair for twenty-five years, was always ready to tell the story of how the Old Baron had given him the money to start his own shop. He greeted Martin with a smile, and in response to his request, pointed him in the direction of the telephone which sat on a short storage counter behind a flimsy curtain.

Irene had barely said hello, when Martin rushed on, "Don't say anything, Irene, just listen and do as I ask. Send Otto or Lothar with the car to my barber on Sonnen Platz. They know where it is. Don't wait. This is urgent. Please, do it now. I'll be waiting."

He left some money to pay for the call, and emerged from behind the curtain. He sat down on the only vacant chair, grabbed a newspaper, and hid himself behind the pages of the *Tagesblatt*. When his turn came for a shave, there were only two newcomers in the barbershop.

To the barber's routine question if he had had a busy day, Martin replied in a joking fashion, that he had a great day. "Within three minutes, without haggling over the price," Martin confided in a stage whisper, "I sold my business, including the building, to Adolf Hitler and the German Reich. Just think, how thoughtful the Gestapo is," he mocked, "they even deposited the credit draft in a new kind of a bank account for me. They call it a *frozen account*. I guess something has to melt, before I can get my money?" He winked at the barber in the mirror, trying to catch his eye.

Johannes wasn't looking. Cold fear rushed over Martin when he realized that he said the wrong things, at the wrong place, at the wrong time. How foolish, he berated himself; how careless!

"You are done," the barber announced curtly. He yanked the protective cape from Martin's shoulders, and twirled the barber chair around so fast, that Martin almost sprawled to the floor. With a closed face and his eyes averted, Johannes took the handful of money Martin pushed into his hand, and turned his back on his old customer.

"Just joking, old friend. Just joking," Martin addressed the stiff back. There was no reply.

As luck would have it, Otto had pulled up in the car across the street and gave a short toot on the horn. Relieved, Martin ran out of the barbershop, dashed across the street, and jumped into the car next to Otto.

"So, where's the fire? What's the rush?" Otto joked. When he looked at Martin, he knew that bad news was waiting behind every one of the tense and taught lines on his face .

The floodgates of his emotions opened when Martin recounted the events of the day. Otto winced as he listened to Martin confess his stupid chatting at the barbershop.

"I think we should hide you for a few days," Otto suggested, "just in case someone from the barbershop has turned you in."

"No! I would put my family and all of you in terrible danger," Martin protested passionately. "I have only made a feeble joke; I have said nothing ugly."

"But Martin, don't you know," Otto was agitated and exasperated, "Nazis don't have a sense of humor when it comes to Jews. It may sound horrible," he apologized, "but someone said that the only time the Nazis laugh is when they torture Jews."

"Oh, I know," Martin groaned, "it was all false bravado. Had I used my head, I would not have said something so stupid! I wish I could take it back. I won't tell Irene, she would be furious with me, and rightfully so."

Irene must have heard the car coming up the driveway and was waiting for him at the door, anxiety written all over her face. "What happened," she wanted to know. "Tell me first and then I have some interesting news for you."

Upstairs in the morning room, in their favorite chairs in front of a cozy fire, Martin quickly told her that finally his business was confiscated by the Gestapo under the well-known ruse of a forced sale. "They took it all." he said, "the plant, the bank accounts, the building and its contents, and the apartment."

Irene froze for a moment. "Oh, my dear, I knew something was wrong when you called. And I had a feeling that was it."

"It's all right; my dear. It's all right. I am surprised," Martin said, working on a half-grin, "that I am *surprised*. I really believed that I had prepared myself for it. After all, the confiscation of Jewish businesses and Jewish wealth is happening everywhere. Just the same, I must have believed that I was going to be the exception," he shook his head.

At a loss for words, Irene kept petting his hand in silence, her stomach churning with anxiety.

"You know, *Liebchen*," Martin sighed, "I am relieved it's over. I am going to spend every breath I take on getting us out of the country. I won't leave a stone, or in this case, a country unturned. It finally got through to me that Adolf Hitler has not missed a step in this program of getting rid of the Jews. He has taken away our identity, our professions, our businesses and our possessions. What do we have left?"

He looked at Irene and saw fear rise into her eyes. "You know it. All we have left are our lives. He will take those too, if we stay here."

Irene held up her hands. "Stop a moment. I may have some good news; something you can move on tomorrow." She hastily told him about Horst's phone call and that faraway place that took in Jews and everyone else.

"Shanghai? China, you mean? Did I hear you right?" Martin's eyes opened wide. His eyebrows seemed to climb up to the end of his forehead and stayed there.

"Oh, yes! Shanghai in China."

Breathlessly, she related the rest of the information Horst had given her and watched a transformation take place. He sat up straight, squared his shoulders, and turned the light back on in his eyes.

"This is great!" he shouted elatedly. "Let's go! Start packing, no more waiting around for America! I will be at the Nord Deutsche Lloyd at eight o'clock in the morning."

Before they went to bed, Irene had traced the long ocean voyage on the pages of their atlas with her finger. They agreed they liked rice and green tea, lotus blossoms and painted silk scrolls. What they didn't know about China, they would learn. They went to sleep holding hands. Outside, a wild March wind whipped the bare branches of the still-wintry trees into a frenzied dance, and heavy rain beat steadily against the windows.

Next stop Shanghai. China.

And then it happened. In the wee hours of the morning, Marienhall woke up with a start. Two cars came boiling through the open gates, their horns blaring all the way, kicking up gravel in their haste. Car doors slammed, fists pounded on the front door. The tall oak wings of the entrance with its ancient lock burst open easily under the onslaught of brute power. Loud voices shouted, heavy boots pounded up the stairs to the second floor. Irene had already stepped into the upper hall outside her bedroom, and watched paralyzed with fear, as eight burly SS men tore past her looking for the man of the house.

On the opposite side of the upstairs hall, in the children's wing, Ursula, awakened by the noise, sat up in bed. Fastening the belt of her housecoat, Fraülein Amanda came flying into the room, yanked the young girl out of bed, hissing " . . . Sshh . . .

sshh . . ." between her teeth. She ran to the big armoire in the far corner of the room. Hastily, she opened the door, groped for the back panel, slid it silently aside, pushed Ursula into the dark, and squeezed in next to her. She wrapped one arm reassuringly around the girl's shoulders, rearranged the clothes, shut the mirrored door of the armoire, and slid the panel back into place.

Near tears, her body pressed against a shaking Fraülein Amanda, Ursula whispered, "Are they coming for my father? Will they be looking for us?"

Before Fraülein Amanda could answer, they heard men shouting again, heard the muffled thumping of heavy footsteps down the stairs, followed by the sounds of nail-studded boots clanking and scraping their way across the marble floor in the foyer. Motors raced, car doors slammed, horns blared, gravel crunched as the men from Hell left Marienhall.

Silence.

No one dared to breathe, not even the house.

Satisfied that the intruders were gone, Fraülein Amanda and Ursula scrambled out of their hiding place and dashed across the hall looking for Irene. They found her in the morning room talking on the telephone in a voice so low, Ursula wondered if anyone could hear her.

Following a soft knock on the door, Maria, Liesel, and Trude tiptoed in, their faces troubled, their eyes bleeding tears. Maria, who swore that hot black tea was life's equalizer which took the rough edges off of bad times, had come prepared and handed out steaming glasses of her favorite Russian tea.

When Irene got off the phone, trance-like, she sat down, reached for Ursula, and, in the silence of the early morning, held her close for a long time. When she let go of her child, she motioned for her to sit down on the hassock beside her, and turned to her.

"Perhaps we haven't been fair to you, Ursula, not talking more about the precarious situation of being Jews in Germany right now. We did not want to burden you with a terror we hoped would go away. I know that Fraülein Amanda has discussed the subject with you."

Irene paused, looked in the upturned face of her girl with the trusting green eyes. "We have to face reality, and we have to be strong. Some wise individual once said that hope is no substitute for judgment. He was so right. We have hoped and hoped far too long, even though we knew it was dangerous. Well," she sighed deeply, tears choking her voice. "The Gestapo picked up your father, accusing him of making remarks insulting the Nazis and the Führer. Someone turned him in. The SS officer in charge of the arrest told me where they are taking him for interrogation— a Gestapo sub-station in the outskirts of Breslau. He also informed me that the only way to have your father released is to bring proof that the three of us are leaving the country. Needless to say, we need a miracle and we need it soon."

When she called Erich and Antonia, turning to them for help, Irene hastily ran through the event of Martin's arrest, preceded by the confiscation of his business. She relayed Horst's news about Shanghai being an open port to Erich, and the need to immediately book passage on the earliest east-bound ocean liner. Erich, first agitated about Martin's arrest, calmed down a bit as he listened to Irene describing the possibility of getting to Shanghai, China, and where to book passage. He promised to be at the doors of Nord Deutsche Lloyd before they opened.

"He said that he knew the director of the Breslau branch of the big shipping line and he believed that it would help. I know China is on the other side of the world," Irene added when she saw the surprise on the faces around her, "but it doesn't matter. We have to save our lives. Just remember, the road that takes us there can always bring us back."

Slowly, Irene regained her composure, assured Ursula that help was on its way, and after hugs and holding on to each other, the women parted. "As soon as I hear from Erich, I'll let you know," Irene promised. "In the meantime, keep busy, go about your day, and pray a lot. I'll be doing the same."

Back in her room, Ursula popped into bed, and asked Fraülein Amanda to sit by her. "I promised Mother I would try to sleep some more, and I would not worry. But I am. Please stay with me and talk to me. I need to know more about life outside Marienhall; I am not a little girl."

After Ursula tucked the quilt under her chin, Fraülein Amanda wrapped herself in a spare blanket and slipped in next to her on top of the bed. The wind had stopped, the heavy rain had turned to a steady drizzle, and the house was still. Fraülein Amanda talked about the arrogant bullies of the world and how beating down and destroying innocent people made them important and superior in their own eyes. She talked about how one man's dream of power can easily become another man's nightmare. "But I also know that for every evil deed there is a good deed, for every villain, a hero," she mused. "Enough for now. Close your eyes and get some sleep. I have a feeling we have a big day ahead of us."

It was early afternoon when Irene burst into the schoolroom, eyes alive, bubbling over with excitement. "Sorry, Fraülein Amanda, school is out for a moment. Good news! We have tickets for Shanghai! We are leaving exactly one week from today. Erich just called and told me the most astonishing story. Luck is on our side! Remember when I said we needed a miracle? Well, thank God, we had one. I still can't believe it, but here's what happened.

"Erich arrived at Nord Deutsche Lloyd precisely at nine o'clock. He was amazed to see a throng of people, a block long, three deep waiting in line. He got out of his shiny black and chrome Mercedes and the first strange thing happened. He said the crowd parted, like the Red Sea and made a path for him to the front door of the shipping company." Irene paused for second, smiled and continued.

"Can't you just see him? His imposing figure, tall and erect, walking with that purposeful, military stride of his, dressed by the best tailors in dove gray. One glance at his handsome features with that imperial look demanding attention, and people know that he is *somebody*. He always gets away with it. Thank heaven, it worked again."

Irene went on to say that bidding the crowd a cheerful "Good Morning," he walked into the ticket office, heading straight for the door that announced in gold lettering: Hans von Steglitz, Director. He knocked, and not waiting for an answer, he strolled in. The distinguished-looking man behind the desk was talking on the telephone, looked up, recognized Erich, smiled, and gestured for him to be seated.

"Here comes the miracle part," Irene could barely contain herself and hurried on, "The director hung up the telephone and came around his desk to greet Erich. Waving a fistful of papers in one hand, he explained that a German journalist, with his wife and two young sons, had booked first-class, round-trip passages to Kobe, Japan on the Nord Deutsche Lloyd's *Gneisenau*. The ship sails from Hamburg at midnight, tonight. Well, the journalist was rushed to the hospital early this morning with a bad appendix. The director was going to the outer office to announce the availability of these tickets," Irene stopped and took a deep breath.

"Guess what? Erich said he reached for his briefcase, dumped bundles of marks on the man's desk, and told Director Steglitz to help himself to the amount he needed. The tickets are ours! We are going to Shanghai."

"If the ship leaves tonight," Ursula who had been all ears, questioned, "how can we get to Hamburg before midnight?"

"I hadn't come to that yet," Irene smiled at her, "it is another part of the miracle. It takes the ship eight days to sail from Hamburg to Genoa, Italy. We have that week to get ready and take the train to Genoa, where we will board her. Erich is on his way here and he will fill us in on the details. And now," she grimaced, closing her eyes as though in prayer, "we still have to get Martin released—today, if at all possible. The sooner the better; every minute counts."

She left to call her mother and Lucy. "I'll be back with Erich as soon as he gets here, and we will find out what to do next." On the way to her room, euphoria changed to sadness. Eight days, Irene talked to herself, just eight days—no time for tears and painful goodbyes. How do you say goodbye to a lifetime, to the loved ones you leave behind? For a split second, she even felt guilty at having found a way to safety. Quickly, she put her thoughts away. No use creating phantoms, Martin would say. He was right. She would need all her energy for dealing with reality.

At four o'clock in the afternoon, Erich stepped out of his car, looking as dapper and fresh as though he was on his way to tea with the queen. Irene met him at the door and brought him to the schoolroom, where Lothar and Trude were waiting with Ursula and Fräulein Amanda. Dark clouds swollen with unshed raindrops had settled over Marienhall, and only the rosy light from several lamps eased the gloom.

"Young lady," Erich held out his arms to Ursula, who made a run for the shelter of his love, "you have quite an adventure waiting for you. You are going to China. What stories you will have to tell us when you return. But first," he let go of her and joined the others seated around the school table, "we have some work to do."

From his briefcase he retrieved a big Manila envelope. "Here are your tickets to China, and some instructions. I have been told by the shipping company's director that another new decree has been issued by the Party," he paused, shaking his head in disbelief.

"This latest one," he continued, "prohibits porters at train depots and docks from helping Jews with their luggage," he sighed. "So, pack only what you each can carry—no steamer trunks; just a regular suitcase. One piece each," he emphasized. "Not only that," he added, rubbing his his face, as though waking up from a bad dream, "but you will do the packing under the eagle eyes of a so-called 'Packing Inspector,' another invention of pure Nazi chicanery. That Hitler thinks of everything! The inspector will seal the luggage with official stickers. You cannot open your suitcases until you are out of Germany."

Erich handed Irene another official-looking, swastika-adorned paper. "I went to the Finance Bureau to get Martin's Tax Obligation Release, which you need to leave the country. Keep it with your passport. Luckily, the man in charge was eating his lunch and was in a hurry to get back to his meal. He quickly gave me the release, but not without tossing a few insults my way for helping a Jew, And that brings me to the last and biggest task: getting Martin out of the hands of the Gestapo and who is going to do that?"

He looked around the table. "I know," he said, "that any one of us going into the lion's den could get into deep trouble. An Aryan helping a Jew is not a popular thing to do. So, my dear," he turned to Ursula, a slow smile playing around his mouth, "we shall send a child to do a man's job. Actually," he petted her hand, "you are not a child anymore. You've been a grown-up young lady for a long time. You are eleven years old and as tall as your mother. You are smart, you have poise and a quiet self-assurance about you way beyond your years."

Erich got up, pulled Ursula to her feet and, placing his hands firmly on her shoulders, he said, "Now, here's what you do. Believe me, it is simple and I know you can do it. Walk into the building and tell the guard at the front desk your name and that you came to ask for the release of your father, Martin Blomberg. Say you've brought proof of leaving the country in seven days," he stopped to catch his breath. "Hand him the tickets to Shanghai. Say no more. Don't be afraid; you'll be fine. They are not used to dealing with young people. It will work. Lothar will drive you there in the old car he uses for his hunting trips, and I'll be here when you return with your father," he assured her.

Fraülein Amanda jumped to her feet. "No matter what you might say, Herr von Warteburg," her tone was strangely terse, even commanding, "I am going with her. There are a few more things she needs to know, and what to expect. You get the car, Lothar, I'll get our coats."

Lothar nodded, a bit dazed, and left. No one else spoke.

Like the swift wind that had crept up again with rain-bearing gusts, Fraülein Amanda was back wearing her hat and coat and helped Ursula with hers. Erich handed the governess the manila envelope. "Guard it with your life," he said hoarsely, "and go with God."

In the dark of the early March evening, Lothar kept a steady pace as he drove on the rain-soaked country road, splashing through puddles and avoiding mud traps. In the backseat, Fraülein Amanda held class. After explaining some Nazi ideologies, she grabbed Ursula's hands, turned her to bring her face to face, and began telling her what might be waiting for her.

"Nazis are no more than overgrown bullies, dangerous, of course," she started, "and they are going to use terrible words to insult you and make you feel inferior. Don't listen, don't be afraid. Be modest and humble, keep your poise, and answer their questions. Don't let them rattle you . . . "

On and on she went for the next hour, until Lothar located the Gestapo compound on a lonely area at the edge of a Breslau suburb.

He stopped in front of the small guard post that looked like a large toad, jutting out from the high, shard-topped brick wall. With the manila envelope in hand, and with Fraülein Amanda's prayers and God's blessing in her ears, Ursula got out of the car.

In an unsteady voice, Lothar added his blessings, "Good luck, my darling. I am going to park the car at the corner," he pointed to his right, "away from these floodlights. I'll be watching for you and come roaring back as soon as I see you."

Always a child of imagination, making up her own stories of heroes and princesses, villains and evil witches, Ursula made believe she was on her way to rescue her prince from a wicked monster who lived in the villain's dungeon.

She walked up to the SA man on guard and told him her mission. The man just grunted, astonished at seeing a young girl, opened the gate, and pointed to a well-lit building. "Go through that door, and up the stairs. The officer on duty on the second floor will take you to Major von Ketzler."

Carefully stepping over the slick, pillow-like cobblestones of the courtyard, she reached the gray stone building. The door opened with a hollow groan and revealed a brightly lit hall with two unoc-cupied desks squatting under the watchful eyes of Hitler's portrait, flanked by huge Nazi flags. The dull cement walls seemed to breathe stale, damp air at her and she could hear the echo of voices and doors slamming coming from the far end of the hallway.

Her imagination took her up the stairs looking for the monster's lair. She addressed her request to the elderly man (surely a villain's assistant) behind a desk on the second floor. Surprised at seeing such a young person, he motioned her to follow him down a narrow hall, where he knocked on a door, and entered with Ursula behind him.

"*Heil Hitler,* Herr Major! Please forgive the interruption, but this Jew girl needs to see you. She wants to get her Jew father released; they are leaving Germany. Good riddance I say, Herr Major."

Major von Ketzler wore the death-black SS uniform of Hitler's elite corps, decorated with silver eagles and other insignia. He was a big man with broad shoulders, thick steel-gray hair, and pale ice-cold eyes beneath bushy eyebrows. The arrogant expression on his features matched the tone of his voice. "Let me see what you have, Jew girl; bring it to me."

Ursula, her heart skipping a beat, approached his desk and handed him the precious contents of the manila envelope. Careful not to come in contact with her hands, Major von Ketzler gingerly picked up the papers between two fingers, and turned his back to her. An oppressive silence clung to the room, as minutes ticked by. Finally, the SS officer turned sharply on his heels and with a wild move of his arm, sailed the documents across his desk to land at her feet.

"Pick them up, Jew girl and get out of my sight," he snarled. He then addressed Ursula's escort, "Give this little Jew whore her Jew father. China is a good place for them," he laughed obscenely, "I heard that the Chinese people eat pigs and dogs."

Ursula quickly gathered the papers and returned them to the envelope. The SA man snapped a crisp *Heil Hitler!* at the Major, grabbed her roughly by one shoulder, and propelled her ahead of him, shouting, "Let's go Jew swine, let's go!"

Back in the hall, he looked furtively around to see if they were alone. Satisfied there was no one in sight, he whispered, "Don't be scared, young lady. I just sound bad, I have to. I know your father; he is a good man. My son was an apprentice at your father's shop."

They had reached the first-floor hall, when from somewhere (in the dragon's dungeon) there came an animal-like howling of unbearable pain that defied anything she had ever heard.

The man at her side ignored the sounds of terror, opened the entrance door, and pushed her outside into the rain. "Wait here, I'll get your father."

Ursula tucked the envelope inside her coat and shrank against the wall, trying to escape the steady drizzle that came on the breath of a brazen March wind. She kept painting pictures in her mind of going home. Hand in hand with her father, step by step putting more distance between them and the monster, they walked home.

Home.

After what seemed an eternity, her SA escort appeared in front of her, clutching the top end of a big burlap bag in one hand. "Here, Jew pig, here's your Jew father. Now get out of here."

With that, he transferred the bag into her hands, gave her a shove that almost toppled her over, and for all to hear shouted, "Get moving, Jew whore."

As she grabbed the tied-up end of the big sack in both hands, she heard him whisper, "Good luck! I'll help you soon."

Bewildered, she started to drag the heavy burden through the courtyard in the direction of the guardhouse. Each time the bottom of the bag connected with a cobblestone, a soft moaning reached her ears. She stopped, relieved that her father was alive, she knew that each foot gained would cause him great pain. Storm troopers were watching her struggle, ready with insults and crude encouragements.

Suddenly, the man who whispered that he would help was at her side. He picked up the blood-streaked sack in his arms and carried it toward the gate, yelling at her, "If we wait for you to get out of here, we'll be here all night, you stupid Jew pig." The guard opened the gate, the man dropped his burden on the dark street, and without a look back, he walked away and closed the gate behind him.

Ursula started to shiver and was near tears, when she heard a car approach and stop, dimming its headlights. Lothar rushed up to her, picked up the big sack, and as gently as he could, dropped it on the back seat by Fraülein Amanda. He came back for Ursula, hustled her into the seat next to him, got in the car, and drove away into the black of the night under a starless sky.

Fraülein Amanda quickly removed one of the knives Lothar used on his hunting expeditions from its restraining leather strap, and carefully cut through the burlap. Stark naked, his knees tucked under his chin, his arms hugging himself, Martin was breathing in shallow gasps. She assured Ursula and Lothar that he was alive, and that the blood seemed to have come from superficial scratch-like wounds. She tossed a warm lap robe over him. When she forced a few drops of brandy from Lothar's flask down his throat, Martin spit and sputtered, opened his eyes, and came alive.

"Are they gone? Where are we? What has happened?" his voice was hoarse and strained.

"We are in the car, Lothar is driving. You are safe and we are going home," Ursula answered quickly, her head turned, trying to get a glimpse of him.

"What is the child doing here? Why is she here?" Martin asked, confused and trying to get on his feet.

Fraülein Amanda gently pushed him back against the seat, "We'll talk later. Right now, please rest, be still. And just so you can rest easier, Erich was able to book passage to Shanghai; you are leaving next week."

"He did?" Martin stammered, "how wonderful." Exhausted, he leaned back, pulled the lap robe snugly around him, closed his eyes, and murmured a weak, "Thank you, Fraülein Amanda."

When Lothar drove through the gates of Marienhall, he gave the horn two sharp taps, and by the time he stopped the car at the house, lights were on, the front door opened, people ran out. Eager arms carried the blanket-wrapped Martin into the house.

Irene grabbed his blood-streaked hand, "Oh, my dearest! What did they do to you?" she gasped, "What happened to you?"

"They kept my clothes," he answered, squeezing her hand. "But I am all right; just sore. I shall not talk about it ever. I have already forgotten what has been done to me. Please, don't ask me again. It's over. I just want a bath and some sleep."

In the hall, he shook hands with each of the assembled Burdachs whose anxious faces relaxed considerably at the sight of him. Martin was beginning to wear down and was grateful when Otto deposited him in a chair in the quiet of his bedroom with Irene at his side.

Ursula and Fraülein Amanda had stayed back, waiting for Martin to be taken care of. Barely inside the door, Ursula flew into Erich's open arms. Unashamed tears trickled down his cheeks. He cupped her face into his hands and shook his head in wonder, "I am so proud of you; my heart is bursting. I am so proud. I knew you could do it. You can do anything!"

Shedding her hat and her coat, Fraülein Amanda took charge of Ursula. "Enough for tonight," she announced firmly, "she needs to unwind and put this night behind her. She can tell you all about it at breakfast."

Sitting up in bed, sipping one of Maria's life-saving cups of hot tea, Ursula turned her puzzled face to her governess who sat by her side, "Why do people hurt other people; people they have never seen before, people they don't know? Why?"

Fraülein Amanda shook her head in silence. A wild gust of wind rattled the tall windows, chasing raindrops up and down the glass panes. "Maybe the wind has the answers," she murmured, "I wish I knew."

Straightening the quilt around Ursula, she kissed her good night. "You have been so courageous today. I am proud of you. Forget the ugliness of people, believe in the goodness of life. Dream happy dreams."

Ursula looked up at the spot on the ceiling over her bed, where Fraülein Amanda, years ago, had painted a golden star.

"This is your Wishing Star," she had explained, "before you close your eyes, look at the star and make a wish."

The gold glitter of the Wishing Star twinkled as it listened to her wish.

Chapter Twenty

MARCH 1939

H OW MUCH LIVING can I squeeze into five days?" Irene
asked Trude, her face a painful question mark. "How
many goodbyes can I say without breaking my heart?"

Trude looked at her best friend, her own heart heavy and
sad. "You will do what you have to do. That's the good part of
being a woman. Men react and cause problems, women act
and make life happen. And, don't forget," Trude smiled,
"count your blessings. You were given the miracle for which
you asked: you are able to leave Germany. Live and breathe
on that. And," she advised lovingly, "keep your goodbyes
brief; the longer you tarry, the harder it gets. That goes for
me too."

Irene nodded, grateful for Trude's company during the
difficult chore of choosing what to pack and what to discard.
They were going through drawers and closets, armoires and
storage boxes, admiring favorite gowns, fur wraps and silken
shawls, dancing shoes and glittering evening bags, recalling the
festive events for which Irene had worn them. Except for the
memories, these things would stay behind. Otto had set up
Ursula's ping-pong table under the windows of the second floor
hall, and while Martin was resting, Irene and Trude were
arranging the items for inspection.

"We really don't know what Shanghai is like," Irene pondered, frustrated, holding up a simple linen suit, "just that the summers are hot and humid and the winters are chilly and humid."

Looking at the size of the suitcases she had brought down from the attic for their journey, she realized how little they would be able to take. During the three days before the arrival of the Packing Inspector, Irene changed, eliminated, and replaced things several times until she finally gave up, nervous and exhausted. In between she took care of Martin, keeping him sedated and quiet.

Two days before leaving Marienhall, the Packing Inspector, a tough-looking young Nazi, arrived, full of importance, arrogance and foul language. He checked the suitcases for false bottoms and hidden treasures. He took a pencil-thin stick, ran it first through a tin of brown shoe polish, then through a jar of Irene's face cream, leaving brown streaks of polish. He broke two chocolate bars into tiny pieces, making sure the almonds were not diamonds. He watched Irene pack each approved item into its designated suitcase, cursed the Jews, cursed her. Three hours later, he sealed the luggage with a blob of red wax over a swastika-imprinted red ribbon, let fly with a string of Jew curses and left. In the foyer, he aimed a swift blow at the big crystal vase on the hall table and sent it crashing to the floor. "Hey Jew," he yelled, "now you have your own *Crystal Nacht*." His obscene laughter bounced from wall to wall.

Irene and Martin huddled together in the morning room at the end of the day. "One more step accomplished," he sighed, "and unless the Nazis invent another hurdle tomorrow, we'll be on board the *Gneisenau* in less than forty-eight hours."

"As hard as it has been, as sad as it all is," Irene said softly, "I can't wait."

Since the train for Genoa was scheduled to depart early in the morning from the Breslau main station, Irene arranged to spend the last night in Lucy's tiny place in the city. "I don't want to leave from Marienhall, it would be too hard," she said to her sister, holding back the tears. "Also, I want to spend a little time with you. Maria is preparing a basket of farewell delicacies, wine, bread, and pastries for dinner. We can sit and talk."

The Breslau depot which served all corners of Germany, as well as the border-sharing European countries, was crowded with travelers. The three Blombergs stationed themselves near the big glass doors that led to the tracks, put down their suitcases, waiting for their train to be announced. A couple with two young girls arrived and dropped their heavy luggage with their prominent swastika seals in a tight circle a few feet away from the door. Jews, no doubt.

Several SA men made their way through the crowd, loud and crude, they were obviously looking for trouble—at least to harass and frighten departing Jews. When they came near the family of four, one husky fellow whipped out a crowbar on a short rope, let it fly to land on the broad side of the woman's bulging suitcase. The hook bit into the leather, the man yanked hard to free the crowbar, causing the leather to rip, and out rolled a handful of gold coins. The gold pieces twirled and slid and danced on the granite floor, coming to rest at the shiny boots of the Nazi bullies.

Shouts of *Jew! Filthy Jew! Jew Pig!* brought his comrades to the scene, clubs raised. Within seconds, hard blows rained on the head and shoulders of the two adults as the little family was hustled out of the depot with their luggage and the offending coins.

Irene clutched a hand over her mouth to stifle a silent protest, and Martin crunched his teeth so hard that Ursula could hear it. Horror reflected in her eyes, as she witnessed for the first time an act of Nazi brutality, and made her body shiver. The busy chatter around her stopped. In the tomb-like silence of the big train station Martin pulled his child protectively against him. What next? he worried.

It seemed an eternity before the train to Genoa was announced for boarding on Track Three. Weary and out of breath, they found the first-class compartment Erich had purchased for them, heaved their suitcases onto the racks above the seats, slid the door shut, and collapsed against the green, velvety upholstery. Punctual to the minute, the train whistle sounded, the wheels turned, and the train moved slowly out of the station.

Martin leaned back with a deep sigh. "Oh, this feels good," he said. "Wake me when we are in Italy." No sooner had he closed his eyes, he fell asleep.

Forcing a smile all the way from her mouth up into her eyes and adopting a light tone, Irene turned to her daughter. "Here we are, on the first leg of our journey. Let's make believe we are on holiday. You have been such a help in getting us here. I cannot tell you often enough how proud we are of you—how much we love you. I am looking forward to the sea voyage; just the three of us together and time to talk. Right now, let's do what your father is doing and get some sleep. It's a long way to Genoa."

Ursula snuggled close to her mother, resting her head next to hers. "Fraülein Amanda said that I was getting older by the minute, and to make sure to enjoy this trip. I already miss her," she said, her voice small and forlorn.

"Shhh, shhh," Irene stroked her daughter's head, "she will always be in your heart, and that's pretty close. Absence or even death does not diminish a person. You are taking along all the gifts Fraülein Amanda has given you. And who says you are not going to see her again?"

Ursula nodded sleepily and the two shut their eyes against the world. Ursula was asleep in no time, but Irene's mind replayed the last moments at Marienhall with the Burdachs and saying goodbye to her mother. The latter never ceased to surprise Irene; she had changed so drastically over the years. With her face serene, her voice gentle and void of self-pity, Toni looked at her daughter's weepy eyes.

"Look," she said, "I have already lived a lifetime, and a good one at that. I cannot count all the blessings that have come my way. Knowing that my children are safe means everything to me. I just pray to God that Lucy and Arthur will be able to join you soon. Ana Marieke and I will be fine. We are two old war horses out to pasture. We have our memories and we have our dreams. God will take care of the rest. So, go in peace and be well."

"Thank you, Mother," she whispered in the stillness of the compartment; and in one of her rare conversations with God, Irene again asked the Almighty for the courage to stand by her heart.

The last time Erich and Antonia visited Marienhall, they assured Irene they would return to say their farewells, but when the time came, they stayed away. Irene was not surprised when Antonia called, confessing to take the cowardly way out and to say goodbye on the telephone. Hedwig was so upset that she locked herself into her room, refusing to see anybody.

Irene's vision then settled on the pitiful sight of Ursula clinging to Fraülein Amanda and the distraught faces of the assembled Burdachs. Lothar had turned out all the lights in Marienhall, and the venerable manor house loomed tall and stark in the darkness of the evening sky.

Quickly, he helped his passengers into the waiting automobile, and climbed behind the wheel. As he approached the gates, he twisted his head slightly, and thick with emotions, he said, "Marienhall will be waiting for your return, and so will we. Don't look back, you'll get a stiff neck and a stiff mind. Look ahead and live." Irene would never forget his words.

"Don't look back," she murmured and gave herself over to the rhythmic sound of the wheels on iron tracks, and the swoosh of the wind as it met the train.

By the time Ursula and Irene woke up, the scenery outside had changed and brought the majestic snow-capped mountains of the Alps into view. It wasn't long before the train slowed down, pulled into the station, and came to a stop. Martin shook himself awake. "We are on the Brenner Pass," he announced, "the border between Germany and Italy; another milestone."

Suddenly, compartment doors flew open, SA poured in asking for passports, followed by the hateful words "*Juden raus!*" (Jews get out!)

"What do they want now? Is there ever going to be an end?" Martin shivered as he straightened his tie and jacket. His hands were shaking a little; he was still drowsy from the sedatives, and not too steady on his feet. Irene hoped the crisp mountain air would breathe a bit of new life into his lungs. She held on to his hand all the way.

Out on the platform, yelling their customary cruel insults and brutal threats, the storm troopers prodded the Jewish passengers, like cattle, with their night sticks, into lining up against the wall of the depot. Two tough-looking SS officers appeared, strolled down the line of frightened people, peering at faces, as though inspecting troops at the parade ground. On their way back up the line, one of the officers jabbed his swagger stick at an occasional man or woman, who had to take two steps away from the wall. To Martin's great concern and visible agitation, Irene and Ursula were among them.

Giving his hand a firm, reassuring squeeze, Irene took Ursula by the arm and followed the few other chosen ones into the building. Men and women were separated. A storm trooper pointed to a door near the entrance, and with a calculated sneer in his voice, told the cluster of eight women that someone would conduct a body search for hidden gems.

A moment later, the door opened, a heavyset woman with plain features, a ruddy complexion, and piercing dark eyes beneath heavy eyebrows pointed to the well-dressed lady next to Irene. "Follow me, Jew whore," she rasped, "and the rest of you, keep your mouths shut. Not a word out of you!"

Apprehension and fear settled over the waiting women and clung to them like a second skin. Silence. A touch of relief registered on their pinched faces when the lady stepped out of the room after a few minutes, seemingly calm and unharmed. Irene was next, and when she reappeared, she flashed a quick smile of encouragement at everyone. With a rude gesture of her thumb, the woman came for Ursula, pointing at the open door. The room was big and gloomy and looked a bit like a doctor's or a dentist's examination room. A few glass cabinets a dentist chair hugged one wall. A table covered in black oilcloth, with strange metal contraptions at one end, dominated the room. The air was dank and unpleasant, thickened by a layer of a strong disinfectant and human fear.

"Face the table, pull up your skirt, pull down your underpants, bend over, spread your legs, put your face down on the table," the woman snapped harshly.

Embarrassed and unsure of what to expect, Ursula did exactly as she was ordered, wondering if the woman was a doctor. The oilcloth smelled of lack of care and felt gritty against her face. She shifted her head sideways to avoid her mouth coming in contact with the filthy cloth, when the rough hands of the woman started to roam over her slender body. Up and down and all over, those searching fingers kneaded and punished the girl's soft skin. Suddenly a stubby finger, causing a hot, stabbing pain, explored Ursula's backside, and then settled in the most private part of her body—poking, pinching, and rubbing, all the while the brawny woman was breathing hard. What seemed an eternity later, the woman moaned loudly and finally pulled her hands away from Ursula's body.

"Get yourself together, you Jew pig and get out of my sight," the woman panted and turned away from her. Bewildered, hurting, and feeling soiled, Ursula hurriedly rearranged her clothing, and tore out of the room. Back on the platform, she boarded the train. Two anxious parents, all emotions spent, greeted her when she entered their compartment.

"Thank God you're back," Irene swallowed a sob. "What did that awful woman do to you? Did she hurt you?" her eyes probed her daughter's face. With wisdom beyond her years, Ursula knew instantly not to put another burden on her parents. She was not sure just what had happened—she didn't have a name for it—but she knew it was ugly and shameful. She would put the obscene act out of her mind and let it die.

"Oh," she answered lightly, her eyes clear and innocent, "the woman asked if I had any jewels hidden on me. She poked in my ears, pinched my nose, and looked between my toes. Then she let me go." Satisfied, Martin and Irene relaxed considerably. In barely a whisper, they commented on the Nazis' total commitment to rob, demoralize, and finally destroy the Jews of Germany.

"Now that the blinders are off," Martin mused, "I can't believe I waited this long . . . "

He was interrupted by the sound of the conductor's sharp whistle, the answering tooting of the engine, and the familiar clanking, squeaking, and rattling as the train started to move. The red-and-white striped barriers on both sides of the border were raised to let the train pass.

"Welcome to sunny Italy," Irene raised an empty coffee cup in a mock toast. "I feel better already."

"Sunny or not," Martin, replied dryly, "we are still in a Fascist country. *Il Duce* is Hitler's ally and that makes me uncomfortable. I'll relax in Shanghai, strange as it will be."

The conversation came to a halt. Weary of the subject, drained and exhausted, they nestled back into their seats. Their eyes shuttered against the world, and with the rushing notes of the wind's song in their ears, they lost themselves to their thoughts and visions of their own making; alone with themselves.

Blue skies and friendly faces greeted the travelers in sunny Genoa. Outside the terminal, Martin hailed a taxi to take them to the dockside of the *Gneisenau*. The handsome mop-haired taxi driver, expressing the lively characteristics of his Mediterranean heritage, swerved and dipped in and out of traffic and through narrow streets in a death-defying manner. When the harbor came into sight, the sleek bow of the *Gneisenau* rose high above the water dominating the scene. Within a few minutes, Martin, Irene, and Ursula walked up the gangplank of the big ship that would take them to the other side of the globe. Was it real? Irene pinched herself, or was it a dream?

A kind and chatty cabin steward, by the name of Guenther, settled them into their quarters, telling them he would see after all their needs. Attached to the spacious and elegant main cabin was a small one, just right for young travelers. Sensing his new passengers' frayed nerves and need for solitude, Guenther suggested they take their meals in the cabin, until they were ready for the bustling atmosphere of the dining room. Gratefully, Irene accepted his offer.

The *Gneisenau* sailed promptly at midnight to the music of the ship's band playing a popular German farewell folksong over and over again. Not wanting to recall the painful lyrics, Irene shut the portholes in the cabin, and relaxed to the soft rolling motion of the big ocean liner heading out to sea. Sleep did not come to her that night, and at two o' clock in the morning she slipped quietly out of the cabin and made her way to the deserted upper deck.

A starry sky of rich midnight blue tented high above the Mediterranean sea. Waves splashed softly against the side of the ship and the white foam of the ship's wake left a wide streak of light on the dark waters. Irene leaned against the ship's rail, her face turned into the salty breeze and with her eyes fixed on the firmament, she lost herself in the beauty of the moment. Taking deep, hungry breaths of the cool ocean air, she felt clean again, and whole.

"Oh, the Greatness of it all, and the smallness of me," she spoke to the sky. To herself, she added, "Evil can destroy what man has built, but it cannot touch the magnificence of the vast Universe and the Greatness that exists beyond time and space."

Irene pulled her wrap snugly around her shoulders and crossed her arms to keep it in place She welcomed the deep knowing that she belonged to Greatness, and that she carried within her very soul the strength and the courage to meet life's demands—enough for Martin, the love of her life and for Ursula, the child of her heart.

The ship with its cargo of eternal strangers plowed steadily toward the horizon where the ocean met the sky. Beyond it, there lay a land and a promise.

Epilogue
AUGUST 1945

IT WAS OVER. The fighting, the bloodshed, and the senseless murder of millions of innocent people. Finally. It was over. Hitler's dream of a Thousand-Year Reich ended in its twelfth year. But those twelve years, those shameful years, have cost so much.

Only Lucy, Max, and Inge, with the help of Erich von Warteburg, were able to make it to China.

Arthur Burger, with his wife Rosa, and their two children lost their lives in the gas chambers of Auschwitz.

Toni Burger and the faithful-to-the-end Ana Marieke died in Theresienstadt, victims of crude, experimental surgeries on women.

Ida Bohne (only two weeks before the fall of Berlin) was betrayed to the Gestapo for hiding Jews in her home, and was locked into a cattle car with several hundred Jews. The train was on its way to the death camp, Ravensbrueck, but was left on the tracks locked and unattended, when the train's crew fled from the oncoming Russian army. No one unlocked the doors of the cattle cars.

Helene Schreiber, elegant woman of the world, moved to Wiesbaden, where she learned to drive a small truck. Loaded with vegetables as camouflage, she smuggled Jewish children into Switzerland. On her fourteenth run, she was picked up at the German border and sent to the Warsaw Ghetto.

Eugene Blomberg was arrested in Prague and also shipped to the Warsaw Ghetto. Brother and sister died in the often written-about terrors of the Ghetto uprising.

Erich and Antonia von Warteburg survived the war. When the Russian armies came too close for comfort, and having heard the horror stories of the rapings and killings by Soviet soldiers, they fled on foot. Leaving everything behind, they walked more than eight hundred miles to Koblenz am Rhein, where old friends took them in. Warteburg was destroyed.

Maria was the only Burdach who lived to see the end of the war. Marienhall, situated at one end of an airfield, was taken over as a *Luftwaffe* headquarters, and was eventually bombed to rubble by Russian planes. Instead of fleeing the new enemy, the Burdachs chose to stay at Marienhall and they died with it.

Having had a home for the first time in their colorful vagabond lives, Woyczek and his gypsy family never left Marienhall.

Fraülein Amanda visited her family in London. She was killed in an air raid shortly before the end of the war.

Horst von Brunnen managed to get to Switzerland. He never returned to Germany.

The eighteen thousand or so Middle European Jewish refugees who made it to China, came to be known as the Shanghai Jews.

But that is another story.

About the Author

URSULA BACON FLED Nazi Germany with her parents in 1939 and landed in Shanghai, China, along with eighteen thousand other middle-European refugees. The family spent most of the war years in a Japanese-controlled "Designated Area," often referred to as a ghetto. She married a young refugee in Shanghai and came to the United States in 1947 where she settled in Denver, raised two children, and lived the American Dream. Today, Ursula lectures and conducts writing and publishing workshops. She is a frequent keynote speaker at women's conferences and other educational events.

Suggested Topics for Reading Group Discussions

1. Do you think that there still is open parental opposition today to people of different faiths contemplating marriage—especially between Jews and gentiles?

2. The married life of Martin and Irene was idyllic, without quarrels, strife, or fights. According to Irene, it is mostly the woman who makes a relationship work smoothly. Do you agree?

3. In today's world, wealth is all around us. Many children are raised in families with an undisguised show of affluence, in contrast with the years of Ursula's childhood, when youngsters were often not made aware of their parents' wealth and were brought up with great modesty. Of the two, which is healthier?

4. The whole Blomberg clan believed that wealth is a responsibility, something to be shared to ease the lives of other people. What is your take on that?

5. Had you lived during the 1930s, would you have given more credence early on to Hitler's vicious and inflammatory threats against the Jews, which contributed to the basis of the Nazi policy?

6. How do you feel about Lothar Burdach's dark deed? Was loyalty carried beyond friendship? Could you have done it?

7. Do you believe it is possible to promote hate and prejudice against a people in present-day America? Are there signs of neo-Nazism and are they spreading?

8. Considering the planting of seeds of hate against Jews and Christians in the fertile minds of many young Muslim children by their elders, could we be facing a dangerous threat to our freedom and our lives?

9. Can the Holocaust happen again on a large, global scale?

10. What can we do to live in peace with the world?